THE MISEDUCATION OF THE WEST

How Schools and the Media Distort Our Understanding of the Islamic World

EDITED BY JOE L. KINCHELOE AND
SHIRLEY R. STEINBERG

Reverberations: Cultural Studies and Education

Westport, Connecticut
London

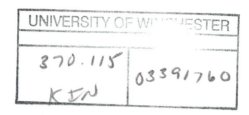
Library of Congress Cataloging-in-Publication Data

The miseducation of the West : how schools and the media distort our understanding of the Islamic world / edited by Joe L. Kincheloe and Shirley R. Steinberg.

    p. cm.—(Reverberations : cultural studies and education)
    Includes bibliographical references and index.
    ISBN 0–275–98160–6
    1. International education—United States. 2. Multicultural education—United States. 3. Islam—Public opinion. 4. Public opinion—United States. I. Kincheloe, Joe L. II. Steinberg, Shirley R., 1952– III. Reverberations (Praeger Publishers)
    LC1090.M49 2004
    070.4'4990909767—dc22   2004003790

British Library Cataloguing in Publication Data is available.

Library of Congress Catalog Card Number: 2004003790
ISBN: 0–275–98160–6

First published in 2004

Praeger Publishers, 88 Post Road West, Westport, CT 06881
An imprint of Greenwood Publishing Group, Inc.
www.praeger.com

Printed in the United States of America

The paper used in this book complies with the Permanent Paper Standard issued by the National Information Standards Organization (Z39.48–1984).

10 9 8 7 6 5 4 3 2 1

To those who have been imprisoned, persecuted, or killed as a result of the miseducation of the West—particularly those who have died needlessly in George W. Bush's War on Iraq.

Contents

Chapter 1

Introduction

Joe L. Kincheloe

In the Western tradition of writing about, researching, and representing Islam, Europeans have consistently positioned Muslims as the irrational, fanatic, sexually enticing, and despotic others. This portrayal, as many scholars have argued, has been as much about Western anxieties, fears, and self-doubts as about Islam. In this book the editors and authors are fascinated by these representations in light of the events of the early twenty-first century. After 9/11 and the wars in Afghanistan and Iraq the ways images of Islam have been embedded in the Western and especially the American consciousness become extremely important to everyday life. With these concerns in mind the editors and authors examine the educational practices—defined broadly to include both schooling and media pedagogy—that help construct these ways of seeing.

Grounding the Miseducation: The Trouble with Difference

Central to any description of this miseducation is the West's effort, especially after the Scientific Revolution of the seventeenth and eighteenth centuries, to depict its own superiority. In the first decade of the twenty-first century it is high time to clean up the historical distortions developed centuries ago and passed down across the generations. If the United States is to become a great nation guided by a moral compass, it can do so only by way of its relationships with other nations and cultures. Nations, like individuals, develop a self-image in their interaction with others. Christopher Stonebanks's chapter in this volume offers compelling insight into this issue. Through a respectful interaction with those different from ourselves, we come to new modes of consciousness. We gain a chance to see ourselves as the other sees us—indeed, our familiarity with ourselves is made strange. Only when a nation gains this view of itself can it move toward maturity.[1] Such a view in no way dictates a particular response to an atrocity such as the 9/11 attacks, but it does help a nation reflect on larger social, cultural, and historical dimensions of why groups such as radical Islamists might hold the United States in contempt. In its maturity the nation acquires the disposition to learn from tragedy.

The mature culture/nation is dedicated to learning from difference. In such a nation's schools, for example, citizens come to understand that schools are contested public spaces shaped by diverse forces of power. See Yosef Progler's compelling historical view of Napoleon's French schools in Egypt and the power relations involved in this pedagogical situation in his chapter in this volume. In this context learning from difference means that teachers are aware of the histories and struggles of colonized groups and oppressed peoples. Such teachers would understand the complicity of educational institutions themselves in such oppression. Many scholars maintain that the classroom is a central site for the legitimization of myths and silences about non-Western and often non-Christian peoples. If educators who value the power of difference were to teach about the history of Islam, they would have to rethink the canonical history of the West. Indeed, when school texts distort the history of Islam, they concurrently distort all history. Teachers and educational leaders who act on the power of difference forge such recognition into a politically transformative mode of education. Such a pedagogy understands Western societies as collectivities of difference where the potential exists for everyone to be edified by interaction with the other and the ways of knowing he or she brings to an encounter. Of course in contemporary America, such respect for difference is viewed by many as an anti-American position.

Because of its transformative power, difference in contemporary America must be not only tolerated but also cultivated as a spark to human solidarity and creativity. This is what this book attempts to do: to think about the power of difference in relation to Western-Islamic interactions and their portrayal in educational institutions. Any description of a rigorous education needs to include an understanding of the power of difference that nurtures a critical sense of empathy. Cornel West contends that empathy involves the ability to appreciate the anxieties and frustrations of the other, never to lose sight of the humanity of the marginalized no matter how wretched their condition—and I would add no matter how much some of them may express their hatred for us.[2] The point emerging here involves the pedagogical, ethical, and cognitive benefits derived from the confrontation with difference and the diverse vantage points it provides us for viewing the everyday world. As I have written elsewhere,[3] educators who value difference often begin their analysis of a phenomenon by listening to those who have suffered most as a result of its existence. These *different* ways of seeing allow educators and other individuals access to the new modes of cognition—a cognition of empathy. Such a perspective allows individuals access to tacit modes of racism, cultural bias, and religious intolerance that operate to structure worldviews.

There is little doubt that this valuing of difference or understanding of the miseducation of the West would not end the terrorist activities of groups such as al-Qaida. But such understandings put into action over the long term will operate to change the nature of the United States' relationship with most of the Islamic world. Given the dominant political consciousness of the Bush administration and its diplomatic and educational operatives, such views of difference are being challenged and discredited at every opportunity. The epistle to America's teachers by right-wing educator Chester Finn's Fordham Foundation, "September 11: What Our Children Need to Know" pushes this discreditation in the educational realm in profoundly disturbing ways.[4] As Finn puts it, he had to act because so much "nonsense" was being put out by the educational establishment. What Finn describes as nonsense can be read as scholarship attempting to provide perspective on the long history of Western-Islamic relations. Finn's use of "so much" in relation to this "nonsense" is crass exaggeration. Most materials published about 9/11 for educators were rather innocuous pleas for helping children deal with the anxiety the attacks produced. Little elementary or secondary school material devoted to historicizing or contextualizing the Islamic world and its relation with the West appeared in the first two years after the tragic events of 9/11.

Reflecting the viewpoints of the Bush administration on how to properly educate Americans about the Islamic world, the Fordham report illustrates the traditional Western tendency to promote its own moral, political, and cultural superiority whenever it has to deal with Muslim societies. As Victor Davis Hanson puts it in one of the essays included in the report,

Not all cultures are equal in their moral sensibilities; few dictators, theocrats, tribal leaders or communists welcome the introspection and self-criticism that are necessary for moral improvement. So before we seek guidance from others abroad or adjust our policies to an apparent international consensus Americans must first ask of other nations in the world: do their people vote, do they respect women, do they enjoy freedom, and can they express themselves without audit or censorship?[5]

Other authors in the Fordham report write about "teaching nonsense" and "foolishness" in a way that many would interpret as references to pedagogies that question American superiority and infallibility. The editors and authors of *The Miseducation of the West* are promoting foolishness when we argue that it is necessary for Americans in this era to study how individuals from Islamic nations understand the world, themselves, their histories and cultures, and the West. Teaching such understandings is not foolishness; it is an effort to understand the peoples of the world so we can interact with them in more culturally sensitive and equitable ways. In the case of the diverse peoples of the Islamic world, Westerners, Americans in particular, need to contemplate why it is that so many of them are angry about both the historical and the contemporary relationships between the Islamic world and the West.[6]

Again the Fordham Foundation's opposition to such types of understanding manifests itself. Chester Finn writes that educators take values such as "tolerance and multiculturalism" and carry them "to extremes."[7] These nebulous educators (I think we are the types Finn and the other Fordham authors are referencing) are totally unconcerned with history and civics. The world is rather black and white, Finn suggests, and there is no need to understand diverse points of view. In the post-9/11 world our children need to clearly understand the difference between " heroes and villains," "freedom and repression," "hatred and nobility," "democracy and theocracy," and "civic virtue and vice."[8] Such pronouncements remove Americans from history, while in their lack of specificity vilify the Islamic other. "They" were after all the ones who attacked us—"they" referencing Islam as a whole. In the name of teaching "true history," Finn and his fellow Fordham authors move America to a historiographical Disneyland where all of our intentions are good. American history becomes the happiest history on earth.

The propaganda-like teaching of American history signaled by the Fordham report connotes more than merely a jingoistic response to 9/11. It represents a return to a 1954 view of America as the bearer of the democratic torch to the antidemocratic forces of the world. Concurrently, and more importantly, it signifies a larger effort to use 9/11 as the referent for an American Empire freed from the need to understand the rest of the world in any way outside imperial military necessities. A critical education must counter such tendencies and work to conceptualize 9/11 in a variety of contexts.[9] Without this critical challenge the effort to simply appreciate the perspectives of individuals from other cultures, other social systems, and other religious heritages can be dismissed as irrational, anti-American, and even anti-Christian. Haroon Kharem's chapter in this volume on the European miseducation about the Moors illustrates a specific effort to dismiss the contributions of Islam to Western civilization.

In the context of the ideology of the George W. Bush administration and supporters of its educational agenda such as the Fordham Foundation, works such as *The Miseducation of the West* become socially unacceptable knowledge. The Fordham report is ideologically complicit with advancing the power of the new American Empire and in this role must avoid humanizing "the enemy." In this context disinformation becomes the rule of the day, as generalizations about the monolithic Islamic world proliferate. The power of difference in this ideological frame is dead. As is stated numerous times in Fordham's "September 11: What Our Children Need to Know," such forms of understanding and celebrating difference are dangerous to the future of America.

Miseducation and the Invisibility of the Operations of the Empire

In many ways 9/11 was a profound shock to millions of Americans who obtain their news and worldviews from the mainstream, corporately owned media and their understanding of American international relations from what is taught in most secondary schools and in many colleges and universities. Such individuals are heard frequently on call-in talk radio and TV shows expressing the belief that America is loved internationally because it is richer, more moral, and more magnanimous than other nations. In this mind-set those who resist the United States hate our freedom for reasons never quite specified—jealousy, maybe. These Americans, the primary victims of the miseducation, have not been informed by their news sources of the societies that have been undermined by covert U.S. military operations and U.S. economic policies.[10] Many do not believe, for example, the description of the human effects of American sanctions on Iraq between the First and Second Gulf Wars. Indeed, the hurtful activities of the American Empire are invisible to many of the empire's subjects.

The complexity of the relationship between the West (the United States in particular) and Islam demands that we be very careful in laying out the subtle argument we are making about the miseducation. The activities of the American Empire have not been the only forces at work creating an Islamist extremism that violently defies the sacred teaching of the religion. But American misdeeds have played an important role in the process. A new critical education based on an appreciation of difference can help the United States redress some of its past and present policies toward the diverse Islamic world. While these policies have been invisible to many Americans, they are visible to the rest of the world—the Islamic world in particular. Ignoring the *history* of the empire, Fordham report author Kenneth Weinstein writes that the Left "admits" that differences exist between cultures

but paradoxically downplays their violent basis through relativism and multiculturalism. It views cultural diversity and national differences as matters of taste arguing that the greatest crime of all is judgmentalism.[11]

Weinstein concludes this paragraph by arguing that Americans are just too nice and as such are naïve to the threats posed by many groups around the world.

Weinstein and the other Fordham authors set up a classic straw man argument in this context. The Left they portray equates difference with a moral relativism that is unable to condemn the inhumane activities of particular groups. Implicit throughout "September 11: What Our Children Need to Know" is the notion that this fictional American Left does not condemn al-Qaida and its crimes against humanity. This type of misrepresentation is an egregious form of miseducation. It is the type of distortion that equated opposition to the Second Gulf War with support for Saddam Hussein's Iraqi regime. How can these malcontents oppose America, the Fordham authors ask. Their America is a new empire that constantly denies its imperial dimensions. The new empire is not like empires in earlier historical eras that overtly boasted of conquest and the taking of colonies. The twenty-first century is the era of the postmodern empire that speaks of its moral duty to unselfishly liberate nations and return power to the people. Empire leaders speak of free markets, the rights of the people, and the domino theory of democracy. It is an empire whose public relations people portray it as the purveyor of freedom around the world. When its acts of liberation and restoration of democracy elicit protest and retaliation, its leaders express shock and disbelief that such benevolent actions could arouse such irrational responses.

With all of their concern with teaching history, the authors of the Fordham report and other right-wing perspectives often ignore the warnings of past American leaders such as George Washington about the temptations of empire building. As President John Quincy Adams put it in the 1820s: "If America were tempted to become the dictatress of the world, she would be no longer the ruler of her own spirit."[12] As the American Empire spends massive sums of money on its foreign excursions, it finds it more and more difficult to designate money for democratic essentials at home such as education and infrastructural needs. The costs of the empire consistently undermine the promise of domestic democracy and economic justice.

In my chapter on Iran I deal with the inability of American leaders to understand the impact of empire building in the Persian Gulf on the psyches of those personally affected by such activities. In the case of Iraq in the Second Gulf War American leaders simply disregarded the views of nations around the world, the Muslim world in particular, as they expressed their opposition to the American invasion. History was erased as Saddam Hussein was viewed in a psychological context as a madman. References to times when the United States supported the madman were deleted from memory. The empire thus could do whatever it wanted, regardless of the impact on the Iraqi people or the perceptions of others (irrational others) around the world.

An epistemological naïveté—the belief that dominant American ways of seeing both America itself and the world are rational and objective and that differing perspectives are irrational—permeate the Fordham report. As John Agresto writes:

It is not very helpful to understand other cultures and outlooks and not understand our own country and what it has tried to achieve. What is it that has brought tens of millions of immigrants to America, not to bomb it, but to better its future and their own? What is it about the promise of liberty and equal treatment, of labor that benefits you and your neighbor, of an open field for your enterprise, ambition, determination and pluck? *Try not to look at America through the lens of your own ideology or political preference but see it as it really is.* Try, perhaps, to see the America most Americans see. That can be a fine antidote to smugness and academic self-righteousness. [emphasis mine] [13]

Studying the Fordham Foundation's ways of looking at and teaching about America with its erasures of history deployed in the very name of a call to teach history, we are disturbed. When this is combined with an analysis of media representations of the nation's war against terrorism and the Second Gulf War, we gain some sobering insights into America's future. The inability or refusal of many Americans, especially those in power, to see the problematic activities of the "invisible" empire does not portend peace in the world in the coming years. The way knowledge is produced and transmitted in the United States by a corporatized media and an increasingly corporatized/privatized educational system is one of the central political issues of our time. Yet in the mainstream political and educational conversations it is not even on the radar. One of the purposes of *The Miseducation of the West* is to help put this issue on the public agenda.

The Politics of Knowledge: Power and the Representation of Islam

Americans—as well, of course, as other peoples around the planet—are victimized by the new American Empire's politics of knowledge. In the contemporary electronic world saturated by the information of corporate knowledge producers, many Americans simply are unaware of knowledge constructed by diverse groups and individuals. I spoke with several Americans who sought diverse information sources in relation to the Second Gulf War. Other than the Pacifica Radio Network and programs such as Free Speech Network News and Democracy Now, it was very difficult to find alternative news of the war. Such alternative news attempted to transcend the outlawing of the history of U.S.-Muslim relations promoted by mainstream information sources. Such historical erasure is central to the miseducation of the U.S. public, as it subverts the democratic process. Without the benefits of historical context the society is depoliticized, for all political positions involve particular historical interpretations. Combined with the confusion caused by the cacophony of hyperreal information saturation, dehistoricization produces depoliticization and its telltale characteristics: nihilism, cynicism, apathy, and escapism.[14]

In the Fordham report's contribution to this oppressive politics of knowledge any historical study of Western-Islamic or U.S.-Islamic relationships is off-limits. The history that needs to be studied, insist Fordham authors Lynne Cheney and Gloria Sesso and John Pyne, are patriotic documents such as Thomas Paine's *Common Sense,* the Declaration of Independence, *Letters from an American Farmer,* the Gettysburg Address, Franklin Roosevelt's "Four Freedoms" speech, and Reagan's statement to the country after the *Challenger* explosion.[15] While I would not question the value of any of these documents, the call to study them in lieu of histories of Islam and Western/U.S. relations with Islam in this context is perplexing. The message of Lynne Cheney in her short piece in the Fordham report and in her chilling American Council of Trustees and Alumni's *Defending Civilization: How Our Universities Are Failing America*[16] is that any historical study of Islam or American relations with Islam is anti-American. Why anti-American? Because it implies that the United States did something to incite the attacks of 9/11.

To historicize and contextualize, the right-wing story goes, is to fail to condemn the terrorist acts of 9/11. Such scholars, former secretary of education William Bennett argues in the Fordham report, are the "fools" who have argued "that there is no such thing as evil."[17] Thus, understanding complexity in foreign affairs and international relations is viewed as a form of irredeemable relativism. The issue of U.S.-Islamic relations in this right-wing politics of knowledge is quite simple and requires little analysis: the United States has played a passive, innocent, and benevolent role in the Muslim world and then without warning was hit with an inexplicable attack.[18] To argue that this is a crass oversimplification of a complex story is not to justify on any level the acts of the 9/11 terrorists. What the right-wing positions delineated here actually do is shut down democratic conversation about the new world situation in which the United States finds itself.

The right-wing story about the contemporary world situation conveniently omits the last 500 years of European colonialism, the anticolonial movements around the world beginning in the post–World War II era and their impact on the U.S. civil rights movement, the women's movement, the antiwar movement in Vietnam, Native American liberation struggles, the gay rights movement, and other emancipatory movements. In other work I have maintained that the right-wing reaction to these anticolonial movements has set the tone and content of much of American political, social, and educational experience over the last three decades.[19]

Using Aaron Gresson's concept "the recovery of white supremacy," referring to what was perceived to have been lost in the liberation movements, I have studied dominant cultural groups' attempts to reclaim cultural and intellectual supremacy by positioning themselves as victims of the so-called "oppressed."[20] The attacks of 9/11 fit quite well into this discursive construction of white/European victimization. In the years following the attacks much has been made of alleged Muslim persecution of Christians in Islamic countries from Iran to Palestine.[21] In the same context persecution of Muslims by Europeans and Chinese has been virtually ignored. It the post-9/11 context it is obvious who the innocent victims are in the racial and cultural conflicts around the world in the discourse of victimization: white European Christians. The American Empire has no choice—it must discipline these barbaric forces.

How is it in a free society that such a politics of knowledge can go unchallenged? The answer to that question is extremely complex. And while it is one of the key issues this book addresses, it is far broader and more complicated than the scope of this work.[22] For the most part such a politics of information is not imposed by the U.S. government but is more of a self-censorship by the media. Over the last several centuries knowledge about the Islamic world in the West has been produced with conquest and control as objectives. If such a politics of knowledge remains unchallenged, as Edward Said accurately predicted in *Covering Islam* (1981),

we will face protracted tension and perhaps even war, but we will offer the Muslim world, its various societies and states, the prospect of many wars, unimaginable suffering, and disastrous upheavals, not the least of which would be the birth of an "Islam" fully ready to play the role prepared for it by reaction, orthodoxy, and desperation.[23]

The Right-Wing Politics of Knowledge: Objective Portrayals of Barbarism and Irrationality

The right-wing politics of knowledge intersecting with the political-economic dimensions of globalization and geopolitical needs of the American Empire have rendered Said's words eerily prescient. This politics of knowledge with its American assumptions makes for a world where reality is perceived across a great chasm of misconstruction.[24] Distorted pictures of an irrational and barbaric people shape decision making in areas of foreign policy, economics, and education. Scientific ways of seeing in the cultural sphere while claiming neutrality are profoundly shaped by discursive, ideological, linguistic, social, cultural, political, economic, and historical contexts. Islam has been seen and continues to be viewed on a certain horizon and within particular contexts. In the Second Gulf War reporters for the major TV networks denied that their coverage was framed by a particular American perspective toward the war. Television in the United States was objective and fair while Qatar's al-Jazeera was biased and characterized by low journalistic standards.

One of the lessons scholars around the world learned in the last third of the twentieth century was that no knowledge is disinterested. All information is produced by individuals operating at a particular place and a specific time—they see the world and employ methods for viewing the world from a particular point in the complex web of reality. Understanding, for example, a speech by an Islamic cleric about his revulsion in relation to American culture's influence in his nation or region involves a different type of contextualized and historicized analysis than a mathematician solving an obstinate mathematical problem. Those from the West who study and examine the words of the Islamic cleric must

- understand the unique interpretive circumstances of a Western student engaging with an Islamic text,
- be sensitive to the power relationships between the interpreter's culture and the culture of cleric, and
- be aware of the purposes for which the interpretation will be used.

Thus, a key dimension of the miseducation of the West assumes that Western knowledge of Islam and the Islamic world is objective and disinterested. The West's distorted view of Islam, labeled by Said as Orientalism, has reemerged in the last couple of decades of the twentieth century and the first decade of the twenty-first century in a new and more dangerous version. Postmodern Orientalism is now promoted by TV news, film (see Shirley Steinberg's chapter on Islam and Hollywood), edutainment CD-ROMs, and video games. A distorted, demonized view of the Islamic world is passed along by a pedagogy much more powerful than traditional academic scholarship. The new cultural pedagogy colonizes consciousness via the pleasure of the entertainment media. No matter how horrible the Second Gulf War may have been, it was damn good entertainment for many back home. A colleague of mine described a conversation between himself and two of his male university students before the outbreak of the war:

Professor: So you understand the reasons many people oppose the war in Iraq?

Student 1: Yeah, the arguments make a lot of sense but still, you know, uh, uh…

Student 2: What we're saying is that it's going to be so much fun to watch on TV. We can hardly wait.

Such a powerful politics of knowledge wins the consent of individuals to dominant American power along an axis of pleasure even when their logical facilities might resist. Despite its new attire and high-tech modes of transmission, postmodern Orientalism still relies on traditional Orientalism's medieval images of Islam as a barbaric and derivative theology of sodomites. Some of the comments of fundamentalist Christian theologians such as Jerry Falwell and Franklin Graham in the post-9/11 years have echoed such medieval images with a vengeance. Recent CD-ROMs that cover Islam include *Microsoft Bookshelf*, *Microsoft Encarta*, the *Compton Interactive Encyclopedia*, *Hutchinson History Library*, and Dorling Kindersley's *History of the World*.

In all of these multimedia works Islam—and the rest of the world, for that matter—are seen through the geopolitical interests of the American Empire. America becomes the barometer for all human civilization, with the alumni of the Harvard Business School occupying the highest link of the civilizational food chain. Muhammad is a minor character in world history here; the *Microsoft Bookshelf*, for example, grants him less than a paragraph: "Islam has enshrouded Muhammad's life in a mass of legends and traditions."[25] Civilization and human accomplishment in these contemporary sources are exclusively European phenomena, and the contemporary world is viewed through a U.S. Cold War and post–Cold War national interest perspective. In the post–Cold War framework the icon of the Muslim terrorist represents the general Islamic threat to U.S. global dominance. After the fall of the "evil empire" of the Communist bloc, the Islamic threat fills the *enemy vacuum* quite effectively. From these and countless other Western sources on Islam one would learn that not only did Islam promote ignorance but also there was no role for Islam in a grand universal history of mankind.[26]

So when educators with a critical consciousness of the consequences of colonialism and the distortions of the right-wing politics of knowledge began to construct pictures of Islam that considered different ways of seeing the world, right-wing scholars were angered. Although such representations rarely find their way into elementary and secondary curricula, right-wing scholars—especially after 9/11—asserted that they did and attempted to scare their constituencies with allegations that these perspectives were taking over the field. Teacher educators, Chester Finn asserted, were especially guilty of such un-American offenses:

The second chapter of this unhappy story was written by education experts who have opined in scholarly journals about the "educational meanings of September

11th." The good news is that few firing-line educators read such journals. The bad news is that the people who write in them are also, characteristically, the men and women who prepare future teachers in our colleges of education.[27]

The antidote to this distortion of the facts, the contributors to the Fordham report argue, is readily available. Teachers, they contend, should simply quit teaching lies and instead teach factual knowledge about America. There is nothing complicated about social, cultural, political, historical, philosophical, and economic data about the world. Everyone knows what is right. Teachers must simply start telling the truth about America. Researchers writing about the miseducation of the West would not need to discuss such simplemindedness in regard to the complexity of the knowledge of the social sciences and humanities except for the realization that in the political/educational world of the twenty-first century, this is the argument being made by right-wing groups such as the Fordham Foundation and the American Council of Trustees and Alumni. Scholars or analysts such as ourselves cross the ideological line in the sand when

- we question the benevolence of the use of American military power,
- we connect a people's contemporary anger with their colonized or historically colonized status, or
- we maintain that U.S. textbooks and media representations possess an American bias that blinds Americans to the reasons that many people around the world criticize the United States so vociferously.

In this right-wing context Douglas Kellner's assertion in his chapter in this volume that the American media after 9/11 "performed disastrously, whipping up war hysteria, while failing to provide a coherent account of what happened, [and] why it happened" is not the type of analysis necessary in a media-dominated, electronic democratic society. The Finns, William Bennetts, and Lynne Cheneys of the contemporary landscape view such critique as inappropriate and anti-American. Such a right-wing perspective does not respect democratic discourse.

Why Is There Such Mistrust of the United States If America Is So Benevolent?

One dimension of the story we are telling in this book involves the reasons for the hatred and mistrust of the United States in the Islamic world. It is true that not all Muslims around the world in their cultural, political, social, and theological diversity hate the United States. But why is it that so many do? One answer to this complex question is directly related to the miseducation delineated here: so many people in the Islamic world hate the United States because many Americans have no idea why they should harbor such feelings. Many Muslims from around the world express shock at widespread American ignorance of the U.S. role in the world, the U.S. role in Islamic history. When Chester Finn writes that 9/11 presents a chance for Americans "to teach our daughters and sons about heroes and villains, about freedom and repression, about hatred and nobility, democracy and theocracy, about civic virtue and vice" the American blindness to colonial and neocolonial atrocities around the world is revealed.[28] Also, there is a degree of cowardice in Finn's Manichaean binarisms, for he never simply states that Muslims are the villains, repressors, haters, theocrats, and purveyors of vice—he simply implies it over and over again in order to maintain plausible deniability of racism.

Finn and Fordham, Bush and the Cheneys, and other purveyors of the right-wing politics of knowledge simply refused to recognize that 9/11 in part reflected the rage toward the United States pulsing through the veins of many Muslims. The indifference many U.S. policy makers displayed toward the suffering of everyday people around the Islamic world fanned the flames of this anti-American fury. In Iraq, for example, the indifference of American leaders to the effects of the sanctions put into place in 1991 after the First Gulf War angered millions of Muslims around the world as well as the Iraqi people.[29] This is one of many reasons that when U.S. and British forces invaded the country in March 2003, they were not met with the flowers and kisses of a grateful people as promised by George W. Bush. Despite their disdain for Saddam Hussein, most Iraqis obviously did not see the Second Gulf War as the War of Iraqi Liberation.

Moroccan scholar Loubna Skalli in her chapter in this book captures the nuance of these Islamic sentiments so well.

Fundamentalists...are a generation of Muslim youth in revolt. They are in revolt against the imposed colonial projects of modernization in their countries and the unfulfilled promises of their postcolonial political regimes and national elite. They are in revolt against the unequal distribution of wealth and resources within and among nations, against their own socioeconomic and political exclusions, as well as against the widening circle of the disenfranchised classes from which most of them come. They are in revolt against their own sense of powerlessness in the face of all the global forces that threaten their religious and cultural identity.

More important, perhaps, fundamentalists are in revolt against the traumatic legacy of Western colonialism that continues to destabilize the core of their social and cultural fabric—a process kept alive, if not exacerbated, by American hegemony and its perceived homogenizing materialistic values.

Compare Fordham author John Agresto's view of these same Islamic fundamentalists with Skalli's:

The anniversary of September 11th gives us the opportunity not to preach the usual pap about diversity—that different cultures see the world in different but equally valid ways. Rather, we now have the opportunity to show that there are people and cultures with ideas radically and fundamentally different from our own. Different even on the most basic givens we take for granted as the basis of civilized life—that, for example, the ends do not justify the means, that innocents are to be treated with respect, that people should not be exploited as means to ideological or religious ends, that the subjugation of women is an affront to human dignity, indeed, that there is such a thing as human dignity. Consider with your students how, despite the fact that human nature may be everywhere the same, political, religious, or economic ideologies might so affect people's outlooks that even the deepest principles of civilized society are to some easily rejected.[30]

Agresto makes no effort to humanize "the enemy," to understand the forces—many constructed by Western and U.S. colonialism—that shape the fanaticism of some Muslims. Just as importantly, he fails to distinguish the fanatic from the angry but reasonable majority. The use of the word "civilized" denotes an absence of civilization in Islamic culture that can be corrected only by learning from the rational West. Skalli's description differs from Agresto's in that while she may not agree with many of the beliefs and actions of the young Islamic fundamentalists, she understands many of the forces that have helped create them. Agresto's black-and-white portrait seems in its own way to illustrate a cultural fundamentalism similar to the absolutism of any religious fundamentalist group, Christian, Judaic, Hindu, or Islamic.

The fundamentalism of the right-wing politics of knowledge is central to our understanding of the hatred and mistrust of the West, the United States in particular. Fundamentalism as used in this context is defined as the belief in the inerrancy of America, the American political philosophy in particular as well as the Western scientific creed and its methods for producing objective knowledge. The Fordham report well illustrates this fundamentalism, albeit in a manner that avoids unambiguous statement of its position. The ideology and rhetoric of the report make it a document well worth extended analysis.

The Fordham report assumes from the beginning that this Americana and American political philosophy are monolithic expressions of one culture's social and political values. The United States is not now nor has it ever been monocultural and of one political mind. The effort to construct the assumption that America has a common culture and politics is an attempt to position particular ethnicities and specific political points of view as existing outside the boundaries of true Americanism. When educators focus on diversity, the right-wing logic posits, they are misleading their students and pushing a relativistic agenda where nothing is right or wrong. The epistemological naïveté of such assertions is blatant, as Fordham authors ignore an entire body of social theoretical work that moves far beyond the polar extremes of pure objectivity on one end of the continuum and relativism on the other.[31]

Finn asked the 23 authors of the report to answer this question: "What civic lessons are the most imperative for U.S. K–12 teachers to teach their pupils, as the 'anniversary' of the September 11th attacks draws near, about the United States and what it means to be an American?" In his introduction Finn actually asserts that the Fordham Foundation sought a wide range of responses to the question,

but we did not seek people who would repeat the conventional wisdom of the education profession—there's already plenty of that for anyone who wants it. Nor did we seek people who would psychologize the topic or whose reverence for tolerance dwarfs their appreciation of other compelling civic values. Above all, we sought people who take history and civics seriously, people who take America seriously.[32]

There is something profoundly disingenuous in this quotation. First, Finn and the Fordham Foundation did not seek a wide range of responses—they sought individuals who for the most part offered the same viewpoints about American culture, politics, and education as Finn himself. It's fine to offer a generally homogeneous view. In the name of intellectual honesty, however, it is important to admit that one is doing so. Second, there is no monolithic conventional wisdom of the educational profession. There is as much diversity of belief among teachers and teacher educators as there is in America writ large. Again, there is a level of duplicity at work here. Finn and many of his ideological brothers and sisters have for years been painting the education profession and teacher education in particular as radical, incompetent enemies of true Americanism. The unstated purpose here is to continue to discredit such professionals in order to eventually end public schooling and teacher education as they now exist. Third, tolerance is positioned in a false binarism with civic values. It is simply absurd to assert that promoting the value of tolerance is at odds with the larger notion of civic values. And finally, Finn and his ideological companions continue their efforts to equate disagreement with their perspectives as examples of not taking history and civics seriously and not taking America seriously. The implication here moves us back to equating dissent against this right-wing politics of knowledge with anti-Americanism.

Finn also argues in his introduction that there are teachers who are patriots who "love our country and the ideals for which it stands." Because of their love of country, Finn asserts, these teachers "need no advice whatsoever." They will know what to teach, Finn tells his readers, because of their love of America. The anti-intellectualism and even anti-scientific pursuit of knowledge in this assertion tells us that what to teach about 9/11 is an affair of the heart, not the mind. Thus, there is no reason to study the history of Afghanistan and its relations with Europe, especially the Soviet Union and recently with the United States. There is no reason to explore the colonial history of Iraq and the nation's relationship with the United States over the last 30 years. There is no reason to trace the recent history of Iran, as I do in my chapter "Iran and American Miseducation: Cover-ups, Distortions, and Omissions." Even the best teachers, Finn contends, "may find their resolve shaken, their ideas challenged, their lesson plans disputed when they encounter materials from their peers, associations, professors, [and] journals." Alas, what a problematic situation—an open *democratic* debate might break out around the issues raised here.

The fundamentalism of Finn and the right-wing leaders of the United States in the first decade of the twenty-first century frightens the world in ways that many Americans are only beginning to understand. People around the world are baffled that such scholars seem to believe that there is only one objective history of the world and such a chronicle is constructed from an American point of view. "Do they not understand the arrogance and ethnocentrism of such a perspective?" scholars from Spain, Germany, Brazil, Turkey, Mexico, and many other countries ask me as I travel around the world. When Lynne Cheney[33] argues in her chapter in the Fordham report that in response to 9/11 American teachers need to teach about traditional documents and great speeches of American history—all of which should be in the social studies curriculum, we all agree—she misses some important dimensions of such a pedagogy.

While it is necessary to teach about the historical ideals of the United States, it is also important to study the struggles to *enact* such principles. The devil is in the details of these struggles, endeavors marked by profound successes and profound failures. Contrary to the party line of Finn and his compatriots, the study of the failures is not anti-American but a celebration of one of the central ideals of American democracy. As has been argued by many since the emergence of democratic impulses in a variety of cultures around the world, a society is democratic to the degree that it allows for self-criticism. Self-critique does not seem to occupy a very high rung on the Fordham ladder of democratic values. It is indoctrination that seems at odds with such democratic principles.

Thus, legitimate disagreements about the politics of information around U.S. relations with Islamic nations and about the meaning of 9/11 and the ways we teach about it are quashed by Finn, Cheney, Bennett, and their supporters. The assertion that it is too simplistic to argue that religious fanaticism was the only cause of 9/11 was met with accusations of treason, siding with the terrorists, and "blaming America first" by purveyors of the dominant politics of knowledge in government and the media. Indeed, only enemies ask the United States to consider its past in terms of studying its history in relation to other nations and cultures. The erasure of history takes place in the name of history, as we have seen with the

Fordham report. As Lynne Cheney argues in her American Council of Trustees and Alumni Report, it was not our lack of understanding of Islam that led to the 9/11 attacks.[34]

On one level it is trite to argue that Americans need to know more about the world. But in the context of the right-wing politics of knowledge, progressives must insist on more sophisticated understandings of the perspectives of other cultures, especially about the role of the United States in the world. We must demand higher media news standards—TV and radio coverage that provides multiple perspectives and viewpoints from around the world. The U.S. media must get beyond representing the United States as victim in international relations and provide insight into America's role in the complex system of world events. In this complex context, understanding and addressing the genesis of terrorism and anti-American sentiments in the world should not constitute a controversial act.

Western Liberation or Western Assault: Historical Dimensions of the Islamaphobic Miseducation

When educators struggle to place the events of the late twentieth and early twenty-first centuries in historical context, do they discern historical continuity connecting the intersection of Western (or Christian) cultures and Islam? Is it a misappropriation of history to trace Western-Islamic relations from the rise of Islam in the seventh century through Charles Martel's victory at the Battle of Tours in the eighth century, the crusades, the Ottoman Empire and the rise of other Islam societies, and European colonialism to the Islamaphobia of the present? Obviously, human beings make selective use of the past to make sense of and rationalize particular dimensions of the present.[35] To some extent all political positions are historical interpretations. These are important questions that educators and policy makers must keep in mind as they attempt to understand contemporary Western and Islamic relations.

In this context consider Ibrahim Abukhattala's assertion in his chapter in this book that despite the contemporary stereotypes of Muslims as intolerant and prone to terrorism and violence, historical scholarship teaches him a very different picture. For example, in Spain from the eighth century to the fourteenth century, Abukhattala argues, the Muslim empire was one of the most tolerant empires in history. Jews, Christians, and Muslims lived and worked together in harmony for 800 years. From the First Crusade at the end of the eleventh century onward, Muslims in the Middle East experienced European entry into Islamic lands as an assault. As the British and French moved into the Muslim world in the eighteenth

century, the assault from the Islamic perspective continued and intensified.

From the Crusades and colonialism the Europeans "learned" that Muslims were barbaric, ugly, zealous, and ignorant. Such perceptions allowed
a moral justification to the European colonial project around the world.
With the coming of European modernity in the seventeenth and eighteen
centuries there emerged a new articulation of European superiority that
positioned the Muslims and other peoples around the world as profoundly incompetent and inferior. Viewing these "inferior" peoples
played a central role in shaping European self-consciousness. In the
medieval period Europeans had been intimidated by what they knew was
the superior learning of the Muslim civilization. After the Scientific Revolution and the birth of modernity Europe was seen by Europeans as most
definitely superior. This notion of European superiority became the foundation for the miseducation of the West.

At the very least we begin to learn from these historical insights that the
Islamaphobic depictions of Western-Islamic relations is more complex
than the right-wing politics of education would have us believe. While
there is no disinterested selection of historical events, we can conclude at
the very least that there exist many versions of this story. The story told in
mainstream media and education cannot be separated from the influence
of historical and contemporary Islamaphobia. What is interesting here is
that these historical and contemporary versions of Islamaphobia intersect
in what we are calling the miseducation of the West. The barbaric images
of Islam developed during the Crusades and colonialism lay in wait,
ready to be deployed when the political climate needed them, such as during the oil embargo of 1973 or the First Gulf War of 1991. When most post-
Enlightenment Western scholars researched Islam through the conceptual
lenses of Western modernity, employing its assumptions about knowledge production, the ways human societies should develop, the nature of
civilization, and the writing of history, they found—not surprisingly—
Islamic culture(s) to be inferior.

Islamic law in these studies was not real jurisprudence and Islamic ways
of making meaning not real rationality. Soon a canon of the Islamic studies
developed, and these ethnocentric assumptions became sanctified as the
findings of the old masters of the field. Scholars of the tradition maintain
that it became quite authoritarian and aggressively resisted criticism both
from within and outside the discipline. Samuel P. Huntington's *The Clash of
Civilizations: Remaking of World Order* is the most popular contemporary
articulation of this scholarly tradition.[36] The thesis is by no means original—
violence and barbarism are central traits of Muslims—but in Huntington's
hands they are turned into a broader ideology. The ideology that there is an
inevitable clash of civilizations between the Western Christian nations and
the Eastern Islamic and Confucian societies is injected into the discourse of

U.S. foreign policy. If the United States does not act decisively, the ideology asserts, bloody Islam will continue its warring tradition against the West. The idea that Muslims have often been victims of Western violence is conveniently omitted from Huntington's thesis.[37]

With the inauguration of the George W. Bush administration the ideology of civilizational clashes quickly became a basic concept in U.S. foreign policy. With the 9/11 attacks the concept was sanctified, and wars against Afghanistan and Iraq quickly followed. This clash-of-civilizations ideology reinvigorates American colonial impulses with its concept of cultural superiority under attack. Islam is represented as posing a threat against civilization itself with its inferior ways of seeing and being and its alien values. In this context add Bernard Lewis's best-selling *What Went Wrong: Western Impact and Middle Eastern Response* and we begin to get the idea that Islamaphobic scholarship is thriving in the twenty-first century.[38] Lewis continues Huntington's miseducation, arguing Muslim inferiority, barbarism, and failure as a culture. Having first coined the term "clash of civilizations" in a 1990 article in *Atlantic Monthly*, Lewis argues that contemporary Muslims want someone to blame for their failures and have irrationally chosen the guiltless United States—an America that has never done anything to harm the Islamic world. We now have no alternative to war, Lewis concludes. The United States must fight the Islamic world and establish control over it.

The contemporary Islamaphobic miseducation of the West is guided by this inevitable cultural conflict model. The notion that the United States exercises new forms of economic and cultural colonialism or that the United States has intervened in the internal affairs of different nations to help install governments favorable to U.S. economic and geopolitical interests is forbidden knowledge in these models. The idea that U.S. oil companies might have engaged in corporate practices that were not fair to oil-producing Muslim nations is also erased. The racism toward Muslims sanctioned by such models can be heard in countless media productions. The following is an excerpt from Bob Grant's syndicated radio show on WABC in New York the day after the Oklahoma City bombing—the most listened to radio station in the country at that time.

Grant: Tommy from Brooklyn, hello.

Caller: Well, I'd like to say that it's very amazing that both, as far as the O.J. Simpson trial and this awful tragedy that happened yesterday, people are saying that O.J. is guilty and nobody ever saw nothing. And now they're talking about Muslims and Mr. Salameh and all this, this is what you're saying, and no one ever saw anything. That's just as worse.

Grant: Now—yeah—we did see a lot of things. We saw the Simpson case—Nicole with the throat slashed... In the Oklahoma case, you

klutz, in the Oklahoma City case, we don't know how many more
dead people we need to convince you that somebody did that. And
the indications are that those people who did it were some Muslim
terrorists. But, a skunk like you, what I'd like to do is put you up
against the wall with the rest of them, and mow you down along
with them. Execute you with them. Because you obviously have a
great hatred for America, otherwise you wouldn't talk the way you
talk, you imbecile.[39]

To avoid misunderstanding, let us pause for a moment to review the
argument being made here. The miseducation of the West emerges from a
long history of distorted Western knowledge production about Islam. In
the contemporary post–Cold War era we witness a new period of Islamaphobia fanned by numerous scholars and the media. What the editors and
authors of this book are *not* arguing is that Islamic nations have no responsibility for intolerance, fundamentalist zealotry, and inhuman terrorism.
What we are maintaining is that all of these traits can be found in all cultures and religions and that Western scholarship and education has often
painted a Eurocentric black-and-white picture of who is "civilized" and
who is not. For example, the anti-Jewish sentiment expressed in many
parts of the Islamic world is racist and frightening. Of course, anti-Jewish
sentiment and actions are not the exclusive province of Muslims. None of
our arguments for a more reasoned, balanced, and contextualized view of
the Islamic world should be connected to the anti-Jewish sentiment to be
found in particular Muslim locales. The Israeli-Palestinian question, as
Mordechai Gordon writes in his chapter in this book, is profoundly complex. While we do not support many of the policies of Israeli governments
over the last decades, this disagreement should in no way be viewed as an
anti-Jewish sentiment. We are vehemently opposed to anti-Semitism of
both an anti-Jewish and Islamaphobic variety.

The Diversity of the Islamic World:
Understanding Power on a Complex Terrain

A key point that we have already alluded to involves the understanding
that there is no essentialized, unified Islamic world about which we can
make uncomplicated generalizations. Of course, one of the failings of
Finn, Lynne Cheney, Huntington, and Lewis and many others involves
their depiction of a monolithic Islamic world. The portraits of Islam delineated by Orientalists both old and new never existed and do not exist in
the first decade of the twenty-first century. The perception of Islam as the
"enemy" is a social construction of Westerners—especially Americans. As
argued previously, rejecting this enemy status does not mean that we

should affirm all actions of Islamic peoples and societies.[40] When, however, a secondary-school textbook such as *World Cultures* by Petrovich, Roberts, and Roberts chooses a picture of Muslim men praying with their guns beside them out of the millions of photographs of Muslim men praying, a critical education of Islam "calls out" such fear-mongering.[41]

Obviously, some elements of the Islamic world, specifically, some individuals often referred to as Islamic fundamentalists—have made violence a central duty of true believers. These individuals often allude to traditional Western/U.S. colonialism and its new economic and cultural varieties as *al-Salibiyyah*—the Crusade. This new Crusade, while less violent, has exerted a more powerful impact on the Islamic world than did the medieval invasions by Christian warriors. In the new crusade of economic and cultural colonialism the Muslim world has been positioned as dependent on the United States, and major cultural displacements have resulted from modernization and economic development programs. In the Muslim world—as well as in the societies populated by other religions—individuals have been taken aback by the secular dimensions of the new colonialism. In response they have turned to a literal and insular fundamentalist version of their faiths. As they fight back against those they perceive as the infidels, they replace the central values of generosity, love, and justice with more and more strident forms of intolerance and hatred.[42] The Western/U.S. retaliation for the violent acts that come out of this fundamentalist intolerance increases the cycle of hatred and violence.

Recognition of this complexity and diversity in the Islamic world and the one-dimensional representations of the politics of knowledge we are referring to here as the miseducation demands a pedagogical revolution. Such a revolution would involve

- understanding the United States from the perspectives of diverse groups around the world,
- gaining a historical awareness of the relationship between the United States and the rest of the world, and
- appreciating the reasons many individuals around the world claim that the U.S. population is historically and politically uninformed.

Without these insights, without an understanding of the nature of the way U.S. power operates in the world, America is entering into a dangerous period where wars with perceived threats to the American Empire will be the order of the day. We do not believe that the United States, like many militarily overextended empires before it, will survive such a future. As a result of the miseducation, the United States encounters every new international circumstance as if it is a totally new situation, completely unrelated to colonial histories and global political and economic issues. This is analogous to the tragic Alzheimer's patient who wakes up every morning to discover yet again—as if for the first time—that her husband has died.

A complex and rigorous education ignores the right-wing call to dispose of multiculturalism and diversity in our schools.[43] A rigorous and critical education analyzes both the United States and the world as well as the U.S. relationship to the world. Teachers, students, and citizens must understand how knowledge is produced about these subjects as well as the ways that power shapes the types of knowledge to which we have access. The questions of where we get our knowledge, how is it produced, and whose interests it serves grant us access to one of the most important concerns of our time—the politics of knowledge in an age of electronic media. When the advocates of a right-wing politics of knowledge openly discourage us from exploring diverse knowledge and perspectives, our mendacity detectors should detonate. Such a policy is not compatible with a democratic society, not to mention a democratic education. A key dimension of a democratic education involves a literacy of power that enables an individual to explore the relation between power and knowledge, to expose the imprint of power on the knowledge that confronts us. "Inevitable civilizational conflicts" has a Fascist ring to it, as it forces us into direct conflict with Islamic others. If the conflict is inevitable, then we might as well go ahead and take their oil fields, because they're just going to use the oil money to attack us anyway. I suggest a preemptive strike—we have no choices.

An Education for the New American Empire in the Twenty-First Century

A literacy of power helps us understand that the United States has entered a new phase in its national development. The American Empire in the first decade of the twenty-first century stands ready to use military action to defend its economic and geopolitical interests whenever necessary. Under the rhetorical cover of fighting for democracy and liberation, the United States seeks a new form of global domination. Most of the time it will avoid directly ruling a nation, opting instead for installing friendly governments that allow U.S. economic and cultural domination. These friendly governments face few restrictions around issues of democracy or human rights as long as they create friendly business climates for American corporations. In these good business climates the nation's land, labor, markets, and natural resources are open to exploitation by transnational corporations.[44]

In the name of democracy the United States has supported dictators and tyrants in the Islamic world, including Saddam Hussein before the First

Gulf War and Osama bin Laden in the Afghan fight against the Soviets. Wrapped in the flag of freedom the United States has insisted that Muslim governments silence the voices that criticize American policies in the region.[45] Such contradictions are repressed in the mainstream media and in the right-wing politics of knowledge in general. As William Damon writes in his chapter in the Fordham report,

To understand that freedom and democracy must be defended, young people need to know three things: 1) What life is like in places that honor these ideals and in places that don't; 2) How these ideals have come to prevail in some places and not in others; and 3) Why some people hate these ideals and what we must do about that.[46]

If it were only that simple and free from contradictions. Damon's first two points reference the simplistic binarism contrasting those who support freedom and democracy (the United States) and those who don't (the despotic Muslims). His third point deals with the mission of the twenty-first-century empire: Those who hate these ideals must be dealt with so the empire can function more efficiently.

Despite the power of the U.S. corporate media to produce an information environment that refuses to refer to the American Empire or give credence to alternative views of U.S. relations with the Islamic world, many Americans still protested the Second Gulf War with Iraq. In speeches I delivered after 9/11 that explained some of the reasons for the anger many Muslims have felt toward the U.S., even politically conservative audiences were interested in the alternative information and perspectives I was providing. Audience members wisely asked why they had not heard the information I was providing. We live in an era of depoliticization where public discourse around political questions slowly fades away in a world of ideologically charged entertainment. In such a cosmos a literacy of power becomes more and more important, as we struggle to counter the miseducation that continues to shape American views of the world.

Chapter 2

September 11, Terror War, and Blowback

Douglas Kellner

On September 11, 2001, terrorists hijacked an American Airlines flight from Boston to Los Angeles and crashed it into the North Tower of the World Trade Center in New York City. Within minutes a second plane hit the South Tower. During the same hour, another hijacked jetliner hit the Pentagon, while a fourth plane, perhaps destined for a White House crash landing, went down in Pennsylvania, possibly at the hands of passengers who had learned of the earlier terrorist crimes and struggled to prevent another calamity.

The world stood transfixed at the graphic videos of the skyscrapers exploding and discharging a great cloud of rubble, while heroic workers struggling to save the people inside were themselves victims of the unpredictable collapse of the towers and shifting debris. The World Trade Center's twin towers, the largest buildings in New York City and potent symbol of global capitalism, were gone, and the mighty symbol of American military power, the mythically shaped and configured Pentagon, was severely wounded. Terrorists celebrated their victory over the American colossus, and the world focused on the media spectacle of America under attack and reeling from the now highly feared effects of terrorism.

Momentous historical events like the September 11 terrorist attacks and the subsequent U.S. response, military and otherwise, test social theories and provide a challenge to give a convincing account of the event and its consequences. They also provide scholars in the discipline of cultural studies an opportunity to trace how the discourses of social theory play themselves out in the media, as well as to test how the dominant media perform their democratic role of providing accurate information and discussion and assuming a responsible role in times of crisis. In these remarks, I first suggest how certain dominant social theories were put into question during the momentous and world-shaking events of fall 2001; how highly problematic positions generated by contemporary social theory circulated through the media; and how the media on the whole performed disastrously and dangerously, whipping up war hysteria while failing to provide a coherent account of what happened, why it happened, and what would count as responsible responses to the terrorist attacks. I also argue that a combination of critical social theory and cultural studies can help illuminate the September events as well as their causes, effects, and importance in shaping the contemporary moment.

Social Theory, Falsification, and the Events of History

Social theories generalize from historical experience and provide accounts of historical events or periods that attempt to map, illuminate, and perhaps criticize dominant social relations, institutions, forms, and trends of a given historical epoch. In turn, they can be judged by the extent to which they account for, interpret, and criticize contemporary conditions, or predict future events or developments. One dominant social theory of the past two decades, outlined in Francis Fukuyama's *The End of History*, was strongly put into question by the events of September 11 and their aftermath.[1] For Fukuyama, the collapse of Soviet communism and the triumph of Western capitalism and democracy in the early 1990s constituted "the end of history." This signified for him "the end point of mankind's ideological evolution and the universalization of Western liberal democracy as the final form of human government."[2] While there may be conflicts in places like the Third World, overall, according to Fukuyama, liberal democracy has triumphed, and future struggles will devolve into resolving mundane economic and technical problems; as a result the future will accordingly be rather mundane and boring.

Samuel Huntington polemicizes against Fukuyama's "one world: euphoria and harmony" model in his *The Clash of Civilizations and the Remaking of World Order*.[3] For Huntington, the future holds a series of clashes between "the West" and "the rest." Huntington rejects a number of other models of contemporary history, including a "realist" model that holds that nation-states are primary players on the world scene and will continue to form alliances and coalitions that will play themselves out in various conflicts, as well as a "chaos" model that discerns no mappable order or structure.

For Huntington, culture provides unifying and integrating principles of order and harmony, and he delineates seven or eight different civilizations that are likely to come into conflict with one another, including Islam, China, Russia, and Latin America. I will argue in this chapter that while Huntington's model seems to have some purchase in the currently emerging global encounter with terrorism and is becoming a new conservative ideology, it tends to overly homogenize both Islam and the West as well as the other civilizations he depicts. Moreover, as we shall see, his model lends itself to pernicious misuse, as I suggest in the following section. I will argue in a later section that Chalmers Johnson's model of "blowback"[4] provides a more convincing account of the 9/11 terrorist attacks that better contextualizes, explains, and even predicts such events and that it also provides cogent suggestions concerning viable and inappropriate responses to global terrorism. First, however, I will suggest how social discourses work themselves into the media as well as public policy debates and can inform or legitimate certain practices.

Social Discourses, the Media, and the Crisis of Democracy

On the day of the terrorist attacks on the World Trade Center and the Pentagon, and the years that have followed, the television networks brought out an array of national security intellectuals, ranging from the right to the far right, to explain the horrific events. The Fox Network presented former UN ambassador and Reagan administration apologist Jeane Kirkpatrick, who quickly rolled out a simplified version of Huntington's clash of civilizations, arguing that we were at war with Islam. Of course, Kirkpatrick was the most discredited intellectual of her generation, legitimating Reagan administration alliances with unsavory fascists and terrorists as necessary to beat Soviet totalitarianism. Her discourse was premised on a distinction between fascism and communist totalitarianism that argued that alliances with authoritarian or right-wing terrorist organizations or states were defensible since they were open to reform efforts or historically undermined themselves and disappeared, while Soviet totalitarianism had never collapsed, was an intractable and dangerous foe, and must thus be fought to the death with any means necessary. Of course, the Soviet Union collapsed in the early 1990s, along with its empire, and although Kirkpatrick was totally discredited by most scholars in political science, she was awarded a professorship at Georgetown University and allowed to continue to circulate her bizarre interpretations of world events.

On the afternoon of September 11, Ariel Sharon, prime minister of Israel, himself implicated in war crimes in Sabra and Shatila in Lebanon in 1982, came on television to convey his regret, condolences, and assurance of Israel's support in the war on terror. He called for a coalition against terrorism, which would contrast the free world with terrorism, representing the good versus the bad, humanity versus the bloodthirsty, the free world against the forces of darkness who are trying to destroy freedom and our way of life.

Curiously, the Bush administration would take up the same tropes, with Bush attacking the "evil" of the terrorists, using the word five times in his first statement on the September 11 terror assaults and repeatedly portraying the conflict as a war between good and evil in which the United States was going to "eradicate evil from the world," "smoke out and pursue...evildoers, those barbaric people."[5] The semantically insensitive and dyslexic Bush administration also used cowboy metaphors, calling for bin Laden "dead or alive," and described the campaign as a "crusade," until Bush was advised that this term carried heavy historical baggage from earlier wars between Christians and Muslims. And the Pentagon at first named the war against terror "Operation Infinite Justice," until they were advised that only God could dispense "infinite justice" and that Americans and others might be disturbed about a war expanding to infinity.

Disturbingly, in mentioning the goals of the war, Bush never mentioned "democracy," and the new name for the campaign became "Operation Enduring Freedom," while the Bush administration's mantra became that the war against terrorism was being fought for "freedom." But we know from the history of political theory and history itself that freedom must be paired with equality, or things like justice, rights, and democracy, to provide adequate political theory and legitimation for political action. As we shall see, the contempt for democracy and self-autonomy that has characterized U.S. foreign policy in the Middle East for the past decades is a prime reason that groups and individuals in the area passionately hate the United States.

In his speech to Congress the week following 9/11, Bush described the conflict as a war between freedom and fear, between "those governed by fear" who "want to destroy our wealth and freedoms" and those on the side of freedom. Note that all of the dominant right-wing and Bush administration discourses are fundamentally manichaean, positing a binary opposition between good and evil, us and them, civilization and barbarism. Such dualism can hardly be sustained in empirical and theoretical analysis of the contemporary moment. In fact, there is much fear and poverty in "our" world, and there is wealth, freedom, and security in the Arab and Islamic worlds—at least for privileged elites. No doubt freedom, fear, and wealth are distributed in both worlds, so to polarize these categories and make them the principle of war is highly irresponsible. And associating oneself with "good" while making one's enemy "evil" is another exercise in binary reductionism and projection of all traits of aggression and wickedness onto the other while constituting oneself as good and pure.

Of course, terroristic and theocratic Islamic fundamentalists themselves engage in similar simplistic binary discourse. For certain manichaean Islamic fundamentalists, the United States is evil, the source of all the world's problems, and deserves to be destroyed. Such one-dimensional thought does not distinguish between U.S. policies, people, or institutions while advocating a jihad, or holy war against the American evil. The terrorist crimes of September 11 appeared to be part of this jihad, and the monstrous acts of killing innocent civilians shows the horrific consequences of totally dehumanizing an "enemy" deemed so evil that even innocent members of the group in question deserve to be exterminated.

Many commentators on U.S. television offered similarly one-sided and Manichaean accounts of the cause of the September 11 events, blaming their favorite opponents in the current U.S. political spectrum as the source of the terror assaults. For fundamentalist Christian ideologue Jerry Falwell, and with the verbal agreement of Christian Broadcast Network president Pat Robertson, the culpability for this "horror beyond words" fell on liberals, feminists, gays, and the American Civil Liberties Union. Jerry Falwell said, and Pat Robertson agreed: "The abortionists have got to bear some burden for this because God will not be mocked. And when we destroy 40 million little innocent babies, we make God mad. I really believe that the pagans, and the abortionists, and the feminists, and the gays and the lesbians who are actively trying to make that an alternative lifestyle, the ACLU, People for the American Way—all of them who have tried to secularize America—I point the finger in their face and say, 'You helped this happen.'"[6] In fact, this argument is similar to a right-wing Islamic claim that the United States is fundamentally corrupt and evil and thus deserves God's wrath, an argument made by Falwell critics that forced the fundamentalist fanatic to apologize.

For other right-wingers, like Gary Aldrich, president and founder of the Patrick Henry Center, it was the liberals who were at fault: "Excuse me if I absent myself from the national political group-hug that's going on. You see, I believe the liberals are largely responsible for much of what happened Tuesday, and may God forgive them. These people exist in a world that lies beyond the normal standards of decency and civility."[7] For other rightists, like Rush Limbaugh, it was all Bill Clinton's fault, and election thief manager James Baker[8] blamed the catastrophe on the 1976 Church report that put limits on the CIA.[9]

On the issue of "what to do," right-wing columnist and poster girl Ann Coulter declaimed: "We know who the homicidal maniacs are. They are the ones cheering and dancing right now. We should invade their countries, kill their leaders and convert them to Christianity."[10] While Bush was declaring a "crusade" against terrorism and the Pentagon was organizing "Operation Infinite Justice," Bush administration deputy defense secretary Paul Wolfowitz said the administration's retaliation would be "sustained and broad and effective" and that the United States "will use all our resources. It's not just simply a matter of capturing people and holding them accountable, but removing the sanctuaries, removing the support systems, ending states who sponsor terrorism."

Such all-out war hysteria was the order of the day, and throughout September 11 and its aftermath ideological warhorses like William Bennett came out and urged that the United States declare war on Iraq, Iran, Syria, Libya, and whoever else harbored terrorists. On the Canadian Broadcasting Network, former Reagan administration deputy secretary of defense and military commentator Frank Gaffney suggested, to the astonishment and derision of the Canadian audience, that the United States needed to go after the sponsors of these states, such as China and Russia, as well. And right-wing talk radio and the Internet buzzed with talk of dropping nuclear bombs on Afghanistan, exterminating all Muslims, and whatever other fantasies popped into their unhinged heads.

My point is that broadcast television allowed dangerous and arguably deranged zealots to vent and circulate the most aggressive, fanatic, and downright lunatic views, creating a consensus for the need for immediate military action and all-out war. The television networks themselves featured logos such as "War on America," "America's New War," and other inflammatory slogans that assumed that the United States was at war and that only a military response was appropriate. I saw no cooler heads on any of the major television networks that repeatedly beat the war drums day after day, without even the relief of commercials for three days straight, driving the country into hysteria and terrifying rational and sane citizens throughout the world.

This was one of the most disgusting and upsetting performances by U.S. broadcasting networks that I have ever seen. The unrelenting war hysteria and utter failure to produce anything near a coherent analysis of what happened and reasonable response to the terrorist attacks put on display the frightening consequences of allowing corporate media institutions to hire ideologically compliant news teams who have no competency to deal with complex political events and who allow the most irresponsible views to circulate. I saw few, if any, intelligent or complex presentations of the complexity of U.S. history in the Middle East, accounts of the origins of bin Laden and his network that discussed the complicity of the United States in training, funding, arming, and supporting the groups that became Islamic fundamentalist terrorists. Nor did I see any accounts that went into the U.S. relations with the Taliban, the multifaceted U.S. role in Afghanistan, or the complications of Middle East politics that would make immediate retaliatory military action extremely dangerous and potentially catastrophic. Such alternative information circulated through the media, including major newspapers, but rarely found its way onto American television, which emerges at this point in our current crisis as a thoroughly irresponsible source of information and understanding.

Fortunately, there is a wealth of informed analysis and interpretation on the Internet, as well as a respectable archive of books and articles on the complexity of U.S. foreign policy and Middle East history. Drawing on these sources, in the following section, I argue that the causes of the September 11 events and their aftermath are highly complex and involve, for starters, the failure of U.S. intelligence and interventionist foreign policy since the late 1970s, and the policies of the Carter, Reagan, Clinton, and both Bush administrations.[11] In other words, there is no one cause or faction responsible for the catastrophe but a wide range of blame to be ascribed. Taking into account the history and complexity of the issues involved, I argue that Chalmers Johnson's model of "blowback" provides the most convincing account of how U.S. policy and institutions contributed to producing the worst terrorist crime in U.S. history, with destructive consequences still threatening.[12]

The Bush Administrations, the CIA, and Blowback

In this section, I will argue that the events of September 11 can be seen as a textbook example of blowback since bin Laden and the radical Islamic forces associated with the al-Qaida network were supported, funded, trained, and armed by several U.S. administrations and by the CIA. In this reading, the CIA's catastrophic failure was that not only did it not detect the danger of the event and take action to prevent it, but that it also actively contributed to producing the groups that are implicated in the terrorist attacks on the United States.

Chalmers Johnson develops the term "blowback" as follows: "The term 'blowback,' which officials of the Central Intelligence Agency first invented for their own internal use, is starting to circulate among students of international relations. It refers to the unintended consequences of policies that were kept secret from the American people. What the daily press reports as the malign acts of 'terrorists' or 'drug lords' or 'rogue states' or 'illegal arms merchants' often turn out to be blowback from earlier operations."[13]

Johnson provides a wealth of examples of blowback from problematic U.S. foreign policy maneuvers and covert actions that had unintended consequences, as when the United States became associated with support of terrorist groups or authoritarian regimes in Asia, Latin America, or the Middle East and its clients turned on their sponsors. In Johnson's sense, September 11 is a classic example of blowback, in which U.S. policies generated unintended consequences that had catastrophic effects on U.S. citizens, New York City, and the American and, indeed, the global economy. As I suggest in the following analysis, U.S. policy in Afghanistan at the end of the Cold War and to the present contributed to the heinous events of September 11. In the useful summary of Alexander Cockburn and Jeffrey St. Clair:

In April of 1978 an indigenous populist coup overthrew the government of Mohammed Daoud, who had formed an alliance with the man the U.S. had installed in Iran, Reza Pahlevi, aka the Shah. The new Afghan government was led by Noor Mohammed Taraki, and the Taraki administration embarked, albeit with a good deal of urban intellectual arrogance, on land reform, hence an attack on the opium-growing feudal estates. Taraki went to the UN, where he managed to raise loans for crop substitution for the poppy fields.

Taraki also tried to bear down on opium production in the border areas held by fundamentalists, since the latter were using opium revenues to finance attacks on Afghanistan's central government, which they regarded as an unwholesome incarnation of modernity that allowed women to go to school and outlawed arranged marriages and the bride price. Accounts began to appear in the western press along the lines of this from the *Washington Post,* to the effect that the mujahideen liked to "torture their victims by first cutting off their noses, ears and genitals, then removing one slice of skin after another."

At that time the mujahiddeen was not only getting money from the CIA but from Libya's Moammar Q'addaffi who sent them $250,000. In the summer of 1979 the U.S. State Department produced a memo making it clear how the U.S. government saw the stakes, no matter how modern minded Taraki might be or how feudal the Muj. It's another passage Nat might read to the grandkids: "The United States' larger interest would be served by the demise of the Taraki-Amin regime, despite whatever set backs this might mean for future social and economic reforms in Afghanistan. The overthrow of the DRA [Democratic Republic of Afghanistan] would show the rest of the world, particularly the Third World, that the Soviets' view of the socialist course of history being inevitable is not accurate."[14]

Thus, a highly problematic U.S. intervention in the late 1970s in a civil war in Afghanistan, which in retrospect appears as the last great conflict of the Cold War, helped create the context for the current crisis. As a response to U.S. intervention, the Soviet Union in 1978 sent in troops to prop up the moderate socialist and modernizing Taraki regime that was opposed by Islamic fundamentalists in the country. After Taraki was killed by Afghan army officers in September 1979, the Soviets invaded in force in December 1979 and set up a government to avoid a fundamentalist Islam and U.S.-backed takeover.

In the 1980s, the United States began more aggressively supporting Islamic fundamentalist jihad groups, and the Afghanistan project was a major covert foreign policy project of the Reagan and Bush administrations. During this period, the CIA trained, armed, and financed precisely those Islamic fundamentalist groups that later became part of the al-Qaida terror network and those Islamic fundamentalist groups that are now the nemesis of the West, the new "evil empire."

In the battle to defeat Soviet communism in the Cold War, both the Saudis and the United States poured billions into Afghanistan to train "freedom fighters" who would overthrow the allegedly communist regime. This was a major project, with some estimates as high as $40 billion going into training and arming radical Islamic groups that would emerge with a desire to fight other great wars for Islam. Among these groups were Osama bin Laden and others who would later form his al-Qaida network.

In 1989, Soviet troops left Afghanistan in defeat, and a civil war continued for the next several years. The Bush administration, in one of its most cynical and fateful decisions, decided to completely pull out of Afghanistan rather than work toward building democracy and a viable government in that country. They had other fish to fry—in particular Iraq, another Bush I administration intervention that had momentous consequences.[15] After arousing the Arab world in hatred against the U.S. military intervention in Iraq at the end of the First Gulf War in 1991, the Bush administration persuaded the Saudi government to allow the United States to continue to position its forces in the holy land of Islam—another fateful event that has generated blowback effects yet to be fully perceived. For it was the permanent positioning of U.S. troops in what was perceived as the Islamic holy land, Saudi Arabia, that especially angered bin Laden and more radical Islamic groups. When Saudi Arabia continued to allow the presence of U.S. troops after the First Gulf War, bin Laden broke with his country and was declared persona non grata by the Saudis for his provocative statements and behavior. It was also reported at this time that the Saudis put out a contract on bin Laden's life, supposedly with the assent of the first Bush administration,[16] although assassination attempts seemed to have failed.

Meanwhile, as civil war raged in Afghanistan in the mid-1990s, Pakistani military and intelligence groups, with the support of the CIA, funded and organized one particularly fanatical Islamic group, the Taliban, which eventually took control over much of the country. With its promises to stabilize the region, the Taliban gained recognition from the U.S. and Pakistan governments, but not the UN or much of the rest of the world, which recognized the National Alliance groups fighting the Taliban as the legitimate representatives of Afghanistan.

Moreover, by the mid- to late 1990s, bin Laden established al-Qaida, an organization of former Afghanistan holy war veterans. In February 1998, he issued a statement, endorsed by several extremist Islamic groups, declaring it the duty of all Muslims to kill U.S. citizens—civilian or military—and their allies everywhere. The bombing of U.S. embassies was ascribed to the bin Laden/al-Qaida network, and the Clinton administration responded by shooting 70 cruise missiles at a chemical weapons factory in Sudan supposedly owned by bin Laden and at camps in Afghanistan that allegedly were populated by bin Laden and his group. The factory in Sudan turned out to be a pharmaceutical company, and the camps in Afghanistan were largely deserted, producing another embarrassment for U.S. policy in the Middle East. Clinton later claimed that his administration also was plotting to assassinate bin Laden but that a change of Pakistani government disrupted the plot. That would make two U.S. administration plots to assassinate the Islamic leader, who was obviously hardened against the United States by such policies.

Though this is rarely mentioned in the mainstream media, the first Bush administration became one of the largest financial supporters of the Taliban, providing over $100 million this year in what it deemed "humanitarian aid," as well as a supplemental grant of $43 million in May 2001 for the Taliban's promise to declare opium production "un-Islamic" and thus to cut back on a potent source of the world's drug trade. Given that the Taliban has allegedly been a major exporter of opium, which is Afghanistan's major cash crop, it raises eyebrows in knowledgeable circles as to why the Bush administration would have trusted the Taliban to cut back on opium production. Moreover, a story is circulating that the Bush administration was acting in the interests of the UNOCAL consortium to build an oil pipeline across Afghanistan. This project had purportedly led the oil company to encourage the United States to support the Taliban in the first place, since they were deemed the group most likely to stabilize Afghanistan and allow the pipeline to be built.[17]

The Taliban, of course, were a highly theocratic and repressive fundamentalist regime that some have described as "clerical fascism" (Chip Berlet) or "reactionary tribalism" (Robert Antonio).[18] Their treatment of women is notorious, as is their cultural totalitarianism that led to the banning of books and media and the destruction of Buddhist statues. Like the Saudis, the Taliban practice a form of Wahabism, a derogatory term applied to a particularly virulent strain of Muslim fundamentalism. The Taliban have also been the hosts of Osima bin Laden and the al-Qaida network since it was expelled from Sudan in 1996 due to U.S. pressure and insistence. Although bin Laden and al-Qaida were deemed enemies of the United States because of their alleged involvement in a series of terrorist crimes, for some reason the Clinton and Bush administrations continued to provide support to and curry favor with the Taliban group that hosted and protected them.

Consequently, the events of September 11 should be seen in the context of support, continuing from the late 1970s through the Reagan-Bush years to the present, by several U.S. administrations and the CIA for the perpetrators of the monstrous assaults on the United States. This is not to simply blame U.S. policy in Afghanistan for the terrorist attacks of September 11, but it provides a framework within which the events can be interpreted. Of course, other flaws of U.S. foreign policy over the past decades have helped generate enemies of the United States in the Middle East and elsewhere. These include excessive U.S. support for Israel and inadequate support for the Palestinians, U.S. support of authoritarian regimes, and innumerable misdeeds of the American Empire over the past decades that have been documented by Chomsky, Herman, Johnson, and other critics of U.S. foreign policy.[19]

Terrorism and Terror War: Operation Enduring Freedom and the Dangers of Infinite Blowback

Though no doubt there were a multiplicity of contributing factors, 9/11 can be read as a blowback of major policies of successive U.S. administrations and the CIA, who trained, funded, supported, and armed the groups alleged to have carried out the terrorist attacks on the United States—and certainly all circumstantial and other evidence points to these groups. The obvious lesson is that it is highly dangerous and potentially costly to align one's country with terrorist groups; that support of groups or individuals who promote terrorism is likely to come back to haunt you; and that it is dangerous to make Machiavellian pacts with obviously dangerous groups and individuals, as the Bush administration is continuing to do.

After several weeks following the September 11 terror attacks, the global community appeared to be building an effective strategy to address the attacks. But on Sunday, October 7, just short of one month after the attacks, the Bush administration unleashed a full-scale military assault on Afghanistan, purportedly to annihilate the bin Laden network and to destroy the Taliban regime in Afghanistan that had hosted it. The unilateralism of the U.S. response was striking. Indeed, leading American newspapers provided a rationale for U.S. rejection of a UN-led or NATO-led coalition against international terrorism:

In the leadup to a possible military strike, senior administration and allied officials said Mr. Rumsfeld's approach this week made clear that the United States intends to make it as much as possible an all-American campaign.

One reason, they said, is that the United States is determined to avoid the limitations on its targets that were imposed by NATO allies during the 1999 war in Kosovo, or the hesitance to topple a leader that members of the gulf war coalition felt in 1991.

"Coalition is a bad word, because it makes people think of alliances," said Robert Oakley, former head of the State Department's counter-terrorism office and former ambassador to Pakistan. A senior administration official put it more bluntly: "The fewer people you have to rely on, the fewer permissions you have to get."[20]

And so on October 7, the United States unleashed an assault on Afghanistan, with minimal British military support, assuring that the United States and Britain would eventually pay for the attack with the lives of their citizens in later Islamic terrorist retribution. Announcing the attack in a speech from the Oval Office, George W. Bush proclaimed that Afghanistan was being attacked because the Taliban had refused to hand over bin Laden, and thus "the Taliban will pay a price. By destroying camps and disrupting communications we will make it more difficult for the terror network to train new recruits and coordinate their evil plans."

Within the hour, in a startling interruption of the mainstream media's pro-U.S. military intervention in Afghanistan, the networks released a video feed of a speech from bin Laden and his chief partners in crime, obviously fed to the Qatar-based al-Jazeera network in advance. Playing to an Arab audience, Ayman al-Zawahri, the Egyptian doctor who many believed to be a major political and strategic force in the al-Qaida terrorist network, described U.S. support of Israel; failure of the United States to help produce a Palestinian state; the U.S. assault against Iraq in the First Gulf War with a subsequent stationing of U.S. troops in Saudi Arabia, the Arab Holy Land; and other Arab grievances.

Then bin Laden himself appeared, in his now familiar turban and camouflage jacket, with an assault rifle by his side and the Afghan landscape with a cave behind him. In ornate Arabic, translated erratically by the network translators who were trying to render his speech into English, bin Laden praised the attack on America that "destroyed its buildings" and created "fear from North to South," praising God for this attack. Calling for a jihad to "destroy America," bin Laden attacked the "debauched," "oppressive" Americans who have "followed injustice" and exhorted every Muslim to join the jihad. The world was now divided, bin Laden insisted, into two sides, "the side of believers and the side of infidels," and everyone who stands with America is a "coward" and an "infidel."

Remarkably, bin Laden's Manichaean dualism mirrored the discourse of Sharon, Bush, and those in the West who proclaimed the war against terrorism as a holy war between good and evil, civilization and barbarism. Both dichotomized their other as dominated by fear—Bush claimed that his holy war marked freedom versus fear, while bin Laden's jihad poised fearful America against his brave warriors, characterizing his battle as that of justice versus injustice. Both appealed as well to God, revealing a similar fundamentalist absolutism and Manichaeanism, and both characterized the other as "evil."

As the U.S. war machine campaign unfolded, the Bush administration backed away from personalizing the conflict as one between Bush and bin

Laden, perhaps recalling how the first Bush presidency collapsed in part because Bush senior was not able to remove Saddam Hussein, the person-ification of evil in the Gulf War who continued to taunt the United States and who many believed supported the al-Qaida terrorist network.

Although I have referred to "bin Laden" throughout my analysis, I think that it is a mistake to personalize the September 11 events, or to con-tribute to the demonization of bin Laden, the flip side of which is deifica-tion, which no doubt is what he and some of his followers want. "Bin Laden" is better interpreted as what Sorel called a "revolutionary myth," a figurehead for a network and movement to which his opponents ascribe great power and evil, while his followers ascribe wondrous effectivity and good to the name.[21] In fact, there appears to be a worldwide radical Islamic theocratic network that has taken up terrorism and "propaganda of the deed" to help produce a holy war between the East and West, and it appears certain that the problems of terrorism will not be solved by the arrest or elimination of bin Laden and top members of his al-Qaida net-work, who Bush put on top of a "most wanted" list on October 10, 2001.

It should also be made clear that al-Qaida's interpretation of Islam goes against a mainstream reading of the Koran that prohibits suicide as well as violence against children and innocents, and that in no way promises sainthood or eternal happiness to terrorists. Islam, like Christianity, is complex and contested, with various schools, branches, and sects. To homogenize Islam is precisely to play the game of bin Laden and his asso-ciates, who want to construct a Manichaean dualism of Islam versus the West. In fact, just as the West is divided into highly complex blocs of com-peting ideologies, interests, states, regions, and groups, so too is Islam and the Arab world highly divided and conflicted. Only by grasping the com-plexity of the contemporary world can one begin to solve intractable prob-lems like international terrorism.

Endless Terror and the Infinite Terror War

As the United States continued its bombing campaign in October and threatened to expand its campaign against terrorism to states like Iraq, wor-ries began to circulate that U.S. military intervention might create more problems than it would solve. When U.S. Secretary of Defense Donald Rumsfeld likened the war on terror to the Cold War, which lasted more than 50 years, the specter of endless war was invoked. Perhaps this is what the Pentagon had in mind when it first named the military intervention "Oper-ation Infinite Justice." Although war throughout the new millennium would keep America's troops fully employed and the Pentagon budget ever escalating, it would keep U.S. citizens in a state of fear from terrorist retalia-tion, for endless war would no doubt generate endless terror.

Indeed, hysteria and fear reigned throughout the United States after it was reported that the Bush administration believed a significant terrorist response to their military intervention was certain. Reports of an isolated anthrax attack in Florida mushroomed when it was reported that a second case had also appeared in Florida, and that the source was a building that housed the *National Enquirer* and other tabloids that had relentlessly demonized bin Laden, his network, and the Taliban. Reports circulated that a Middle Eastern intern who had worked in the building left an email, while another report indicated that the *Sun* tabloid had received a "weird love letter to Jennifer Lopez" with a "soapy, powdery substance" and a Star of David charm in the letter, evoking the specter of an anthrax-infected postal system that could attack anyone.

Throughout the day of October 9, hysteria in the United States escalated. People were calling in the police when powdery substances appeared in letters and offices, while frantic tabloid representatives tried to assure the public that buying their papers would not expose them to anthrax. There was a run on anthrax antibiotics in Florida and elsewhere, and bioterrorism threats closed an Internal Revenue center in Kentucky and a subway in Washington, D.C.[22]

Meanwhile, things were not appearing to go well on the war front. Although the United States could claim to control Afghanistan's airspace, this did not amount to much. Reports of collateral damage were beginning to circulate, including the death of four UN workers killed by the U.S. bombing. Most ominously, from throughout the world came regional reports of potential worrisome responses to the U.S. military adventure. Pakistan was scarred by riots, and there were fears of upheaval and perhaps a long-simmering explosion of tensions with neighboring India. Although British and U.S. TV networks had engaged in relentless war propaganda for the first several days of the bombing, on October 9 both BBC TV in Britain and ABC TV in the United States were remarkably critical, citing civilian damage and the killing of UN workers in the Afghanistan bombing, the anthrax scare and hysteria in the United States, refugee problems in Afghanistan, and protests in the Arab world. The reports also cited problems with the food deliveries that were supposed to legitimate the intervention and construct it as a humanitarian operation to benefit the Afghan people. Aid workers from the UN and other organizations indicated that the U.S. military intervention had made it impossible for agencies to continue their food delivery, that the food dropped by the U.S. was totally inadequate, and that dropping food in mine-laden Afghanistan was highly dangerous to the people.

Worries were also circulating about how the United States could afford its intervention and the impact of the intervention on the global economy. In October it was reported that there would be no surplus for 2001; that the United States would once again plunge into deficit spending, as it had during the earlier Reagan-Bush years; and that the entire global economy was in peril because of the turmoil. In response to calls for government spending to help avoid deep recession, the Bush administration responded by proposing $70 billion in additional tax cuts, most of which consisted of a capital gains tax cut for the rich. This move suggests that the Bush administration was largely a criminal enterprise organized to rob the federal treasury of money to be channeled toward its most wealthy contributors and supporters.[23]

Finally, it appeared probable that, based on the history of its past 50 years, the U.S. military would not solve the problem of terrorism and would probably make it worse. The U.S. military had failed to defeat communism in major interventions in Korea and Vietnam; in interventions in Lebanon and Somalia in the 1980s and 1990s it had retreated in disgrace after some of its troops were killed. And although the $3 trillion First Gulf War had chased Iraq out of Kuwait, it left dictator Saddam Hussein intact while creating Arab enemies that continue to torment the United States. Thus, in assessing the major enemies of civilization and humanity in the new millennium, we need to equally oppose terrorism, fascism, and militarism while seeking new global solutions to such global problems as terrorism.

Against Terrorism, Fascism, and Militarism

In conclusion, I argue that one should be equally against terrorism, fascism, and militarism as three of the great evils of the past century. Indeed, in arguing that the events of September 11 can be read as blowback against specific U.S. policies by specific individuals, groups, and administrations, I am not, of course, wishing to blame the victims, nor do I associate myself with those who inventory U.S. crimes over the past several decades and see the events of September 11 as a payback for these misdeeds. Moreover, I believe that some analyses that see the events as a logical response to U.S. policy and that call for changes in U.S. policy as the solution to the events are too rationalistic in regard to both the perpetrators of the events and logical solutions to the problem.

First, the alleged terrorists appear to be highly religious and fanatical in their ideology and actions, in a way that is hard for Westerners to comprehend. In their drive for an apocalyptic jihad, they believe that they will further their goals by creating chaos, especially war between radical Islam and the West. Obviously, dialogue is not possible with such groups, but it is equally certain that an overreactive military response causing a large number of deaths among innocent civilians in a Muslim country could trigger precisely the apocalyptic explosion of violence that the fanatic terrorists dreamed of. It would seem that the group that carried out the terrorist attacks on the United States desired just such a retaliatory response, and thus to overreact militarily would be to fall into their trap and play their game—with highly dangerous consequences.

Many critics and theorists of September 11 also exaggerate the rationality of the West and fail to grasp the striking irrationality and primitive barbarism involved in the immediate response to the horror by Western politicians, intellectuals, and media representatives, some of which I documented earlier in this analysis. To carry out the retaliatory military response called for by high officials in the Bush administration, crazed intellectuals, and many ordinary citizens, repeated endlessly in the media with almost no counterdiscourse, would risk apocalypse of the most frightening kind. Unilateral American military action has created a divided Europe and America, a new generation of potential terrorists in the Islamic world, an Afghanistan where instability reigns, and an Iraq that in many ways is less safe than before the U.S. invasion in 2003.

Thus, though it is reasonable to deem international terrorism a deadly threat on a global scale and to take resolute action against terrorism, what is required is an intelligent, multifaceted response. This will require a diplomatic consensus that a global campaign against terrorism is necessary. Such a campaign would consist of the arrest of members of terrorist networks; regulation of financial institutions that allow funds to flow to terrorists; national security measures to protect citizens against terrorism; and a global criminalization of terrorist networks that mobilizes international, national, and local institutions against the terrorist threat. Some of these measures have already begun, and the conditions are ripe for developing an effective and resolute global campaign against terrorism. There is a danger, however, that excessive military action would split a potential coalition, create perhaps uncontrollable chaos, and destroy the global economy. We are living in a very dangerous period and must be extremely careful in how we respond to the events of September 11.

Therefore, I would argue for a global campaign against terrorism and not war or large-scale military action. Terrorists should be criminalized, and international and national institutions should go after terrorist networks and those who support them with appropriate legal, financial, judicial, and political instruments. Before the Bush administration's military intervention threw the world into potential chaos and collapse, an intelligent campaign was indeed under way that had arrested many participants and supporters of the bin Laden and other terror networks, that had alerted citizens throughout the world to the dangers of terrorism, and that had created the conditions for development of a global campaign against terror.

I also suggest that another lesson of September 11 is that it is now totally appropriate to be completely against terrorism, to use the term in the arsenal of critical social theory, and to declare it unacceptable and indefensible in the modern world. There was a time when it was argued that one person's "terrorism" was another person's "national liberation movement" or "freedom fighter," and that the term was thus an ideological concept not to be used in politically and theoretically correct discourse—a position that Reuters continues to follow, according to one report.

In terms of modern or postmodern epistemological debates, I am not arguing for absolutism or universalism. At times in history "terrorism" was an arguably defensible tactic used by those engaged in struggles against fascism, as in World War II, or in national liberation struggles, as in the American or various Third World revolutions against oppressive European empires and colonialism. In the current situation, however, when terrorism is a clear and present danger to innocent civilians throughout the world, it seems unacceptable to advocate, carry out, or defend terrorism against civilian populations because of the lethality of modern weapons, the immorality of indiscriminate crime, and the explosiveness of the present situation when terror on one side could unleash genocidal, even species-cidal, terror as a retaliatory response.

It is therefore the time for neither terrorism nor military retaliation, but for a global campaign against terrorism that deploys all legal, political, and morally defensible means to destroy the network of terrorists responsible for the September 11 events. Such a global response would put terrorist groups on notice that their activity is not acceptable and will be strongly opposed, and thus construes "terrorism" as a moral and political malevolence not to be accepted or defended.

I would append that progressives should be now, as previously, against fascism. The supposed perpetrators of the September 11 events were allegedly both terrorists and fascistic Islamic fundamentalists who support a theocratic state that would abrogate human rights and employ torture and murder in the name of supposedly higher theological values. In the contemporary world, such fascism should be opposed, and more democratic and progressive modern values and democratic politics should be defended.

I am reluctant to defend, however, U.S. military interventionism in Afghanistan—not to mention Iraq—on the grounds that the problem of terrorism is largely a global one that requires a global solution through global institutions and not unilateral military action. The U.S. military intervention is likely to make the situation worse and evoke endless terrorist response. Thus, while I support a global campaign against terrorism, especially the al-Qaida network, that could include military action under UN or other global auspices, I would not trust U.S. unilateral military action for reasons already laid out in this study—reasons based on U.S. failures in the region and a sustained history of supporting the most reactionary social forces. Moreover, one of the stakes of the current crisis and of globalization itself is whether the American Empire will come to dominate the world, or whether globalization will constitute a more democratic, cosmopolitan, pluralistic, and just world, without domination by hegemonic states or corporations. Now more than ever, global institutions are needed to deal with global problems. Those who see positive potential in globalization should renounce all national solutions to the problem of terrorism and seek global ones. Consequently, while politicians like Bill Clinton and Colin Powell have deemed terrorism "the dark side of globalization," it can also be seen as an unacceptable response to misguided and destructive imperial national policies that themselves must be transformed if a world without terror is to be possible.

Chapter 3

Loving Muslim Women with a Vengeance: The West, Women, and Fundamentalism

Loubna Skalli

Current Islamic revival, often reduced to fundamentalism and radical politics, has spawned many speculations about its causes, its implications, and the potential threats it poses to the perceived stability in the world. Western popular media frequently depicted fundamentalists as a generation of irrational Muslims full of uncontrolled anger and fury. Their women are victims of oppressive veils and walls of seclusion, awaiting delivery by the West, even if this comes in the garb of "shock and awe" military intervention.

This is clearly an abridged and simplified version of a complex set of phenomena. To talk about Muslim fundamentalism in the singular form is as grave a mistake as treating Islam, the West, and the East as monolithic entities. The tendency to insist on this singularity, then, betrays either an ignorance of or an unwillingness to recognize the intrinsically diverse and dynamic nature of their realities.

In addition, "Islamic fundamentalism" is a problematic concept that obscures the existence of a large spectrum of political positions and ideological expressions within and among Muslim countries.[1] This essay retains the concept, nonetheless, because beyond considerable differences, these religious groups reveal considerable similarities in their misogynist ideas and agendas. They virtually all seek politico-religious legitimacy through an interpretation of the scripture that is inimical to gender equity and women's dignity.

Fundamentalists, then, are a generation of Muslim youth in revolt. They are in revolt against the imposed colonial projects of modernization in their countries and the unfulfilled promises of their postcolonial political

regimes and national elite. They are in revolt against the unequal distribution of wealth and resources within and among nations, against their own
socioeconomic and political exclusions, as well as against the widening
circle of the disenfranchised classes from which most of them come. They
are in revolt against their own sense of powerlessness in the face of all the
global forces that threaten their religious and cultural identity.

More important, perhaps, fundamentalists are in revolt against the
traumatic legacy of Western colonialism that continues to destabilize the
core of their social and cultural fabric—a process kept alive, if not exacerbated, by American hegemony and its perceived homogenizing materialistic values. The West, with America at its head, is unquestionably
omnipresent in the vision, discourses, and agendas of Muslim fundamentalists.[2]

And so are Muslim women. To fundamentalists, both the West and
women are closely and intimately linked.[3] Both are a source of frustration
as well as obsessive fascination. The West is fascinating because of its challenging economic, military, and technological power. Its arrogance and
imperialistic tendencies are humiliating while its cultural values are
judged as threatening to the Muslim moral order. Muslim women, on the
other hand, are key players in preserving the spiritual unity of the Muslim
larger *umma* (community) and guaranteeing the "purity" of indigenous
cultural norms. This makes them a source of obsessive-compulsive fascination to the fundamentalist; Muslim women's tendency to reproduce
Western women's lifestyles, their increasing invasion of the public space,
and their rising feminist demands for equality and emancipation are
gravely disturbing.[4]

Women and the West: Both are linked and intertwined in the logic of
Muslim fundamentalists. Both need to be reformed, contained, and sub-
dued. From Afghanistan to Morocco, from Pakistan to Sudan, fundamentalists hope to regain control over their world by launching a moral
crusade against at least two kinds of enemies: women from within and the
West from without.

The greater the fundamentalists' frustration with and resentment of the
West, with America at its head, the tougher their oppressive measures targeting Muslim women. Strict policing of women's bodies and lives and a
retraditionalization of the Muslim family, both taken as major features of
religious ethical and moral law, are considered by virtually all fundamentalists among the viable strategies for countering Western imperialism and
curbing the impact of its powers. Re-Islamizing an already conservative
Muslim family institution and reclaiming it as the privileged site of male
power is an ambition expressed in all brands of fundamentalism.

Muslim fundamentalists, however, are neither unique nor original in
their strategic use of Muslim women to advance their politico-religious
agendas. In the late eighteenth and early nineteenth centuries, European

colonial powers saw in Muslim women a strategic tool for pacifying Arab-Muslim societies and domesticating the rebellious indigenous population. Both patriarchal ideologies have been strikingly naïve in assuming that Muslim women can be manipulated at ease with great obedience and little resistance.

This essay does not try to reduce all forms or expressions of fundamentalism to gender questions. Nor does it argue that the oppression of Muslim women by fundamentalists should be justified exclusively by colonial history. The main objective is to present a lucid understanding of how Muslim women are caught in the power games of the patriarchal forces in both their secular as well as their religious dimensions, at the local level as well as at global levels. The sections of the paper seek to explain how both women and the West are made central in the political vision and agendas of Muslim fundamentalists; how patriarchal ideology and misogynist practices bring together the most avowed enemies, Western colonial powers and Muslim fundamentalists; and how both traditions depend on Muslim women to further their different political, economic, and sociocultural interests.

At the risk of oversimplifying complex historical processes and ideologies, the first section provides a brief account of the historical context for some of the modern debates and concerns. Most examples are drawn from colonial and postcolonial Morocco, Tunisia, and Algeria (the Maghreb), although occasional references are made to the Arab-Muslim Middle East.

Revisiting the Past

It is not a truism to state today that the inferiorization of the Arab-Muslim man and the demonization of his religion facilitated the European colonialist expansion at the end of the eighteenth and beginning of the nineteenth centuries.[5] The historical implications of Bonaparte's expedition to Egypt (1798) are never overrated.[6] It launched a long chain of profound transformations in the political, socioeconomic, cultural, and ethical orders of Muslim countries. In the process, indigenous peoples were demonized and their cultures misrepresented and devalorized through a plethora of racist theories, some of which have proved to be resiliently enduring.[7]

Variations around images of "barbarism," "backwardness," "sexual promiscuity," and "animalism" characterized Europe's master colonial narrative. The West's distorted gaze has been fully documented in Edward Said's seminal work on Europe's Orientalist project. In brief, orientalism exploited real differences between Eastern and Western cultures and turned them into the logic of the superior versus the inferior race. To the Western superior being, civilized thinking and behaving was opposed by the mysterious, vicious, and inferior Oriental being. In a unique exercise of distortion of historical and cultural realities, the Orientalist project established the "us" versus "them" opposition. A vast corpus of literary, artistic, philosophical, and scientific works contributed to producing and reinforcing an impressive capital of stereotypes, most of which expressed the European white man's fantasies about the Orient more than the realities of the peoples observed.

By inferiorizing indigenous beings and their cultures, the Orientalist project served to legitimize the "civilizing mission" of Western colonialism and provide the moral prop for justifying "the white man's burden." In reality, colonialism worked toward the depersonalization of the Arab-Muslim individual—an alienating process that involves colonizing the minds of the oppressed. On the one hand, their religion and cultural heritage are continuously devalorized and their history distorted; on the other, the colonized are urged to view the "civilizing mission" as the only salutary escape from the oppressive "darkness" of their world.[8]

Muslim women were present in the European white man's fantasies and colonial policies. Women were meant to become a strategic tool for the civilizing mission.

Muslim Women in the Colonial Project

Current debates on the fate of Muslim women have roots that stretch back to the traumatic context of Western encroachment in the Arab-Muslim countries and the painful awakening (Nahda) of these societies to the realities of colonialism.[9] Muslim women were central to both the European colonial project and the Arab-Muslim reaction to it.

European colonialism used women, among other things, as key vectors of change in the process of modernizing the Arab-Muslim world and refashioning it according to the Western model of progress. The Arab-Muslim awakening relied on women to preserve the spiritual essence of the umma by helping to counter the colonialist disruptive forces and launch Islamic-based reforms. The process was never this simple, of course, and women were never entirely the passive puppets in the hands of either their local or their foreign "masters." Muslim women's resistance to divisive colonial policies was expressed through heroic deeds and deaths during the nationalistic movements and wars of liberation. Historians and feminist scholars have increasingly documented this resistance.[10]

Nonetheless, competing ideologies and conflicting politico-economic powers positioned Muslim women in the cross-fire, as illustrated in the following discussion.

The colonial regimes revealed an exaggerated interest in the life and conditions of Muslim women. They professed to educate them and liberate them from the oppressive yokes of their religion and men. The colonialist logic attributed the backwardness of Muslim societies and the inferiority of their cultures particularly to two main observed practices: veiling and seclusion of women. These became the emblem of both women's oppression and their culture's backwardness.

During the 1909–1912 war against the Spanish occupation of Northern Morocco, a Spanish journalist reporting on the events of the day wrote in his dispatch: "How can this miserable people move forward or become civilized when women's only functions are to give babies?"[11] The same journalist would "change [his] mind only two days after making such a statement. He realized that during the observed military operations it was the women who took care of all the support services at the rear. They assisted the injured, carried them away from the field. Years later, he would record in a book that the defeat that has come upon us today…is the result of the decisive role played by Moroccan women."[12]

But such a quick change of mind was the exception that did very little to alter the colonial habit of judging other cultures by their women. The value of the Arab-Muslim cultures was directly linked to the "degradation" of women. Deeply entrenched and historically superimposed patriarchal practices were attributed directly to the core values of Islam. Dominant patriarchal and misogynist interpretations of Islam, on which are based the discriminatory gender practices in establishment Islam, were taken by colonial rulers as the sole and unique interpretation of Islam.[13]

The intrinsic merits of the Muslim faith were thus questioned and vilified. The veil and segregation were taken as an expression of the general backwardness of the cultures, and hence, all the cultural customs and norms need to be cast away and replaced by Western enlightening lifestyles.

Lord Cromer, the powerful figure of British rule in Egypt, sums up this attitude when he explains that the "complete failure" of Islam as a social system lies "first and foremost" in its degrading treatment of women. To overcome this, Egyptians must "be persuaded or forced into imbibing the true spirit of western civilization."[14]

The spokesman of the colonial power in Tunisia, Victor de Carnière, exemplifies this logic by stating that "as long as Mr. Mohamed does not take Mrs. Mohamed unveiled for a walk or to the theater, as long as Mr. and Mrs. Mustapha do not attend French receptions together, and do not in turn invite their French friends for dinner or for a cup of tea, the two races will remain separated by an insurmountable abyss."[15]

Unveiling and accessing public space, as the colonial voice from Tunisia suggests above, were expected to liberate at once the female population and civilize their cultures. While Islam and Muslim cultures were demonized for their gender practices, Western civilization was presented as the only emancipatory and egalitarian alternative. The West was presented in the colonialist discourse of white men as clearly more tolerant toward its women and less misogynist. Debunking such historically ungrounded logic about the West's attitudes toward its women has been, and still is, one of the major tasks of Western feminists.

Meanwhile, feminist scholars of Islam, gender, and the Middle East have aptly demonstrated that the colonial interest in Muslim women was neither genuine nor gender sensitive. If anything, it was the work of misogynist and imperialistic white men who held double standards about women's rights depending on their geographic positioning. Leila Ahmed has revealed that Lord Cromer, who relentlessly waged the feminist stick on Muslim men's heads, was in his Victorian society the founding member, and at times president, of the Men's League for Opposing Women's Suffrage.[16] In other words, the colonial European man was preaching in colonial lands a feminism he could neither practice nor tolerate in his own country.

In fact, he appropriated the language and logic of Western feminism and turned it against the oppressed peoples. "Remarkably," Haideh Moghissi explains, "female domesticity, and sexual purity and chastity, deemed appropriate in Europe and aggressively promoted at home, were presented for Muslim women as 'evidence' of sexual slavery and signs of peculiar moral and religious deficiency in the Other."[17]

The abolition of the veil and segregation became within the colonized Muslim societies gestures invested with more than one meaning. In the colonialist vision and narrative, they became the potent symbol of the civilizational divide between Europe and Muslim societies and the visible markers between the Superior and Inferior races. Broader political, cultural, and racial connotations were thus grafted onto the heads of women and through their movement in space. It is no accident, as Leila Ahmed cogently argues, that the "abandonment of native culture was posed as a solution for women's oppression only in colonized or dominated societies and not in Western ones."[18] No such choices were made or imposed on Western women, for instance.

Colonial gender policies succeeded in trapping struggles over cultural and national identity with much larger struggles over religious identity and nationalistic loyalty. The result is that Muslim women's demands for justice and equality have always been perceived in the Muslim world as an act of allegiance to the Western powers and betrayal of their own cultural group. This complex dynamic is clearly captured in the following statement of Leila Ahmed:

It is evident that the connection between the issues of culture and women, and more precisely between the cultures of Other men and the oppression of women, was created by Western discourse. The idea (which still informs discussions about women in the Arab and Muslim cultures and other non-Western world cultures) that improving the status of women entails abandoning native customs was the product of a particular historical moment and was constructed by an androcentric colonial establishment committed to male dominance in the service of particular political ends.[19]

The implications of this confusion have been disturbing and far-reaching. It is in these two specific areas (veil and segregation) that the struggle over cultural identity and resistance to Western hegemony have been waged and fought. It is through them that the pull of tradition and the push of modernity have been expressed, whether in the early nationalist discourses or in the current Islamization projects of fundamentalists, as the following sections will further demonstrate.

"Let's Get Them Through Their Women"[20]

In reality, the white colonial men understood the pivotal role Muslim women play in the cohesion of their social order; and hence tried to utilize them as part of the larger strategy of "divide and rule." This strategy involved trying to use the bodies and minds of Muslim women in the hope of advancing colonial interests. The abolition of the veil and the encouragement of desegregation, outwardly hailed as requirements for the emancipation of women and their progress, were utilized to destabilize Muslim societies from within.

In Algeria, for instance, a representative of the French regime suggested that if you "give women rudimentary and broad schooling...you would have introduced to the core of the Kabylie (Berber) home, into the farmer's hut, and under the tent of the shepherd, a powerful element of assimilation."[21] From the assimilation of the indigenous population to the subjugation of the whole nation, they saw but few steps. Again in Algeria, one of the French general governors recommended, "If, you convert 100 000 young indigenous girls to our civilization...these young girls, who will naturally become the privileged wives of the most important men of their class, will for ever guarantee the subjugation of the country and be the guarantee of its future assimilation."[22]

In Egypt, however, a different policy was adopted. British rule slowed down rather than accelerated the nationalist initiatives in matters of girls' education. Greater demands for schooling were discouraged simply through the institution of higher tuition fees.[23] Under the French Protectorate in Morocco (1912–1956) nationalists' initiatives to send girls to school were seriously discouraged and early formulations of the reforms of women's conditions frozen. In this context, colonial rule took a decidedly more elitist approach to education since they reserved it for the sons of the national elite. Their attitude toward women and the culture was

more paternalistic. It sought to overprotect in order to better maintain indigenous social structures intact while preserving the country's "primitive" and "exotic" aura, so much celebrated by earlier European travelers, adventurers, and anthropologists.[24]

In general, though, the colonial rule thought that the sensitive issues of women's bodies and sexuality, on which the honor of the entire Muslim patriarchal order heavily depends,[25] would prove to be a more powerful strategy to subdue resistance. Marnia Lasreg's probing into "the eloquent silence" of Algerian women documents ways in which French colonial rule turned prostitution into a tool of social coercion. The female body was used as a weapon against families that refused to collaborate with the new regime.[26] Tactic or strategy, rape was turned into a military weapon.[27]

Campaigning for the pseudo-liberation or modernization of Muslim women did not preclude their exploitation for colonial economic interests. The combined oppressive natures of colonialism and capitalism did nothing to improve the conditions of women, particularly those from the lower social strata. If anything, colonial economic policies were the foundation for the emerging feminization of the proletariat and feminization of poverty. Masses of unskilled and uneducated rural women were exploited as housemaids, field-workers, and cheap labor in fishing and canning factories. In addition, colonial capitalistic interests competed with and severely displaced the small income-generating activities of poor women.[28]

A comprehensive history of the colonial policies toward Muslim women in the Maghreb, at least, has yet to be written. Nonetheless, existing documentation already points toward the long-term legacy of such a policy on gender relations and discussions in the Muslim countries.

In the Shadow of Eternal Reforms

Daniel Rivet, a scholar of colonial North African history, states that colonization has exacerbated the masculinity of Maghrebi men. Denied an opportunity to celebrate his own history, the indigenous man sought refuge from colonial humiliation in his religion and in sexuality.[29] No doubt, religion and women have never been loved with such an obsession since.

If colonialists made Muslim women's veil and segregation central "feminist" themes in their regimes, the indigenous elite reproduced, ironically, a similar schema to combat colonialism and rebuild the emerging nation. That is, unveiling and accessing public space (through schooling mostly) became *the* mobilizing themes in the reformist campaigns and the progressive discourses of the often Western-educated male nationalist elite. In the first case as in the second, Muslim women were neither directly consulted nor involved in defining the terms of the reforms targeting them.

They were made central figures, as it were, on these agendas without their consent, and as such, they did not enjoy the full privileges that the position of centrality normally bestows. Centrality then acquires meaning only when explained within the context of the patriarchal ideology of male reformers, indigenous or otherwise.

To the nationalist elite, then, women came to represent a refuge from colonial humiliation, a symbol of national resistance and affirmation of identity, a guardian of cultural as well as religious values, and a vector of modernization of the Muslim society. In a word, women were expected to act as agents of both change and continuity. Veiling or unveiling? Segregating or desegregating? Educating or not educating? The answers to these questions would greatly depend on the class distinctions, ideological leanings, and projects of past and present male nationalists and political elites.

Although women's issues are still hotly debated in many Muslim countries, it is as if the whole burden of the wounded Islamic umma, and the hopes for a dignified present and future, rest entirely on women's heads (literally) and on their shoulders.

Realistic or not, this project seems to encapsulate the anxieties of the traumatic and posttraumatic experiences of colonization in Muslim countries. Women are expected, through their garb and spatial considerations, to answer probably one of the most challenging questions facing Muslim reformists since the nineteenth century: how to reconcile tradition and modernity. Put differently, the question is how to compete with the West's economic, scientific, and military powers while preserving the "essence" of Muslim historical and spiritual identity.[30]

Generations of Muslim intellectuals and reformists have, since the Nahda of the nineteenth century, been struggling with this central question. Various conflicting currents of Muslim thinking have emerged since, each with a specific vision for large-scale reforms affecting virtually every aspect of Muslim life, including women's conditions.

Two such currents have been and still are influential: the Islamic reformist current and the traditionalist conservatives. The reformists, mostly an urban-based male elite, believed that the moral rebirth of the Muslim umma requires a return to Islamic sources through a rigorous reinterpretation of the scriptures (Ijtihad) in order to purge Muslim societies from the effects of centuries of stagnation and contamination. The reforms envisioned would cover all areas of political, economic, religio-ethical, and social life. Theirs was a serious effort to reconcile the urgencies of modernization with the spirit of religion. Women's liberation from male oppression was among the important steps toward rebuilding a just Muslim order. With varying degrees of modernism and progressivism, representatives of this current promoted women's sociopolitical equality with men, especially in matters of education, marriage, divorce, and child custody. The works of such reformers as Jamal Eddine el Afghani, Mohamed Abdou, Rifa'a Tahtaoui, and Kacim Amine have been extremely influential in launching the debates around women's issues in the Middle East.[31] They have impacted the work and reformist vision of such figures as Allal el Fassi and Mohamed el Hajoui in Morocco and Tahar el Haddad in Tunisia.[32]

The traditionalist current adopted an overtly defensive stance toward modernity, perceived as Westernization and cultural contamination. The project of this current is preserving and reinforcing the stable structures of established tradition, which, according to their reading, stipulate female legal inequality with men enshrined in *shari'a* (classical Islamic law).[33] Representatives of this current are mostly conservative religious scholars who see in any potential social change a threat to their legitimacy and to their centuries-old monopoly over the interpretation of the scriptures.

Considerable differences unquestionably exist within and among these currents. All of them, however, positioned women and the West at the center of their vision and reformist agendas. Through the dialectic of difference and sameness, the West would determine for them the nature of the political, social, economic, and moral order of society. This, in turn, would define the roles and duties Muslim women would be assigned to play in some, all, or none of these areas.

Islamic reformists and the nationalist elite have done a great deal to improve the status of women. Yet, it is important to underline that their efforts were in many ways motivated by the pressures and necessities imposed by the colonial powers. Hardly any improvement in women's conditions was dissociated from or discussed outside of the greater benefits it would provide to the larger umma and the nascent nation. The education of girls was not celebrated for its intrinsic value or for the benefits it might have for women as independent individuals. Education was promoted precisely because it would make women good daughters, good wives, good mothers, and good servants to the nation.

The abolition of the veil was encouraged by the urban elite not merely because of the realization that the long tradition of misogynist misinterpretations of the scriptures stripped women of their rights. Rather, removal of the veil would be, like the colonialists wanted it to be, a symbol of the modernization of society and the progressive attitudes of their male political elite. In fact, it would the barometer for measuring the success or failure of modernization.

Further, and with respect to education, there were many restrictions even in the modernist and progressive expressions of reformism. In Morocco, as in Tunisia and Algeria, when the nationalists' calls for the education of girls were formulated, they often recommended that the education of girls be limited to Arabic language, indigenous culture, and religion. The teaching of European languages and science, though desirable in the case of boys, was severely restricted in the case of girls. These subjects were deemed dangerous to the larger noble mission with which women were entrusted: preserving national and religious values to be transmitted to future generations. Thus, while the form and content of girls' education was shaped by the nationalistic dictates, the level of education most tolerated for them was primary schooling for the most part, and secondary schooling in the most progressive agendas.[34]

Now clearly there is a central contradiction in this logic. Trusting women with the heavy task of defending and preserving the integrity of the entire Muslim umma might suggest a valorization of the capacities of women. This is obviously not the case. Women are in fact judged more vulnerable and frail than men since they are more likely to succumb to the perceived external corrupting influences—hence, the selection of the knowledge and language to which they would be introduced.

But neither education nor unveiling went uncontested in colonial and postcolonial Muslim societies. Staunch resistance to both came from traditionalist circles across class and gender lines. If abolition of the veil and seclusion are encouraged by the reformists, and easily adopted by members of the elite class, they are decried by conservatives as an open door to corruption and disruption of the inner structures of Muslim society. Conservative circles tried to place even greater restrictions on the bodies and minds of their women.

The legacy of colonial policies, as discussed earlier, put such high symbolic value on women's bodies and sexuality that it became nearly impossible to discuss women's conditions without the twin concerns over colonialism and nationalism. The family laws promulgated by most Arab-Muslim countries after their independence all reflect the timidity with which earlier progressive calls for women's emancipation were to be translated. In North Africa as elsewhere in the Middle East, postcolonial regimes had little hesitation to modernize many laws related to such sectors as economy, education, commerce, and politics. Except the family law.

There has been practically no change in the legal status of women since the texts were initially drafted to reproduce the patriarchal views of establishment Islam. Family laws, or personal status code as it is commonly called, constitute the cornerstone of the entire patriarchal system and masculinist privileges in establishment Islam. They define the rights, duties, and responsibilities of Muslim women in the public and private spheres. They translate the extent to which male order has been preoccupied with women's sexuality and moral conduct.

Thus, when it comes to changes in women's rights, religion and theology are immediately invoked, and defensive attitudes build up against Western influences of such "undesirable" intrusions as human rights and women's rights. Anxieties over Muslim identity and cultural authenticity acquire an exaggerated proportion as soon as the status or rights of Muslim women are questioned and the legal texts are proposed to undergo the rigorous exercise of Ijtihad.[35] Such reactions come from virtually all circles in society, including the progressive ones.

The interesting literature on nationalism and feminism demonstrates that the female body has been a site of competing claims and discourses in postcolonial countries in at least three different ways. It has been the site for (a) testing out the success or failure of modernity and the strength of tradition, (b) the mythic cultural and national unity in the face of fragmentation, and (c) countering the challenges posed by "Westernization"—often read as women's liberation.[36]

Fundamentalists will push this logic to its extreme.

Of Fundamental Disillusionment

Patriarchy is a powerful ideology. It reinvents itself, ceaselessly. It appropriates grand causes and turns them against the oppressed in order to guarantee its survival. It was partly through the emancipation of Muslim women that European colonialist regimes carried out their much-celebrated civilizing mission. In the process, they made issues of culture and nationalism inseparable from those of gender. It was in the name of a much needed Arab-Muslim renaissance and all-encompassing national reforms that the indigenous elite encouraged the education and unveiling of their women.

With the struggles for independence nearly over for most Arab-Muslim countries, virtually all postcolonial regimes have marched toward the process of nation building with a cohort of male elite. The female population, only the minority of which has been educated, is still struggling to fit in the big national scheme.

Now, in the name of "purifying" the Muslim nation from internal corruption, and in the name of countering the oppression of Western imperialism, religious fundamentalists posit women as key players in their whole project. Their re-Islamization of contemporary Muslim societies, they argue with words and whips, cannot take place without women. Once again, women are seen as part of both the problems and the solutions.

Scores of researchers have already traced the multiple expressions of Muslim fundamentalism to the historic accumulation of frustrations and existential anxieties. Some of these are related to the increasing cultural and political challenges as well as to the economic, socio-demographic, and ethical problems in postcolonial Arab-Muslim countries. A close analysis of these is beyond the scope of this text. Some aspects of the links between the West and women in the fundamentalist politico-religious agenda are underlined.

To virtually all fundamentalists, Islam has been subject to a series of assaults, the last of which have come from external and internal sources. The external sources are colonialists and world powers, while the internal sources are the Westernized national elite, women included.[37] The local elite is accused of having internalized an inferiority complex toward Europe and reproduced a Western model of development and progress, both of which have had deleterious effects on the Muslim umma. They have increased the dependency of Muslim societies on the West, exacerbated class divisions and injustices, and accelerated the dissolution of the Muslim identity.

Their Islamist call is about decolonizing not only the land of the Muslims but also the spirits and minds of the believers, who increasingly pay allegiance to the colonizers and to their products. The role of Western media is considered instrumental in this. They are responsible for spreading immoral values and spiritual barrenness around the world and promoting perverse individualism as well as the dictatorship of consumerism.

Most fundamentalists seem to transfer the sum of their historical misfortunes, present miseries, and future uncertainties on women. Women are the targets of their frustration with poverty, unemployment, corruption, and their sociopolitical exclusion.

With every humiliation Muslim men feel at the hand of postcolonial powers, Muslim women would pay a higher price. With every assertive step women make, and with every right wrenched by feminists, the backlash would be even bigger.

Muslim women are found guilty for having blindly reproduced the Western model of femininity and feminism. Muslim women's increasing visibility, mobility, as well as intellectual independence are all perceived as fundamentally undesirable changes in the social and moral order. The access of women to public space, in particular, is responsible for the disintegration of the family structure and the erosion of its sacredness. These changes are perceived to be the major problems facing "decadent" Western societies.

Accusing women of inner depravity, weakness, and sexual promiscuity, fundamentalists establish ties with a long tradition of misogynist writings that see the Muslim woman's body as the instigator of all chaos (*fitna*) and social disorder.[38] This explains the need to cover it, police it, and regulate its impulses and movements. Rights denied include again education, despite the fact that no single reference is made to this end in the Qur'an or the *Sunna* (prophet's saying and deeds).

In reality, changes in women's lives constitute a serious threat to the foundations on which masculinity is defined in the establishment Muslim order: economic power and control over women.[39] Women's work is a development that threatens both dimensions of this "masculinity." Violence is the language of the weak: perpetrated against women it becomes, ironically enough, a confirmation of their threatening power.

To fundamentalists, violence against women is seen as part of the "post-modern" holy war expected to restore justice, peace, and purity to a corrupt world. In this, they view themselves as the moral conscience of the Islamic world, and the God-appointed "soldiers in Islam's battle against the forces of darkness without and within."[40] Endorsing patriarchal laws and inventing new discriminatory practices allows them to regain control over the family as their absolute kingdom of disenfranchised wife, or wives, and daughters.

Dehumanized and vilified, Muslim women are still entrusted with a tremendous role for which they alone seem to be capable: "religion, morality and culture stand and fall" with women.[41] Despite all the efforts fundamentalists put into purifying society from Western influence, they do not seem to have moved one step beyond the logic of colonialists who trapped the issues of women with the struggles of culture, nation, and religious identity.

Some fundamentalist currents seem to recognize and support women's participation in sociopolitical life. For them, the participation of women in the political scene is justified only if it supports their political agendas and candidacies.

This is not the only level at which the fundamentalists' project and vision remain problematic. Numerous contradictions and flaws abound in their gender policies. First, rejection of the Western world and rage against its hegemony do not include rejection of its technology or military equipment. From audiocassettes, cellular phones, and the Internet to the Swiss-made watch and U.S.-made four-wheel drive, the products of modernization are commonly used and are readily justified as tools for the war against immorality. Feminist scholars also demonstrate that fundamentalists do not hesitate to use modern technology to enhance their surveillance and control over women.

Second, while the political and religious leaders remain vocal about the ills of modernity, they do not hesitate to send their children to modern institutions for schooling and training, whether at home or in the West, depending on which they can afford.[42]

Also, virtually all fundamentalists seem to inhabit an unrealistic time frame. Their problem with time is such that they have frozen their gaze in the past and refuse to face the realties of the present. It is a self-imposed suicide and a premature death they often impose on their women as on others.

Further, in their frenzy to bury their frustrations and anxieties in an imagined "pristine" past, Islamists recuperate traditions and sanction practices that are more patriarchal and misogynist than Islamic. They resurrect them as foundational bases of the Islamic civilization. Brutalizing women, killing them in the name of family honor, sanctioning their rape, and excluding women from education are all reflections of not only a grave misinterpretation of the scripture and the spirit of Islam, but a glaring distortion of both.

Finally, fundamentalists mistakenly believe that the return to the veil will facilitate the return to the just, moral, and classless society of yore. Many non-Muslim observers, scholars among them, also believe that the veil can have no other meaning than women's utter oppression. The veil clearly means this, as it means the rejection of the West. Ample documentation of these meanings is available. But the veil increasingly means many other things as well, as numerous ethnographic studies conducted on women's reasons for wearing the veil seem to suggest.[43]

To some, the veil enables women to experience greater freedom and mobility in the public space without being harassed by unsolicited remarks from men. Many express their dress choice as a mere celebration of their religiosity and as a means through which they can express their identities and assert themselves. Some veiled adolescents identify sentimental problems (love affairs), self-image, and body shape as the primary reasons for their dress choice. To others still, the veil solves some of the financial strains that indigenous and imported fashions put on their limited budget. This is a confirmation that class distinctions remain intact behind the veil. In Jordan, for example, research has revealed that "hiding under the *jilibah* are clothes which are highly diverse, influenced by—if not replicas of—Western styles." In Iran, the wives and daughters of the mullah and the "well-to-do women hide bold European fashions under the *chador*."[44]

Whether imposed or chosen, the veil has certainly acquired diversified meanings that reflect as well as reinforce the contradictory discourses and claims put around women's bodies. The veil seems to be extensible enough to accommodate different intentions while giving to its fervent advocates the illusion that they can eternally lock women into the role of guardian of the patriarchal order.

As this essay has tried to argue, Muslim women are posited as key players in the Muslim relationship with and sentiments toward the Euro-American world. Any progressive changes in women's lives are perceived as acts of allegiance to the West and a threat to the religious and cultural identity of the whole Muslim community. Maintenance of women's traditional status and a return to an "unsullied" past are taken as a triumph over the West and its corrupting forces.

The postcolonial Arab-Muslim debates on the roles, duties, and responsibilities of women are dizzying in their complexity and misleading in their conflicting claims. The cacophony of voices has never been this disturbingly loud. And Muslim women's struggle to resist all forms of oppression has never been more meaningful.

Chapter 4

Iran and American Miseducation: Cover-Ups, Distortions, and Omissions

Joe L. Kincheloe

Before the Iranian hostage crisis of 1979–1981, most Americans knew little about Iran. Many Americans could not locate the country on a map, did not know it was not an Arab nation, and were not aware that most Iranians spoke Farsi, not Arabic. Though many had heard of Persia, most Americans did not equate Iran with Persia.[1] In the analysis of the miseducation of America vis-à-vis Islam, Iran occupies a special place. In the first decade of the twenty-first century American ignorance of Iran continues. Even in the period following 9/11 when the strategic cognizance of Islamdom is given lip service in some quarters, little knowledge of Iran and its most recent history seem to have penetrated the American consciousness. Amazingly, during the 14 months from November 1979 to January 1981 when the United States as a nation was obsessed with Iran, media coverage of the country was superficial, official information was distorted, and historical context was generally deleted from both sources of data.

The standard textbook account of the American coup that overthrew the democratically elected Iranian government in 1953 maintains that the action was necessary to save Iran from communism. There is no evidence that such a possibility existed. The *New York Times* reported a year after the coup that "Moscow counted its chickens before they were hatched,"[2] never considering the lack of evidence of any Soviet involvement. After the coup Americans obtained most of their information about the country from shah-controlled official information sources that provided an egregiously distorted perspective on what was happening in Iranian society. Indeed, when the Iranian Revolution broke out in 1979, even most Iran experts in the United States were taken by surprise. The shah's information providers had told them nothing about the opposition to his rule coming from various social locales, the religious community in particular. Obsessed with American geopolitical interests and Western modes of analysis, Iranian experts in the United States focused on modernization programs, military power, and communist sympathizers. Because of these blinders, they missed the important story emerging right before their eyes: the rise of political Islam. The American misunderstanding of Iran provides unique insight into the miseducation of the West.

The Colonial Setting

The effort to understand the miseducation of the West demands awareness of the colonial past of most Islamic nations. Of course, much transpired before the coming of the European colonists, but that important history is the subject of another volume. Europeans first came to Iran in the early 1500s. During this period diverse groups in the region were sufficiently united to withstand colonial assaults. After the fall of the Safavid rulers, however, the region was subjected to a series of tribal and feudal conflicts that weakened Iran and thus opened it to colonial penetration. By the nineteenth century Iran's inability to resist Russian and British colonization eventuated in a loss of Iranian independence and self-determination. By the 1820s Russia controlled the north of Iran and by the 1850s the British controlled the southern region. Both Russia and Britain promoted technology and modes of economic development that contributed to their own economic interests, in the process rendering Iran an impoverished and dependent state. Neither nation was interested in even granting formal colony status to Iran until oil was discovered in the early twentieth century.

The history of Russian colonial domination of Iran reads as little more than a series of commercial and political agreements that financially rewarded Moscow while punishing the Iranians. In the late nineteenth century the Russians restricted the flow of goods to Iran, thus rendering the country more and more dependent on Russian economic concerns. In this same period Britain's trade with Iran amounted to less than half of the Russians'. Britain's main concern with Iran in the last half of the nineteenth century involved its status as a protective buffer to Britain's colonial interests in India and the Persian Gulf. Nevertheless, Britain exacted a wide range of economic concessions from the Iranians: immunity from Iranian taxes; monopolies over railroad construction, mining, and banking; a sole right to print currency; a monopoly over tobacco production, sale, and export; and legal jurisdiction over all British nationals in Iran, to name merely a few. In 1901 the British demanded the sole right to explore for and produce oil in any part of Iran that the Russians had not already claimed.

Under Russian and British colonialism Iranian efforts to construct a self-directed modern economic system were crushed. The political, social, and economic domination by the colonists and the Iranian rulers' inability to do anything about it led by the turn of the twentieth century to a profound sense of national shame. As such shame morphed into anger, the Iranians staged numerous rebellions. These revolts led to the Constitutional Revolution of 1906. Viewed by Iranian historians as a profound turning point in Iranian history, revolutionary leaders established a constitution grounded on democratic principles and representative government.

Buoyed by expressions of British support, the constitutional democrats rejoiced with the successful establishment of a popular government. The British, however, by 1907 met with the Russians to formally divide Iran into colonial spheres of influence and to support the reestablishment of the absolute monarch, Mohammed Ali Shah. Both nations had concluded that the democratic constitutionalist movement with its claim to self-determination by the Iranian people could undermine their imperial geopolitical and economic interests in Iran and other nations in the Middle East, India, and various parts of Asia. When Russian diplomatic pressure failed to destroy the constitutionalist government in 1907, the Russian Cossacks attacked the Iranian assembly (the Majlis) in Tehran and targeted constitutionalist supporters. The constitutionalists fought back, capturing Tehran and deposing the shah. At this point, in 1911, the Russians and the British sent in military forces to quash the democratic movement.[3]

With the support of the colonial powers the reinstalled shah embarked on a program of modernization and de-Islamization. No longer could Iranians wear Islamic dress, veiling was prohibited, and the hajj[4] was outlawed. When believers protested against the dress laws, the shah's militia killed hundreds of them. Maintaining tight control and enforcing his secularization policy, the shah continued his rule throughout the 1910s, 1920s, and 1930s. In 1939 Iran declared its neutrality in World War II. The allied powers demanded that the shah allow use of Iranian territory to transport troops and supplies to the Russians in their fight against Nazi Germany. The shah refused, and in August 1941 British and Russian forces invaded the country. Forcing the abdication of the shah, the British and Russians helped install the shah's son, Mohammad Reza Pahlavi, to the throne. Mohammad Reza Pahlavi would become known to the world as the shah of Iran and rule until 1979.[5]

The Postwar Context: The Last Gasps of the British Empire

After World War II numerous Iranians insisted that when it came to European domination, enough was enough. Britain's power and influence over Iranian political and economic life continued to grow as a result of its control of the oil industry and its vast profits. The shah was viewed as a puppet of the British and in that role had refused to speak about the unfair profiteering on Iranian oil. In this context many Iranians began to push for two measures:

1. a transfer of political authority from the shah to the Majlis,[6] and
2. increased Iranian management of and profit from its oil business.

In 1949 these measures became even more important when the shah's government announced a new oil agreement that continued to favor the British disproportionately as well as the exposure of the shah's efforts to rig the Majlis elections. The Iranian public was outraged, and massive protests rocked the country. In the wake of demonstrations a political movement bringing together a variety of political parties known as the National Front surfaced to lead Iranian resistance to the shah and the British. Emerging as its leader was Muhammed Mossadegh, who in 1950 was elected as one of eight National Front candidates to the Majlis. Mossadegh and the National Front, who were predominately middle class and Western educated, viewed themselves as the rightful heirs to the constitutionalist movement.

The British saw Mossadegh as their worst nightmare. Fearing that he might be elected prime minister, the British urged the shah to install the pro-British Sayyid Zia in the position. By late April 1951, the Majlis had elected Mossadegh as their leader. Before becoming prime minister, however, Mossadegh began negotiations with the British to win Iran a more favorable position in the division of oil profits. The better position he offered was a 50–50 split of all oil revenues—an offer deleted from many school textbooks on the subject.[7] In March 1951, soon after the British rejection of the offer, Mossadegh submitted a bill to nationalize the oil industry. The bill quickly passed, and one of his first acts after assuming office was to sign it into law on May 1. Even though the nationalization act still provided the British with 25 percent of oil profits, they continued their efforts to install Zia as prime minister after Mossadegh's democratic election.[8]

In response to Mossadegh's nationalization the British navy was sent to show force and intimidate the Iranians. This flexing of military muscle opened the door to a British-led international blockade, a boycott of Iranian products, and a freeze on Iran's oil exports. The British actions pushed the Iranian economy to the brink of collapse. In this context the British made impossible demands of the impoverished Iranians, including payment for the assets of the Anglo-Iranian Oil Company (AIOC) and that company's work in constructing the oil fields. Mossadegh and the Iranians argued that decades of inflated British profits on Iranian oil had long ago paid for these investments. By June 1951, with Mossadegh still in power, Winston Churchill and Anthony Eden, leaders in Britain's Conservative Party, were arguing that the British, with American assistance, should overthrow Mossadegh in a coup. Throughout the summer they demanded that the shah help in the ouster of the new prime minister.[9]

The Changing U.S. Role in the Islamic World: The Coup

In 1951, as the British pushed their plan to overthrow Mossadegh and reestablish total control of Iranian oil production, higher-level operatives in the Truman administration's CIA, Allen Dulles and Kermit Roosevelt in particular, favored the coup. Concurrently, lower-level employees in the agency opposed it, arguing that the United States should not support British colonialism. President Truman and his close advisors thought it important for the Iranians and the British to resolve the oil dispute and made promises that the United States would not intervene in Iran's domestic affairs. They urged the British to give lip service to the concept of nationalization but accept Mossadegh's original 50–50 oil profits offer.

Such suggestions were not received well by the British and in historical retrospect seem disingenuous given our present knowledge of American covert activities in Iran since the late 1940s. The United States had initiated covert activities in Iran to subvert national politics, spy on the Soviets, and counter what it perceived to be communist influences in the country. The American fears seem exaggerated and even paranoid in light of the release in the 1990s of Soviet-era archives that indicate the USSR's primary objectives in post–World War II Iran involved achieving oil concessions from the country.

In addition, the United States' caution in the summer of 1951 through the spring of 1952 seems less altruistic when understood in the context of the Truman administration's perception of the geopolitical and military balance of power between the United States and the USSR. By the summer of 1952 a buildup in U.S. military capability and a consequent perceived change in the balance of power induced a more aggressive attitude toward both Mossadegh's Iran and the Soviet Union. During this time Truman approved both overt and covert interventions to rid Iran of any uncooperative influences. Simultaneously, the United States put together an oil plan that allowed the biggest American oil companies new access to Iranian oil profits. Mossadegh rejected the plan and scrambled to deal with the increasingly aggressive U.S. attitude. In this context the prime minister could take little comfort in the expulsion of the British from Iran in November 1952. Though the long period of British colonialism had ended, the United States was actively operating to fill the vacuum of colonial power.[10]

With the inauguration of the Eisenhower administration in January 1953, events began to move faster in both the United States and Iran. Newly confirmed secretary of state John Foster Dulles had been working with his brother, Allen Dulles, the director of the CIA, on a plan for an overthrow of the Mossadegh government. Two weeks after Eisenhower's inauguration on February 3, 1953, the Dulles bothers helped arrange a meeting to develop a strategy for the coup. John Foster Dulles was vitriolic in his disdain for Mossadegh. The secretary of state hated the prime minister's unqualified neutrality in the Cold War, his tepid stance vis-à-vis communism, and his lack of respect for the free enterprise system as demonstrated by his nationalization of Iranian oil. In Secretary Dulles's manichaean universe, Iranian oil as well as the nation's 1,000-mile border with the Soviet Union made it too important to U.S. strategic needs to allow it self-determination. The emerging role of the United States as a superpower, as viewed by those administrating and supporting the emergence of the empire, granted it the license to remove and install governments when it saw fit.

In April 1953 Allen Dulles contributed $1 million in CIA funds to be used to overthrow Mossadegh, and by May top British and U.S. officials meeting in Cyprus developed a specific plan. Immediately, the CIA began distributing anti-Mossadegh cartoons and planting negative articles about him in Iranian newspapers. Plans for the coup were finalized in Beirut in June, and Kermit Roosevelt, Theodore Roosevelt's grandson, was sent to Iran to oversee the operation. After President Eisenhower officially approved the coup on July 11, pressure on the shah to take part in it increased. In the minds of administration leaders the biggest obstacle to successfully executing the coup in July 1953 involved the reluctance of the "cowardly" Shah Mohammad Reza Pahlavi to go through with the plan out of fear of retribution. Nevertheless, with or without the shah's cooperation, the work of the CIA and British covert operatives went ahead.

In July and early August CIA agents pretending to be Iranian communist supporters of Mossadegh threatened religious leaders with beatings and murder if they did not support the prime minister. In this same guise they bombed the homes of clerics attempting to catalyze anticommunist and anti-Mossadegh feelings in the religious domain. Much of this information comes from a secret history written for CIA eyes only in 1954 by Donald Wilber, one of the planners of the coup. Not uncovered for public viewing until the *New York Times* published a story about it in April 2000, the secret history detailed the geopolitical and economic factors behind the coup and the specifics of its enactment. Wilber wrote of the "excitement…satisfaction…and jubilation" of the American intelligence community with the success of the coup. The secret history ignored the implications of the coup with regard to longtime protestations of support for democracy and the well-being of the Iranian people. The citizens of

Iran, especially the religious community, would profoundly suffer under the shah's brutal puppet regime.

Methodically implementing the plan, the CIA sent General Norman Schwarzkopf (the father of the Gulf War commander) to help overcome the shah's reluctance to go along with the coup. Understanding the shah's need for reassurance, Schwarzkopf brought Kermit Roosevelt to the palace to placate the monarch's fears. Successfully obtaining the shah's approval on August 11, Roosevelt moved forward. He sent a commander of the shah's imperial guard to Mossadegh's office with a royal decree to remove the prime minister from office. Wanting to get word to the Iranian people of the shah's decree, the CIA planted stories in the Iranian and the U.S. press. Learning of the U.S.- and British-supported military coup to remove him by force, Mossadegh attempted to defend his government. On August 15, when the shah sent forces to arrest him, Mossadegh had them taken into custody instead. The next day Tehran radio announced that the rebellion had been defeated. Roosevelt rallied the CIA and British operatives and the fearful shah's imperial guards, and on the morning of August 19, they struck. Occupying the main squares of Tehran, the telegraph office, and radio stations, speakers supporting the shah announced the success of the coup. Retribution and punishment of all opposition elements began immediately.[11]

The Rising Power of the CIA: Producing Disinformation

Not once in this subversive process did the "pro-communist" Mossadegh—as he was labeled by the Dulles brothers—ask for Soviet help. Not once did the USSR, despite its leaders' knowledge of the U.S. and British instigation of the coup, make a dissenting sound. Contrary to the proclamations of the Cold Warriors, the USSR simply was not interested in taking control of Iran. In the secret history Wilber depicts the CIA as being totally surprised by the success of the coup. As events transpired on August 19, Roosevelt was reluctant to send information to Washington for fear that government officials would think he was crazy. But with the assurance of success, Roosevelt and the CIA rushed to take total credit. By the next year the agency had subverted the government of Guatemala and was giddy with its perceived ability to control events anywhere. Reflecting the power-driven intoxication of the CIA on August 19, 1953, Wilber wrote that "it was a day that should never have ended."[12]

The CIA was only six years old in August 1953. In its infancy, the agency was struggling to find its legs and gain a sense of what it was capable of accomplishing. As Wilber described in his secret history, the CIA, naïve in its use of the press and other forms of knowledge production, lamented its lack of "contacts capable of placing material so that the American publisher was unwitting as to its source."[13] Over the next few decades, however, the spy organization would forge intimate ties with knowledge producers in the U.S. government and the press. By the first decade of the twenty-first century, the TV, radio, and print media would come to serve as compliant spokespeople for the agency's needs. Despite its lamentations, the young CIA in Iran encountered few problems in its efforts to miseducate the world about what was happening in the country.

Operatives consistently planted stories in *Newsweek* designed to unnerve Mossadegh and keep him confused about forces opposing him. The Associated Press was consistently willing to publish CIA plants. For years after the coup, numerous U.S. magazines were more than willing to keep the disinformation alive. Reporters sometimes reflected the bravado of American imperialism. As one reporter for the *New York Times* wrote soon after the coup: "Underdeveloped countries with rich resources now have an object lesson in the heavy cost that must be paid by one of their number which goes berserk with fanatical nationalism."[14] In the 1970s, *Fortune*, for example, printed an article maintaining that Mossadegh "plotted with the Communist Party of Iran to overthrow Shah Mohammed Reza Pahlavi and hook up with the Soviet Union."[15]

In his *New York Times* article on the secret history of the Iran coup, James Risen reflects the CIA's regrets over its inability to use the press for disinformation. He writes:

The CIA's history of the coup shows that its operatives had only limited success in manipulating American reporters and that none of the Americans covering the coup worked for the agency....Western correspondents in Iran and Washington never reported that some of the unrest had been stage-managed by CIA agents posing as Communists. And they gave little emphasis to accurate contemporaneous reports in Iranian newspapers and on the Moscow radio asserting that Western powers were secretly arranging the Shah's return to power.[16]

It seems in this context that Risen documents the CIA's ability to shape media information at the same time he provides examples of the agency's control of the press. Analyzing the CIA's and Risen's references to the CIA failures in this area, it seems that both parties are referring to the fact that no reporters specifically worked for the CIA. If this is the criterion for success, then the bar is too high. The press did not have to be on the agency's payroll to submit to its demands. The press in Iran was more than willing to print planted stories or omit information unfavorable to perceived U.S. interests.

Western European and U.S. correspondents in Iran and Washington during the coup simply never wrote about the CIA's manipulation of civil unrest against Mossadegh. In the years following the coup the uprising was rarely mentioned by American newspapers, radio, or TV.[17] When it was, reports were characterized by an America-as-victim theme. In this discourse the United States was represented as having worked in the best interest of the developing, formerly colonized nations to bring the benefits of modernization. The retrograde elements in Iran (and other nations) in their arrested cultural development were unable to recognize what America was granting them. These premodern elements turned on us, biting the hand that fed them. Emerging here was the image of a long-suffering America in a postcolonial world, paying the price for being the shining beacon of democracy to a cosmos unappreciative of such salvation.

All in the name of democracy, the U.S. coup in 1953 gave America a 40 percent share in an Iranian oil business previously dominated by the British since the discovery of oil in the country. In addition the British were allowed to keep a 40 percent share, and the other 20 percent was divided among other "friendly" countries.[18] As one observer of the day put it, Western countries' advantages in the new oil arrangements were analogous to obtaining a "license to print money."[19] At the same time, however, securing imperial domination of a country on the southern flank of the USSR was deemed one of the greatest victories of the Cold War. The shah provided the U.S. military bases from which to launch missiles and military aircraft against the Soviets and a buffer state between the Soviet Union and the Persian Gulf. The CIA built radar and various listening posts on the Soviet border, while espionage agents used Iranian border facilities and military bases to travel into and out of the USSR on spy missions.[20]

Secretary of State Dulles, like President Truman before him, maintained that Iran was the linchpin to American military interests in the region. With Iran in his pocket, Dulles worked to build a regional alliance against the Soviet Union consisting of Turkey, Iraq, Syria, Pakistan, and, of course, Iran. The shah had been restored to full power by American efforts, his oligarchy functioning to preserve the riches of the elite while granting the United States a free hand in exploiting the country's resources and strategic geopolitical position. For such compliance the shah would receive billions of dollars of U.S. aid—military aid in particular.[21] His American-produced weapons would make him the "policeman of the Gulf"; he would become the leader of the greatest military power in the region.

Daniel Boorstin, Brooks Mather Kelly, and Ruth Frankel Boorstin would represent the events of the early 1950s in Iran in their widely used high school textbook, *A History of the United States,* as an unproblematic victory for the United States. The authors place the overthrow of the Mossadegh government in the context of the larger necessity for the United States to unseat "decadent and corrupt" governments. Indeed, the authors never mention that prime minister Mossadegh was democratically elected. The shah, according to the authors, was returned to his throne—propping up an absolute monarch is good for the United States when his was a "friendly government" that granted our nation "valuable oil concessions." While information concerning the antidemocratic and covert nature of the U.S. and British operation could be found in various publications and books on the region, a young student or an individual who obtained his or her news from newspapers, mainstream news magazines, radio, or TV would be hard-pressed to encounter different perspectives.[22]

The 1953 Coup as Historical Watershed

One of the central reasons that I write on Iran in *The Miseducation of the West* involves how an understanding of the history of Iran in the twentieth century helps explain

- Muslim anger toward the U.S., and
- America's self-miseducation about the reasons for such anger.

Indeed, an analysis of these Iranian dynamics helps Americans in a post-9/11 landscape appreciate that Islamic anger toward the United States involves more than irrational "hatred of our freedom" or our support for Israel. Despite the pronouncements of right-wing educators such as Chester Finn,[23] who argues that "accurate history" will teach America's children that the United States is always a force for democracy, a rigorous exploration of the situation tells us that history is more complex than Finn claims. In Iran, to say the least, the United States did not always act in the interests of democracy and freedom.[24]

From an Iranian perspective, the events surrounding the 1953 coup do not constitute ancient history—they are fresh in the minds of everyday Iranians. Understanding the way U.S. government officials often make sense of the world, Iranians were profoundly shaken by the events of 9/11. Iranians realized the potential way they could be positioned in this American conceptual framework. Their inclusion in George W. Bush's "axis of evil" in the 2002 State of the Union address reflected the framework in question. Many Iranians had already come to understand, as most Americans had (and have) not, that the coup was a watershed not only in Iranian and U.S. history but in world history as well. Obviously, in the Iranian historical context the coup dramatically shaped subsequent events in the country. The anti-American dimension of the 1978–1979 revolution and the hostage crisis are unimaginable outside of the coup's shadow.[25]

Realizing the impact of the coup on Iranian and U.S. relations at the beginning of the new century, elements in both the Clinton administration and the Khatami regime in Iran in 2000 called for friendly meetings between representatives of the two governments. Declaring that the United States wanted a new relationship with Tehran, Secretary of State Madeleine Albright on March 17, 2000, acknowledged the covert American role in the coup. Understanding the Iranian hurt around the topic, Albright knew that such a declaration would open many doors to rapprochement. The coup, she continued, "was clearly a setback for Iran's political development. And it is easy to see why many Iranians continue to resent this intervention by America in their internal affairs."[26] Indeed, in the minds of many the coup was a central event that had to be addressed. On several levels it signaled a new historical relationship between the West and Islamdom—a new era of interaction that continues into the twenty-first century.

This new era of Western-Islamic relations beginning in the years following World War II involves an anticolonial reaction in the Islamic world. Taking place at the same time that other Asian, African, and Latin American nations rebelled against European colonial domination, this anticolonial dynamic played a central dimension in the rise of Prime Minister Mossadegh. Iranians, not the British, he maintained, should direct Iranian affairs and profit from the nation's natural resources. Increasingly, other Islamic nations would come to associate colonial or colonial-inspired modernization programs with a disrespectful secularism. Such an association would in Khomeini's Iran in the late 1970s and in Afghanistan, Turkey, Egypt, and Algeria at various historical moments help construct a powerful religious dimension in these various movements.[27] The U.S. reaction to Mossadegh's government and its moderate anticolonial policies would position the United States as the new agent of a reformulated but still pernicious Euro-colonialism in the Islamic world. The representation of the United States as a colonial power is still difficult for many Americans to understand. Educated to view their country as innocent and standing outside of history, many Americans into the twenty-first century continue to be shocked when faced with its reality.

Because of U.S. actions in the 1953 coup, Iranians and many other Islamic peoples would come to see America as Britain's replacement as the despised Western nation undermining national sovereignty and subverting justice and democracy.[28] The United States would pay for such a designation. Indeed, Chalmers Johnson's term "blowback"—the unexpected consequences of U.S. covert actions around the world[29]—was first used by the CIA in March 1954 in Wilber's secret history. The CIA's concerns that there might be blowback from the coup were on target. Iranians still view the revolution of 1979 as the successful effort to rid the country of American mercenaries and give it back to the children of Iran. In this context the anticolonial movement in Iran and the revolution in which it culminated was not catalyzed by religion. While Khomeini may have employed Islam to justify the revolution, it was the U.S. continuation of British colonialism that drove it. The colonial rebellions of the 1940s and 1950s changed the world. The U.S. resistance to these rebellions in Iran and elsewhere profoundly modified its role in history.[30]

After the Coup: America's Shah

The U.S. response to Iran's anticolonial government included the restoration of the shah, who had fled the country immediately before the coup. Fearful of the forces against him, the shah built a brutal dictatorship that subverted free expression and popular political action. The U.S. spin that the nation had been "saved" from communism was no comfort for the Iranian people. For most Iranians the shah's Iran was a stark land of high poverty, little opportunity for the poor, and torture and terror by the shah's secret police (SAVAK). The United States was more than happy to help the shah with his efforts to squash dissent and retain his firm grip on power. Obsessed with the religious establishment, the shah, with U.S. help, launched attack after attack on religious individuals and groups. SAVAK, the central agent of these assaults, was created by the CIA. Trained by Colonel H. Norman Schwarzkopf, the secret police murdered, incarcerated, and tortured tens of thousands of the shah's citizens.

Despite the shah's totalitarian atrocities and the shocking disparity of wealth that wracked Iran, the monarch and his nation were held up by the U.S. to the rest of the world as the quintessential Western modernization success story. Thus, in the name of modernization the shah mowed down all standing in his way. The modern farm and labor policies moved a huge rural population into the cities, producing a chasm between haves and have-nots. Unrest among the dispossessed was crushed by SAVAK. Such attacks induced Amnesty International to declare in 1976 that Iran possessed the highest death penalty rate in the world, no civilian court system, and an unbelievable incidence of torture. All in all, Amnesty International concluded, the shah's Iran had the worst human rights record in the world. Yet, the United States continued to grant the monarch unqualified support in return for economic and strategic access. The shah was unconcerned with the hardships his industrialization policies were creating for his nation's people. The wealth created went to a small elite whose mansions were built by workers who spent their nights in newly created slums.[31]

Buoyed by legions of sycophants from both the United States and his inner circles at home, the shah began to believe he was an omnipotent leader of a reinvigorated Persian Empire. In 1971, to celebrate his exalted position, the megalomaniacal monarch threw a birthday party to revere the ancient Persian king Cyrus the Great and to celebrate his own royal lineage of 2,500 years. Held amid the ruins of Cyrus's ancient capital of Persepolis, the $300,000 extravaganza included food and wine catered from Paris. As the party concluded, an extravagantly attired shah stood in front of Cyrus's tomb and proclaimed: "Sleep easily, Cyrus, for we are awake."[32] Few of the scholars of Iran from the United States who attended the event noticed the political currents at work in Iranian society. Even overt statements from the exiled Ayatollah Khomeini about the shah as a traitor to Islam aroused little interest among the experts.

American political leaders blinded by the Cold War believed that an absolutist and brutal shah would promote U.S. strategic interests in the region. President Nixon and his trusted national security advisor and later secretary of state, Henry Kissinger, operating on their power-driven theory of realpolitik, were dedicated to this viewpoint. The shah, they reasoned, should get all the weaponry he wanted. When Nixon and Kissinger visited the shah in 1972, SAVAK was in the middle of a period of widespread and violent retribution toward dissidents. Nixon not only ignored the shah's terror against the Iranian people but actually told the monarch that he admired the way he ruled Iran. The shah took the president's words as an endorsement of rule by terror and as a signal that the United States would support him no matter what he did.

The coup of 1953 and U.S. support of the shah's brutality set up in the minds of the Iranian people and many individuals throughout the Islamic world a dichotomy between Pahlavi absolutism and Khomeini fundamentalism.[33] Within Pahlavi absolutism was the modernization impulse to reconfigure Iran as a "civilized" country in the Western tradition. To accomplish such a goal the shah very carefully set out to subvert the foundations of Islamic and Iranian traditions, including the segregation of the genders and the unimpeded functioning of the bazaar. For example, as part of the modernization and industrialization process the shah planned to destroy the bazaar and create in its stead modern stores and supermarkets. Such social and economic reforms placed the shah on a political trajectory bound to crash into the Shiite clergy.

By the late 1960s followers of Khomeini were recording tapes of his speeches pointing to the shah's attacks against Islam and his subservience to the United States and the West. Such assertions resonated with many Iranians, especially among the young, upwardly mobile, and Western-educated sector of the society. To many, a cultural collision between supporters of the shah and followers of the ayatollah seemed inescapable. Khomeini's denouncements of the shah increased with the shah's celebration of 2,500 years of Iranian monarchy. The holy man called for massive demonstrations against the "scandalous festival" and its organizers. He warned the shah, as he had for years, that none of the people around him were his friends and soon his Western allies would abandon him. Slowly, over the years of the shah's rule Khomeini's version of Shiite political Islam emerged in the minds of many Iranians as the only viable alternative to Pahlavi royal oppression.[34]

American experts on Iran—political scientists, historians, economists, sociologists, and anthropologists—for the most part remained ignorant of the power and influence of Khomeini's political Islam. So many of them suckled at the fiscal teat of the Pahlavi Foundation and numerous U.S. foundations intimately tied to the geopolitics and economics of the status quo. Outside of these paradigmatic frames, the Iranologists were blind. Such a scholarly reality offers a quintessential case of the miseducation of America, characterized in this situation by the insidious politics of knowledge production. What we see cannot be separated from where we stand in the complex web of social reality. When the revolution came in 1978–1979 this politics of knowledge production dominated Western media coverage of events. Countless hours and pages were devoted to documenting and dramatizing the seizure of the embassy and the taking of American hostages.

Little about the 1953 coup or the terror of the shah's regime, however, could be found in the voluminous coverage of the revolution. The press was simply too busy fanning patriotic emotions and generating a collective rage toward an Iran gone mad. In this context few Americans seemed to understand why the Iranians were so angry with the shah and the United States. What was all the fuss? Americans asked. In this same mindset many U.S. secondary school history texts that covered the era left out any reference to the brutality of the American-supported Pahlavi regime. In Paul Roberts and Paula Franklin's *Comprehensive United States History*, for example, even as they explained why Iranians called the United States the "Great Satan," the authors make no mention of Pahlavi terror.[35] In various pedagogical domains Americans were miseducated about the Iranian Revolution against the shah's regime and the U.S. role in it.

The Iranian Revolution and Hostage Crisis

The events leading up to the Iranian Revolution were brutal and bloody. By the end of 1977 the revolutionary fire was engulfing more and more Iranians against the extravagance and domestic violence of the shah. Violent encounters between protestors and the shah's imperial guard escalated throughout 1978, resulting in thousands of deaths. The shah was persuaded to leave in January 1979, and by February armed revolutionaries established control over all military posts and the national broadcasting center. The shah's reign was over, as the people of Iran chose Khomeini's political Shiite alternative over the shah's secular nationalism. Like many other religious figures in the nation Khomeini had been attacked, imprisoned, and forced into exile by the shah. Such persecution, along with the shah's killing of his son, elevated Khomeini to the status of a holy martyr who could engender support from a wide range of Iranians, including many secularists and intellectuals. Only Khomeini could command such influence—a power that crushed the shah's elaborate mechanisms of self-protection.

Indeed, Khomeini's was a radical new vision of Shiism, powerful enough to convince thousands to face certain death as they protested the shah's ostensibly invincible regime. Of course, like many literalist views of religions—fundamentalism as referenced in the West—Khomeini's Shia was distorted by its absolutist passions. Most Islamic scholars maintain that the taking of hostages violates what they consider Qur'anic edicts. When the shah's government finally fell, there was euphoria in the streets and rejoicing among many, including Iranian leftists and liberals. The left wing believed that Khomeini would not stay in power very long and that the ayatollahs would soon be replaced by worker and citizen councils with the help of secularized army officers. But this revolution was unique in history. Indeed, it was a revolt against the Western modernist belief in a unilinear history of the Western Enlightenment and Western science bringing light to the world. In this sense it was a rebellion against "progress," the first postmodern revolution, designed to return Iran to the realm of the premodern.[36]

These dynamics were virtually impossible for Americans—who had been misled by the narrow perspectives of media analysts and Iranologists—to understand. All that the experts had constructed about the "true nature" of Iran between 1953 and 1979 evaporated like rain on hot asphalt. The multibillion-dollar army, the research foundations, and the power structures literally disappeared with the massive rebellion that was the Iranian Revolution. The experts struggled to make sense of a revolution that was noncommunist, antimodernist (in the Western sense), and pro-religious. It took a while, but eventually many Western observers would declare that the Iranian Revolution marked the return of Islam. Old stereotypes and gross generalizations began to resurface in the Western consciousness. When one connected OPEC and the oil-price increases of the early 1970s with the Iranian Revolution with its anti-American demonstrations and hostage taking, many U.S. experts concluded, "It's baaack...." If Islam was back, then exactly what kind of Islam was it? Did the Islam of Ayatollah Khomeini represent a monolithic Islam? Lost in the essentialism, the uninformed overgeneralization was the reality that Iran's political Shiism was feared in Muslim countries as well. Dramatic political and theological division wracked the Islamic world in the wake of the Iranian revolution.

Obscuring these dimensions of the Iranian Revolution in the United States was the hostage crisis. On November 4, 1979, about 3,000 revolutionary zealots attacked the U.S. embassy in Tehran. In the assault 54 embassy staff members were taken hostage. The hostage takers demanded that

- the shah—in the United States to seek medical treatment—be sent back to Iran to stand trial,
- the U.S. apologize for its crimes against Iran—a demand typically not understood by Americans, and
- the shah's financial assets be turned over to Iran.

The crisis received more media attention, TV coverage in particular, than any event had in years. The ABC News program *Nightline* was created at this time under the title *America Held Hostage*. It was designed to provide Americans a late-night update on the day's events regarding the hostages. At CBS, anchor Walter Cronkite closed the evening news with the number of days the hostages had been in captivity—"day 329 of Americans held captive in Iran." The focus of the TV news coverage of the revolution and the hostage crisis almost always centered on how to end the crisis and how to get the hostages freed. Rare was attention given to the perspectives of the Iranian people, the larger colonial issues raised by the postmodern revolution. Media analysts and the experts they interviewed could not see the world outside of the effect of Iranian events on American geopolitical position.[37] High school world history textbooks reflected this same narrow perspective, many of them devoting most of their attention concerning the Iranian Revolution to the decontextualized specifics of the hostage crisis.[38]

It is hard to uncover U.S. news reporters who devoted time to covering the significant political activities taking place in Iran at the time of the hostage crisis. Most news agencies ignored the debate over the new Iranian constitution and the diverse social and ideological position put forth by different politicians and groups. In the U.S. press all these players were reduced to the designations pro-American or anti-American. Any ideological or political distinctions beyond this one were deemed irrelevant. The dramatic and portentous changes occurring in revolutionary Iraq were labeled as "Islamic" and subsequently relegated to a domain that was too strange to understand and superfluous to American interests. Writing in the mid-1980s, Warren Christopher, the future secretary of state, argued that the American media during the hostage crisis failed dramatically in the effort to inform the American people about what was happening in Iran and why. Events, he concluded, were reported

outside of any historical framework. At the outset of the crisis, the American people probably knew next to nothing about Iran and its history. While a better perspective on the cultural and political traditions of Iran would not have made the hostage seizure any more acceptable or justifiable, it might have made the episode more understandable and could have encouraged a calmer and more deliberate reaction. In particular, the hatred of the Iranians for the United States could be understood only against the background of gross and prolonged abuses by the

Shah and the history of U.S. involvement with him, and this perspective too often was missing.[39]

The media-driven miseducation did not stop merely with Christopher's charge of decontextualizing and omitting important information. Indeed, the media pounded war drums, maintaining that the Iranians committed an act of war against the United States in taking over the embassy and holding hostages. No one in the mainstream media suggested that the 1953 coup might have constituted an act of war against Iran. No mainstream media efforts to contextualize the revolutionary events in Iran existed—efforts that would have helped Americans understand that many Iranians felt the United States and the shah had held them hostage in their own country for over 25 years. Again, many public school history texts reflect this same conceptual framework on the revolution and the hostage crisis. Roberts and Franklin's *Comprehensive United States History*, for example, provides no explanation of why the Iranian Revolution is labeled "Islamic," why the Iranian revolutionaries "hated the U.S.," or the nature of the context that produced the revolution.[40]

The politics of oil in Iran was rarely covered by TV or other mainstream forms of media. Easily accessible and existing in many locations, information concerning egregious U.S. corporate profits on Iranian oil would have alerted Americans to another reason for the Iranian people's anger toward America. Amazingly, most Iranians saw no revenue from the country's oil industry. The U.S. oil policy was not unique in Iran, as similar practices could be found in other Middle Eastern and Islamic nations. Neither was the United States the only nation involved in such economic exploitation; England and other Western nations enjoyed sweetheart oil deals in Iran and other countries. When clerical and representatives from groups concerned with the negative effects of these U.S. policies in Iran in the 1950s through the 1970s complained about such unjust policies, reporters positioned them as hostile witnesses. When Iranian leaders appeared, they were asked only questions concerning the release of the hostages. Outside of this inquiry, they were allowed little speaking time. More often expert guests on American TV were government officials or intellectuals from think tanks and universities who spoke about the revolutionary events in relation to American national interests.

Another factor in the media miseducation involved the inability of American reporters in Iran during the era to speak Farsi. The thin and dominant ideologically framed reports that emerged from the 300 or so American journalists stationed in Iran were remarkably similar and drawn from the same sources. Crisis management provided a consistent framework, as reporters and journalists of all stripes asked how we could control the irrational Iranians. In this conceptual structure all the Americans were guilty of was too much generosity toward the Iranian ingrates.

Such accounts fueled American outrage and contributed nothing to an overall understanding of events. Even journalists from other Western countries provided a more textured view of Iran and Islam in general than did most mainstream American journalists. The great theological debates among Muslims such as the one between the advocates of *ijtihad* (emphasis on the importance of individual interpretation of the Qur'an) and proponents of *taqlid* (stress on the need for deference to expert interpretation) and its relevance to events in Iran were ignored by the American press. The idea that learning more about Islam was important was not a value expressed by the mainstream U.S. media.

When it came to U.S. dealings with Iran from the 1953 coup to the revolution and hostage crisis, various forms of cultural pedagogy produced forms of mass deception. The belief that only the enemies of the country would call for a social, cultural, psychological, and historical examination of U.S. actions in Iran and the Islamic world was implicit in the massive effort devoted to covering the revolution and hostage crisis. Despite all the time spent in this coverage of Iran and other domains of the Islamic world, events seemed to spiral out of control. In this conceptual vortex Islam occupied a space outside of the radar of Western understanding. In addition to the Islamic revolution in Iran there were troubles in Lebanon, Ethiopia, and Somalia, along with a Marxist coup and a Soviet invasion of Afghanistan. What was happening in the Islamic world, Americans asked. The experts were as surprised by the events as anyone else. The literature and "expert commentary" they presented on TV seemed profoundly out of step with the changes taking place in the Islamic world. The best many of the experts could muster in the midst of the confusion was to argue that there is no rationality to the actions of Iranians and other Muslims.

Indeed, to fill in the lack of understanding of the early political Islamist movements, the representation of Muslim irrationality was combined with vicious depictions of Muslim barbarity. In this context *Newsweek* actually invented stories about the torture of American hostages. Such stories led to grotesque (and ancient) exaggerations about Iran's "war against civilization." The return of the American hostages in January 1981 to the United States was transformed into an extended media-produced ideological event. The conceptual framework involved a celebration of American heroism and Iranian savagery. Sappy stories about former hostages returning to their hometowns were juxtaposed with the new Reagan administration's get-tough-on-Iran policy, a course of action the Reaganites labeled as "the war on terrorism." There were exceptions to these representations, certainly in the alternative progressive presses and even a few pieces in the *Washington Post* and *New York Times*.[41] But in literally overwhelming numbers most newspaper and magazine pieces and TV stories reflected the dominant ideological framework.

The U.S. Inability to Make Sense of Khomeini's Islamist Regime

Only a few months after the revolution erupted, Khomeini was in power and the nature of his regime began to reveal itself. The U.S. media offered little insight into either Khomeini himself or the tenets on which his regime began to operate. Basically Americans learned little more than that he was both stubborn and enraged at the United States for some fuzzy and irrational reasons. As the United States watched the new regime suppress dissent, the bearded ayatollah took on a satanic image in the American collective consciousness. Ayatollah Khomeini's regime was no more undemocratic than the shah's. The difference, of course, was that the ayatollah did not support U.S. interests in Iran and the region. In this context Americans began to feel helpless in their ability to make sense of or shape events in Iran and other parts of the Islamic world. As a central oil supplier for the United States during an era of energy shortages, Iran was always on the American mind. Lost as an ally in America's geopolitical designs, the country became a symbol for the United States's inability to control anticolonial and anti-American perspectives in various locales around the world.

The victory of dark over light and the installation of the "satanic" ayatollah were the dominant constructions shaping the American consciousness. Existing outside of history, culture, and power, the new regime in Iran and the events that led up to it made little sense. Indeed, as an island in time, an aberrant historical event, the Iranian Revolution and the resulting Khomeini government were not meant to be understood. In the irrational context there were no profound lessons to be learned, no insight to be drawn from the experience. President Reagan and the leaders of his foreign policy establishment articulated the closest thing to a lesson from Iran: it's time to get tough with terrorist and rogue states. No moral dimension here, simply a proclamation of power politics. Don't tread on us, because the world is ours to do with what is in our interests. In fact, nothing had been learned since the 1953 coup; this was the same mind-set that shaped U.S. responses at that time. Few commented on the mind-set and the problems such a perspective would produce and continue to produce into the twenty-first century.

Khomeini's extremism played right into the Western representation of him as the satanic ayatollah. The Islamist regime was unwilling to tolerate any political orientation that differed from its own. Soon after taking power Khomeini ordered the arrest of leftists, the Tudah party, Kurds, and Turcomans. Such radicalism was fanned by the memory of the British invasions, the Russian intrusions, and the post–World War II U.S. role in the country. The Iranian response to such Western hegemony was more successful than in other Islamic domains because the Shiite Muslims in Iran were better organized than Sunni groups in other countries. Its zealotry was a direct response to the efforts of the two twentieth-century shahs and their Western allies to destroy Islamic institutions. Khomeini represented the struggle as a total way of approaching life. If we fail to view it this way, he argued, the West will simply steal our resources and turn our land into a market for its products. Thus, Islam, he concluded, must develop not only its theological dimension but its political and economic dimensions as well. This is why Khomeini's brand of revolution was referred to as political Islam and why the United States and its corporate interests began to perceive political Islam as such a threat.[42]

The mainstream media's take on the events in Iran during the era were generally so narrow that the conceptual ability to speculate about what such experiences might tell Americans about future situations in the Islamic world was subverted. For example, many experts from the domain of political science had operated on the theory that rapid urbanization would always undermine traditional loyalties. In this framework the shah's urbanization policies of the 1960s and 1970s should have reduced the importance of religion in the country. Of course, just the opposite was the case, as Islam became the central social structure catalyzing the revolution. When Iranian officials attempted to tell Americans that the United States was perceived to be fighting the colonized peoples of the world seeking to determine their own destinies, U.S. government officials and media spokespeople denied that Iranians and other such peoples possessed worthwhile concerns. Seriously considering such concerns demanded that Americans reflect on the decades of political, military, economic, and cultural intervention in Islamdom—a undertaking the U.S. government during the Reagan administration and the U.S. mainstream media were unwilling to consider. Instead, the nation moved farther to the right, assuming a harder-line stance against the Islamic world, especially in those regions and countries with oil resources.[43] Nothing like the Iranian Revolution and Khomeini's Islamist regime would ever be allowed to happen again.

Containing the Revolution: The Covert Role of the United States in the Iran-Iraq War

The Carter and Reagan administrations, the emirs and sheikhs in charge of the small Gulf states, and the Saudi kingdom feared Khomeini's Islamist revolution. In this context the United States began to court the favor of the Iraqi leader, Saddam Hussein. Along with the Americans the emirs, sheikhs, and kings cut a path to Baghdad to honor the "sword of Iraq." Poems were read to Hussein by a member of the Kuwaiti royal family as the regional leaders spoke of the danger posed to "all of us" by the spread of the Iranian Islamist revolution. As they presented him with money and extravagant gifts, the frightened rulers pleaded with him to crush the radical ayatollahs in Iran. If the revolution spread to Bahrain and Kuwait, they argued, it would not be long before both Saudi Arabia and Iraq, with its majority Shia population, collapsed. Saddam was more than willing to comply but wanted to know what the United States wanted. Upon getting approval from Washington, Hussein ordered his troops to invade Iran in September 1980.[44]

Throughout the war Iraq pursued a relentless propaganda campaign against the Iranians. Financed by Saudi Arabia, Kuwait, and the small Gulf states, the campaign positioned the Islamist revolution as anti-Arab, anti-Islamic, and anti-Sunni. The Iranians were portrayed as the progeny of the fire worshippers of ancient Persia who would have to be freed and converted to Islam in much the same way that Arabs had liberated their ancestors in the seventh century. The United States was so caught up in opposing Iran's political Islam that government officials in the Reagan administration were willing to look the other way when Saddam used chemical weapons against the Iranians. Despite the atrocities of Saddam's military, the United States resumed diplomatic relations with Iraq 17 years after breaking them. The Reagan administration felt that under no circumstances could the United States let the Iranian Revolution spread.

The Iraqi attack on the Iranians pulled the people of Iran together in outrage. What Hussein thought would be a short and relatively easy war took on the character of the trench warfare of World War I, killing by the end over one million Muslims. After a significant Iraqi offensive in the first two years of the conflict, the Iranians counterattacked in 1982, regaining all of the lands overrun by the Iraqis. In the midst of the Iranian counterattack the leaders of the Ba'ath Party met to offer a cease fire that submitted to all Iranian demands. Scholars of the war contend that if this had been accepted, Saddam would have been removed from power. But such an ignominious end for Hussein was not to be. Buoyed by Iranian military victories, Ayatollah Khomeini ignored the generous terms of the cease-fire. The Iranian Revolution, he thought, was on the verge of international expansion. The sword of Baghdad held on to power by a slender thread and continued the fighting.[45]

The massive casualties did not disturb the Reagan administration. Indeed, the administration's strategy was to bleed both sides as much as possible. Former president Nixon writing about the Reagan administration's handling of the situation maintained that Reagan's people did a good job of playing both sides and making sure that neither side emerged as a clear-cut victor. In 1986 this policy took an unexpected twist when the administration began favoring Iran. The reasons for the change are convoluted and muddled but have something to do with American Cold War fears about *possible* Soviet and Iranian ties. A CIA report in 1985 had contended that whatever superpower got to Tehran first would gain a strong strategic position. This helps observers understand the secret U.S. arms sales to Iran in 1985 and 1986. Even before the bizarre shift toward Iran, the United States had been selling the country arms through Israeli intermediaries. This was taking place even as the United States was pressuring allies to stop supplying arms to Iran. When the arms deals were exposed, the Reagan administration faced a serious scandal. Money from the sales had been directed to the Nicaraguan Contras in violation of the Boland Amendment outlawing such support. The exposure of the scam and the double-dealing by the Reagan administration alienated the Iranians and undermined trust of the U.S. in Saudi Arabia and the Gulf States. To cut its losses the U.S. administration turned its "neutral" support back to Iraq.[46]

Such U.S. support helped the Iraqis neutralize Iranian successes and moved the war back to a stalemate. After several massacres of Iranian troops and heavy Iraqi bombing of Iranian civilians, Khomeini agreed to a cease-fire in August 1988. Signing the agreement, Khomeini confided, was like drinking a cup of poison. The defeat marked a watershed in the Iranian Revolution, as many leaders came to understand that uncompromising ideological policies did not always work the way they were intended. The Islamic Revolution could not be exported to other countries in some simple act of transference. A new era was emerging that demanded more pragmatic political, economic, and foreign policies.

These realizations formed the basis on which the Iranian Reformation would be grounded. The unification of all Islamic peoples, Iranian leaders realized, was not possible in the late 1980s, 1990s, or the first decade of the twenty-first century. After Khomeini's death in 1989 Hashemi Rafsanjani assumed the presidency. As a cleric who came from a business background, Rafsanjani embodied the new pragmatism of Iran. He would support modernization policies, industrialization, and even U.S. efforts to replace Saddam Hussein with a moderate Iraqi leader. The Iranians were in the process of creating their own Islamic brand of democracy and modernization, characterized by a more complex interpretation of Islamic law and a more progressive attitude toward women and gender relations.[47]

Khatami's Islamic Civil Society: Liberal Rumblings

Along with the liberalizing influences pushed by President Rafsanjani, Iran continued to ask America to come to terms with its misdeeds in the country. In the 1990s two different but not conflicting impulses pushed Iranian foreign policy:

- a desire to open communications with the United States and pursue a closer relationship; and
- a fear of American economic, political, and cultural hegemony that sweeps away millennia of Persian and Islamic civilization.

Even after all the interventions of the United States in shaping Iranian affairs, from the 1953 coup, support of the shah's brutality, siding with Iraq in the Iran-Iraq war, and the toughening economic sanctions against the country during the Clinton administration to former House Speaker Newt Gingrich's efforts to fund the overthrow of the Iranian government with congressionally appropriated funds, it seems remarkable that forces within the Iranian government consistently worked for closer relations with the United States. President Clinton and other government leaders were very slow to respond to Iranian initiatives throughout the decade.

American officials during this period proceeded cautiously because of their disapproval of numerous Iranian activities, including land disputes with the United Arab Emirates; their hostility (ironically) toward the Taliban government in Afghanistan; and the troubling support of the Palestinian Islamic jihad and Hamas, coupled with a vicious anti-Israeli sentiment coming from the conservative elements of the government and their interest in nuclear weapons. Nevertheless, many observers in the 1990s believed that improved U.S.-Iranian relations were inevitable. After an initial hesitancy, President Clinton in his second term began to take a personal interest in making such better relations a reality.[48]

Coupled with this growing desire for better relations was the sentiment among many Iranian young people that they no longer wanted to be ruled by clerics. The new generation coming of age in the 1990s had experienced clerical oppression and wanted a liberalized, truly democratic government. The election of Sayyid Mohammad Khatami as president in May 1997 was an indication that Iranians had suffered heavy social, economic, and emotional consequences from the Islamist revolutionary fervor. Khatami presented the Iranian people with a vision of an Islamic civil society—one quite different than its Western counterpart. In distinguishing the two visions of civil society Khatami argued that the Western notion traces its genesis to the Greek city-state, whereas the Iranian conception is grounded on the concept of Madanat al-Nabi, the City of the Prophet.

While following different developmental routes, Khatami contended, the two visions are by no means incompatible as both lay claims to a respect for social, cultural, political, and economic liberty. The main difference here is that Khatami's civil society is grounded on theology, whereas the Western version rests on a more secular foundation. Khatami's assertion that the two democratic visions are not incompatible is part of a larger political perspective that is quite liberal in relation to the representations of Iran by educators, media, and government officials. Overtly rejecting Samuel P. Huntington's "clash of civilizations" thesis that positions Islam in a fundamental conflict with the West, Khatami has spoken at length about the interdependence between cultures, nations, and economies. In this same context he has repeatedly called for dialogue among the world's various religions.

Khatami's political philosophy is not well known by Americans. Rarely have his liberal perspectives been a topic for analysis in the mainstream American media. Such viewpoints opened a window of possibility for developing new relationships with Iran in the late 1990s and the first years of the new century. Close ties between the United States and Iran could lay the foundation for a reconceptualized American view of and policy relating to the Islamic world. The Iranians who voted for Khatami well understood these possibilities—liberal democratic reforms at home combined with peaceful coexistence with other countries. Sixty-nine percent of Iran's voters—predominately women and the young—picked Khatami in May 1997 with these hopes in mind. Respect our dignity, these Khatami supporters urged the United States. Recognize the ways you have undermined our efforts to be self-directed and we can become close allies.

It was in this liberalizing context that Albright's remarks were offered. Not surprisingly Iran's foreign minister, Kamal Kharrazi, provided a friendly official response to the secretary of state. If "the United States," he posited, "is really for an improvement of ties with Iran, it should take practical steps in this regard and show that it has abandoned its hostile policy."[49] While Kharrazi was making his statement Iran attempted to show its good faith to the U.S. in a pragmatic gesture. In the early spring of 2000 Iran captured numerous Iraqi ships that were thought to be smuggling oil. By these actions Iran signaled to the United States that it was ready to play the role of a security guard for the Persian Gulf—a policeman who would administer UN sanctions in the region. In the wake of the attacks of 9/11 thousands of Iranians held candlelight vigils, lasting for weeks, designed to show solidarity with America and sympathy for its losses in the tragedy. Day after day crowds congregated and shouted in unison, "America, condolences, America, condolences." Too busy running scenes of Palestinians celebrating American losses at the World Trade Center and the Pentagon, American TV ignored the tapes of the Iranian vigils.[50]

Just Ask the Axis: The Contemporary Iranian Curriculum

Ever since the revolution and the hostage crisis the American media has taught an Iranian curriculum that has made the nation and its Islamist

government known to Americans. The educational power of the media—
a central concern of *The Miseducation of the West*—with its constant volley
of pictures and information representing everything from Islam to peanut
butter, is the great storyteller of the contemporary era. Power-wielding
media conglomerates with an economic agenda have great influence in
shaping our understanding of people, places, and things. The contemporary media curriculum on Iran created such a negative image of the country and its people that recent surveys maintain that Iranians are one of the
nationalities the American public hates most. When asked about their
images of Iran, Americans speak of terrorism, religious zealotry, primi-
tiveness, political repression, and an absence of respect for human life.[51]

These anti-Iranian images were fueled by popular culture. One popular
song in the early 1980s was entitled "They Can Take Their Oil and Shove
It." Movie producers found new bad guys in Iranians. In *The Hitman*
(1991) indigenous rival mobsters join together to decimate an Iranian mob
moving in on their territory. In many movies Iranians slowly morph into
Muslims from other countries. They all have the same culture, characterized by belly dancing, hummus, and oil money. In May 1997 CBS presented an episode of its drama *JAG* in which Palestinians speaking perfect
Farsi take over a hospital. Such distinctions did not matter to the producers of American media culture. One of the lowest points of media representation came with the 1990 release of *Not Without My Daughter*. An
Iranian doctor takes his American wife and daughter back to Iran for a
visit. Once in Iran he "returns" to his Islamic heritage and refuses to let his
wife and daughter go back to the United States. In her chapter on media
representations of Muslims Shirley Steinberg expands on this analysis.
The image of the evil Iranian plays out in every frame of the movie.

Of course, such depictions are dehistoricized, as American connections
to any source of Iranian anger are erased. Images were substituted for
explanation and contextualization of the nature of U.S.-Iranian relations
after World War II. Eurocentric reason raised its insolent head in this context as Iranians were represented as being incapable of Western rationality: they don't understand cause-and-effect or the relationship between
words and reality because of their "bazaar mentality," many Americans
maintained through words and images. It is no wonder that after being
closed for 22 years the American embassy was reopened in 1991 by the Iranians under a new name—the Museum of Arrogance. Iranians flocked to
the building to view many rooms filled with exhibits depicting American
intervention around the world and other examples of American arrogance. As many Iranians point out, the old embassy is a large building and
there is more than enough arrogance to fill it up.[52]

Despite the arrogance, Khatami pushed ahead with his call for a "dialogue between" the countries, not a "clash of civilizations." After 9/11
international leaders met in Bonn, Germany, to put together a new post-

Taliban government in Afghanistan. Iran played a central role in the Bonn negotiations in late 2001. Indeed, observers noted that the "U.S. and Iranian delegations were practically hugging and kissing each other. They were going around arm-in-arm doing everything together."[53] It seemed to those present that a new day had dawned in the domain of U.S.-Iranian relations. Then, to the surprise of the world, only a month and a half later President George W. Bush presented his State of the Union address with its reference to Iran as a partner in the "axis of evil" along with Iraq and North Korea. All of the efforts toward good relations between the two nations broke apart like the *Columbia* over Texas. Immediately, in the Iranian streets observers witnessed American flag burnings and marchers chanting "death to America"—sights and sounds that had faded in the Iran of the late 1990s and the immediate years before the February 2002 speech.

President Khatami, in a tone previously unheard during his tenure, urged Iranians to protest Bush's insulting depiction of Iran as evil. The axis of evil speech had initiated a sea change in Iran. Leaders of hard-line religious politics as well as democratic reformers called for protests against "Bush's threat," as they perceived it. Iranians from different socio-economic classes were profoundly upset by Bush's words, as women from wealthy North Tehran homes marched alongside religious zealots to express their disgust. One liberal young woman in support of democratic reforms told an American reporter: "I didn't hate Bush before, but now I really hate him...He's damaging everything. He has hurt the reformers, and is bringing the hard-liners together.[54] Khatami's speech provided no further reference to the dialogue between civilizations. Calling Bush "immature," Khatami proclaimed that "the time for bullying is over." "Those running the U.S. consider themselves masters of the world, and define their own interests in contradiction to the world's. And since they have power, they use force...today, in an immature and ridiculous way, they are playing with you and your revolution."[55]

The democratic reformers were profoundly discouraged by the axis of evil speech. Many Iranian liberals proclaimed that Bush killed Khatami's reform movement. Ayatollah Khamenei is the Supreme Leader of the Islamic Republic of Iran—an unelected but powerful position of spiritual and political power. A religious hard-liner, Khamenei addressed the nation on national TV after the State of the Union. "America," he maintained, "is neither sincere in its claim of combating terrorism, nor is it qualified to assume a position of leadership in such a war." In light of Bush's proclamation that "you are either with us or with the terrorists," Khamenei stated that "we are neither with you nor with the terrorists."[56]

The Bush administration had missed a golden opportunity to enter into a close relationship with Iran in the war on terrorism as well as in relation to other political, economic, and social concerns. We have been and still are working hard to cooperate with the United States in relation to Afghanistan and al-Qaida, official Iranian spokespeople maintained, but look how President Bush responded. He has not produced trust between the two countries, officials proclaimed, but has generated mistrust. Indeed, in the months following the axis of evil speech Iranian leaders began to fear that U.S. troop deployments against Iraq would ultimately be used to settle America's score with Iran. To deter such a threat hard-liners are working to restart the Iran nuclear weapons program. After the Cold War and 9/11 there are only two major forces in the world, many Iranians argue: the industrialized West led by the United States and the oppressed East led by the Islamic Republic of Iran. Thus, relations between the United States and Iran become more and more polarized in the first decade of the twenty-first century. The words of President Khatami become more and more defensive, as he consistently warns the Bush administration against military action against Iran. The mainstream American media continues to report these events outside of the historical context provided in this chapter.[57] Along with many other Islamic nations and groups, Iran is represented with renewed enthusiasm as an enemy of the United States. The miseducation continues.

Chapter 5

Consequences of Perceived Ethnic Identities

Christopher D. Stonebanks

Three male medical students walk into a restaurant in Florida—a Pakistani, an Iranian, and a Saudi Arabian. While they are waiting to order their meals, an American woman in another booth eavesdrops on their conversation and claims to hear them plotting in Arabic and English about committing terrorist activities. Are you waiting for the punch line? Well, sadly, there isn't one. Before September 11 this little scene would have sounded like the opening to a typical bad ethnic joke that I would have had to politely smile my way through. Now it is part of our lives, a scenario that anybody who pays even the remotest attention to the television news has witnessed over and over again. It is a reality. But it is a reality that goes far beyond three American medical students of "Eastern" origin being detained for possible terrorism for 17 hours on a stretch of highway. It is more significant than simple vigilance against further acts of terrorism because their detention was based on someone's purely imagined account, an account that was derived solely from their appearance. The perception of who this woman believed these men to be was so strong that an otherwise average American citizen could imagine in her own mind three men, whose only common language was English, speaking Arabic. It is yet another example of how North American perception of people from the East is being continuously created, based not on facts and objective observation and research but on the miseducation about the East through a variety of sources.

How is it that an Iranian, a Pakistani, an Indian, a Sikh, an Afghani, or any other dark-skinned person from this vast region have all become "Arabs, or perhaps more accurately, Arabs with possible links to terrorism? Are we witnessing the creation of some sort of Pan-Arabism or Pan-terrorist-Arabism in the West, a forced construction of the image of the dangerous Arab that pays no respect to the rich linguistic, historic, cultural, political, geographic, religious, and ethnic differences among these diverse people of the so-called East? With racial profiling becoming increasingly used and abused, I ask myself what effect this has on the individual who is now being constructed and perceived in this "Pan-Arab" model. The person from any of the multitude of diverse countries of the "Middle East" has become a sort of Pan-Arab creature, devoid of any diversity in language, religion, culture, history, or sometimes humanity. In this new post–September 11 world, Iranians, Pakistanis, and whoever else from that "other" place seem to have lost control in creating their identities. Ethnic identity formation for people of the East has now become a construction of various sources of education and the often more influential media, which is fueled by hysteria to find answers to the otherwise complex situations in the world.

My concern lies with the implications to the youngest victims of this created perception within North America, namely, elementary-school-aged children of imagined and constructed Pan-Arab origin, and all the innuendos and assumptions that go hand in hand with it. I write this chapter for student teachers, teachers, and administrators with the intention of creating awareness of this perception and getting them to think about how schools in North America, Canada, and the United States should manage it. Through the use of personal narratives, I expect to create a dialogue, for the reader to use both internally and with colleagues, that will bring these stories from those who experience them into the shared understanding of our teaching profession.

Often, student teachers, teachers, and administrators complain that academic writing in the field of education is just that—academic, with little relevance to the real world. As a lecturer within the faculty of education at McGill University, I come across many students who share this grumbling, and to a large extent, I agree with them. So, in response to this common criticism, I begin by assuring the reader that this chapter will be practical in nature and based on experience; after all, it was practical experience that fashioned my own motivation for writing it. Much of this work will be based on events and observation. It is narrated by an educator and a student as well as an adult and a child, all of whom lived through and continue to live with many of the consequences that result from being perceived as someone from the East.

Educational research from the personal perspective, or in this case narratives from members of the school's community, always seem to be the most appreciated research within the teaching profession. The practicality and reality of personal experience gives greater depth to the issue being discussed and is all the more relevant when dealing with the narration of "counterstories" by minority groups.[1] These counterstory narratives give a voice to those who otherwise are marginalized and permit those of us within the education profession to hear what these voices have to say. However, for the narrative to be truly revealing and successful, it is important for the writer to reveal all that is relevant about himself or herself in relation to the writing. Drawing from Norman Denzin's truism that "value-free research is impossible"[2] and the principles of Elliot Eisner,[3] with his emphasis on the importance of acknowledging one's values and subjectivity within one's examinations, the understanding grew that academics and researchers, at any level, bring their preconceived notions about the subject to be studied. This is even more important when discussing people who are considered "other."[4]

Said's concept of the other is more than just the prejudices and stereotypes of another ethnic group. It is the dominance of one ethnic group over the other's identity, in both creation and perpetuation. What may have been the creation of the East, or as Said refers to as the Orient, through literature and painting can be easily seen through the modern forms of disseminating information, such as television[5] and film,[6] and even within the highly influential, and overlooked, world of comic books.[7] Later in this chapter I will discuss how modern media continues to miseducate the West because I do appreciate why this concept is often difficult to understand; the complexities of how an identity is created by another and then imposed upon the other is often the source of frustration to many student teachers and teachers alike. It is, however, an essential concept that must be understood not only within the confines of this writing, but also as a means to creating understanding toward and dialogue with the East, not only for people who are from the East but for North Americans of so-called Eastern descent as well.

Most of us from this perceived (real or imagined) Eastern ethnic background have at one time or another experienced this created identity. I can remember an early incident of this happening in my youth. A childhood friend's mother responded with enthusiastic description to her cousin, who had queried my ethnic background. With a genuine smile she said, "Oh, his mother is from the East. You should see her, she's beautiful and *very* exotic!" She then proceeded to do a little dance, combined with shaking her head from side to side, darting her eyes, and waving her hands across her eyes, doing her best to evoke the "dance of a thousand veils." I remember looking up at her from the floor and thinking, "Is that supposed to be an imitation of my mom?" Although I am sure she meant absolutely no harm, I, along with my mother and siblings, had been turned into some creature of the mystical East and "othered" into some kind of mysterious people from a mysterious land; an imagined identity born of romance novels, movies, and myths had been created for us. Some readers may think to themselves, "So what? I'd *love* to be considered exotic!" But think about those three medical students in Florida. Think about the imagined identities that were created for them. Shaheen's exhaustive review of Arab portrayals within cinema reveals that this othering takes on a new, more pervasive form, one that is distinctly more negative and more violent than my friend's mother's dance of a thousand veils. This is the current danger in which we find ourselves—the imagined identity that has been created for us has been born of too many Hollywood "Arab" villains,[8] news channels of questionable authority,[9] and various other media sources, repeated and reinforced in staff room conversations and seemingly validated by the events of September 11.

These issues of perception and the imposed identity creation of minority groups have always been a personal interest of mine. More than likely that is because most of us who carry out research from the student's perspective do so because we ourselves, through our own interactions, have become sensitive to the condition of the individual within the institution of schools. This is indeed my experience, as I can easily recall a series of defining moments in my early elementary years that influenced my interest in studying the social aspects of school and its relationship with minority students. Most of these incidents revolved around the issue of racial intolerance that quietly permeates schools in North America. These events left me so perplexed about the social dynamics of those participating within the "normal" order of the school system that I slowly went from being a child who sought to belong to a group to an individual who relegated himself to the sidelines—in essence, from participant to observer. The defining moment, in my experience, occurred when the social injustice of elementary school racism transcended from childish bullying to what amounted to institutional approval of such actions by staff members—all of which was based on ethnic assumptions and accepted ignorance.

At this point in a narrative endeavor, the author is encouraged to reveal his or her identity. Such a confession, so to speak, reveals any prejudicial motives of the author and enriches the reader's understanding about who is writing and for whom. I don't put forward my own cultural identity and ethnicity with any feelings it will be understood, as I have always found that my heritage is difficult for others to comprehend. In fact, I envy those who come from a monolithic culture and have often, foolishly, imagined how easy it would be to just be white or black. I am a product of a complicated mixed-ethnic marriage (I purposely avoid the subject of race). My father's parents were British and Italian, each holding onto their respective Methodist and Catholic religions. My mother is an Iranian, whose parents' roots differed with religions of Judaism and Islam but, in opposition to the antagonism constantly portrayed in the media, were fiercely loyal and loving to each other. My father, born in colonial Egypt, enjoyed all the advantages of a privileged gentleman's life, the result of his British father's steadfast belief in imperialism (he was, after all, an officer in the British army). Left with little choice of occupation, my father would later fight in three wars for England and, seriously injured twice, suffer the physical consequences of "defending the interests" of a country he had never really known. My mother is his polar opposite. We always used to joke about how my father, despite his early years in Egypt, didn't know the difference between Arabs and Iranians when he married her, fantasizing of Said's Oriental image of the submissive and exotic Arab woman. Instead, he had to deal with the sharp tongue of a politically savvy woman who was very aware of how England, France, the Soviet Union, and the United States were all fighting for possession of her country's precious resources. An interesting mix that, as I grew up in a predominantly Anglo-Saxon neighborhood in Montreal, Canada, presented me with many challenges. When you come from a mixed ethnic and religious background and grow up in a predominantly homogeneous neighborhood, encountering racism was something you dreaded on a daily basis. This, sadly, is not uncommon given that most newly arrived minority groups usually endure such conditions when they move to communities that are culturally and ethnically homogeneous and different from their own.

Although I was born in England, I came to Canada at the age of two and grew up as most Canadians do. With the exception of summers spent in prerevolutionary Iran, my mother gave up all customs of her heritage, choosing not to teach us Iranian culture or language. This was done not out of shame for her own culture, but because there were absolutely no Iranians within our community with whom to share any of these facets. Again, I don't put forward my ethnic background with any sense of fortuity. I do believe, however, that it has given me a unique position of always being a participant observer. The role of being within a group, somewhat accepted by the group, to greater and lesser degrees, but always seeing the event and interaction from another perspective, has always been a part of my life. In the post-9/11 setting, I have an added benefit of having grown up with an Iranian mother who always discussed issues of imperialism that plagued her native country and a British father who always had difficulty seeing how colonialism could ever be perceived as negative. When you come from this kind of mixed background and participate in education and debate regarding issues of politics and basic human rights and conditions, it is maddening to witness the simplicity with which influential "authorities" like Samuel P. Huntington, author of *The Clash of Civilizations* (1996),[10] shape the media and, therefore, the general population's perspective on the East. For instance, creating this belief that there actually is an "Arab world," perhaps floating around somewhere between Venus and Jupiter. How better to dehumanize a culture and a people than to create a world for them, apart from our own Western world? Perhaps more maddening is when academics and even Arabs use this term. It is symbolic of a divide of people that is not based in reality but is created. I try hard to believe that no malice is intended in the creation of these kinds of myths; it is simply symptomatic of the difficulties of dialogue when people know so little about each other.

I've witnessed the dance my parents have engaged in too many times, between the colonial soldier who inadvertently fumbles words that presume the well-meaning but misguided notion that indigenous people need to be somehow "guided," and my proud, indignant, and rebellious Eastern mother who seethes at the comments, fueled by her country's history of imperial manipulation. Most of the time, my mother would laugh off the idea that people from the East were somehow perceived as less than human, but sometimes she would ponder that perhaps it was true. Now that I am a father, I realize she did this with the intention of not wanting to validate her children's uncertainties about their own self-worth and identity. However, the constant sweeping depiction of "people from the East" within film, television, and other forms of mass media was too powerful for us not to feel less than human. In compiling an exhaustive review of the portrayal of people of the East within the media, Shaheen noted that only Native Americans have been more relentlessly smeared.[11] Having experienced this ethnic slurring from an Eastern perspective, I have a great deal of sympathy for the unfortunate group that would have the dubious honor of receiving even worse treatment. As a result of this ethnic background and heritage, I have a firsthand understanding of both perspectives, but I don't admit that with any feelings of good fortune or misfortune. It is simply there, just like the trials and tribulations that accompany people's reactions to and attitudes about who or what they believe you are.

During my childhood, confrontations about my presumed racial background would sometimes degenerate into fighting. The fighting would inevitably lead to myself and the other child sitting in the principal's office awaiting our punishment. The punishment always revolved around the aspect of fighting, and it was usually the position of the principal or teachers that the reason that caused the fight was unimportant. The underlying message was always that fighting was not acceptable regardless of the series of events that led to it. I can remember, on most occasions, meekly attempting to explain to the principal that I was fighting with my classmate due to a racial insult, perhaps coupled with physical intimidation. However, the usual response from the school's authority figure was a curt cut-off and a disapproving shake of the head, declaring that he or she didn't care what reason was behind the fight. The issue of racial discrimination was never addressed, so I always assumed that the school's priority was nonviolence ahead of all other issues, even bigotry.

I never concluded that the adult authority figures within the school had any opinion as to the racial dilemma that I faced on a seemingly daily basis, because that dilemma was never addressed. A single incident, however, that occurred when I was in an early grade proved to be the first time an adult authority figure, in this case a schoolteacher, seemingly approved of the discriminatory actions of another child. This incident would forever alter my impression of the way schools functioned.

It occurred on an early spring afternoon, shortly after school was let out for the day. An older child, a fifth-grader, commenced following me in the school's hallway, venomously jeering after me, "Paki, Paki, PAKI!" The term Paki referred in a derogatory way to people from Pakistan, the assumed origin of my darker complexion. The child commented on my darker skin color, making insulting remarks such as, "You smell like crap because that's the color of your skin." During this entire time, I simply kept my head down, trying to avoid the situation, as the other children laughed at his words.

I remember momentarily feeling relief as he left, I assumed, to retrieve his belongings from his cubby. I did so as well, hoping to get home as fast as possible. Much to my horror, as I exited the school, the fifth-grader was waiting outside, standing with a group of students congregated around him in a half circle facing me. Keep in mind that this was a child two years my senior, and there was quite a size difference between us. Needless to say, I was scared. Realizing that any attempt to deal with this dilemma would probably be futile, I attempted to simply walk past the crowd.

As I pushed through the children, the older child started pushing at me and continued to verbally insult me, and then he spat on my head. I was incensed. It did not matter that the other child was older and stronger than I; the humiliation of being spat upon as if I was some lower form of life in this child's eyes was unbearable. Enraged, I threw my entire body upon the startled child, throwing my fists and furiously rubbing the shame of his saliva off my head and into his clothes. That's the one sensation I recall with the greatest vividness—the feeling of pressure as my head pressed against his torso, head pressed to nylon with my hair acting as a weak border between the jacket and my skin as the wetness of his saliva came into contact with my skin and intertwined in my hair. The other children roared with excitement, and in a moment my teacher had us both by the collars of our shirts and dragged us into the school.

Immediately, she started yelling at us about our disruptive behavior. I was in tears; I felt dirty and ashamed at being spat upon, and the other child simply stood silently in front of my teacher as she continued chastising us, threatening us with detentions. It was too much to bear that I would be penalized for reacting to such a degrading act; I spoke out through the tears. I explained what he had said and what he had done, but the teacher stared back at me with amazement and contempt. "Why," she said, pausing briefly, as her mouth searched for words, "do you have to make such a big deal about what other children call you? So, he made fun of the country you're from; stop making a big deal about it!" In essence, she validated his actions.

I never fully trusted another authority figure within the elementary or secondary school system again. As the other child stood smugly listening to my teacher scolding me, I realized those teachers, principals, and parents held the same contemptuous attitudes that their children and students did. I realized that bigotry was not something that just children indulged in, but that it was an adult vice as well. As an adult, I realized that these children's perceptions and values were completely derived from their families, perhaps as a result of overhearing their parents' fears of losing their jobs to "Paki" immigrants, or the value of their homes diminishing if, God forbid, a family moves into the neighborhood. The fears in England of an invasion by "Western Oriental gentlemen" from countries like Pakistan may have been more overt, but the same sentiments were alive in England's predominantly white commonwealth countries as well.

My ethnic heritage was not Pakistani, but that fact was quite inconsequential. My teacher knew this; I had been in her class a year and had told her where my parents were from. After that incident, I never thought it was appropriate that I explain my heritage to future bigots and never denied that I was from Pakistan or India or wherever the focus of their hatred stemmed from. It wasn't important. Their learned hatred, from whoever influenced them, did not care about geography; their hatred simply cared about differences. In a few years my true country of origin, Iran, would oust Western foreign influences and take a group of Americans hostage for 444 days. This would be enough to quell comments of hatred about other countries, and bigots would at least hate me for the country my mother actually came from.

After that incident, school became a place where classmates were to be avoided and authority figures were not to be trusted. As years passed into secondary schooling, although I was able to grow beyond a distrust of my peers and enjoy a very social lifestyle, I never did fully trust again the school's staff until I entered the College of General and Vocational Education (CEGEP) system. This incident was by no means the worst our family experienced; other incidents included a rock being thrown through our home's window; anonymous phone calls threatening that we should go back where we came from; and, more frighteningly, presumably the same bigoted hoodlums attempted to set our house on fire. University courses in the sociology of education provided a theoretical vehicle to allow me to understand the actions of people within schools. And the incidents that I endured as a child left me with a sensitivity and commitment to work, above all, with students within their schools and to make the relationship between the two more just. The community where this incident occurred has changed; there is a greater diversity in the community and greater tolerance.

In 2000 my wife, our children, and I moved back to the community, and I openly marveled how different the neighborhood had become since I left in 1988. Then September 11 occurred. A few days later, while glued to CNN, I heard a commotion as two vehicles screeched to a halt outside my house. A Sikh man in a turban was angrily pleading at a white man in a pickup truck, "What is your problem?" The white man in the truck yelled back profanities at the man in the turban. Unfortunately, I couldn't hear everything the white man had to say, but his contorted, angry, hateful, spiteful gestures and mannerisms were all too familiar to me. I raced out the front door and bellowed, "What the hell is going on?" The white man looked startled as I took a step off my front stoop and began approaching his truck, and he immediately drove away. The man in the turban stood in the middle of the road, frustrated, angry, and confused. "What the hell is going on?" I repeated. He then proceeded to tell me that this man simply drove by his house, stopped his truck, accused him of being a terrorist, and said he would be back to "take care of his family." Incensed, the Sikh man had jumped in his car, chased down the white man's truck, and pulled in front of him, forcing him to stop. After he explained to me what had happened, he paused in confusion and said, "I'm not even an Arab, I'm Sikh!" "It doesn't matter," I responded with a feeling of dread in the pit of my stomach. "We're all the same to them. Now more than ever." My heart sank. "It" had returned.

Are we Easterners or Middle Easterners all the same? If you are reading this chapter and you are not of what you consider to be Middle Eastern or Eastern descent, do you believe we are all the same? For instance, can you see the differences, hear the differences, and acknowledge the differences in history or even pick up the different cultural mannerisms? Are you open to the reality that they, or we, are not all the same? Consider North American history and its forgotten plight of the Native Americans. At one time their diversity, their very individuality, at least by their own perception, was unquestioned. It is without argument that prior to the colonization of America, the Native tribes were as diverse as they were numerous. North America's vast magnitude was reflected in the multiple cultures, languages, politics, and beliefs of its Native people, much like the so-called Middle East. Before the European colonization of North America, the Native tribes probably considered themselves as distinct from each other as do European countries within Europe. European colonization and the conquest of the American continent and its indigenous people changed that. It is the European view of the Native tribes and people that ultimately changed their own perceptions of themselves and the relationships the Native tribes and people had with each other. It is the very perception that the majority of white people held of the Natives as a group that encouraged the genesis of a Pan-Indianism identity.

In Fredrick Barth's 1969 anthropological publication *Ethnic Groups and Boundaries*, he formulates that ethnicity evolves from a unison of socially

ascribed designation and group self-identification. This process is not
unlike many social theories that contend that the individual is shaped not
only by how he or she perceives him- or herself but by how others see him
or her as well. According to Barth's perspective, ethnicity is decided from
both the group's view of themselves as well as how those outside the group
view them.[12] Joane Nagel (1996) further expands on Barth's theory, making
convincing arguments that the arrival of the white Europeans gave the
Native Indian tribes the first sense of themselves as a collective against for-
eigners.[13] In many ways, it gave them a forced sense of "us against them."
Or, as Nagel contends: "Despite differences, there is an overarching sense
of "we" (and of "they") that emerges when collective fates and interests are
at stake and when the larger group confronts outsiders."[14]

White people of this century, even those who think of themselves as liberal and
somehow romantically attached to the Indian cause, seldom understand that
being "Indian" is something forced upon people of cultures as different as Chinese
and Italian. Totally different languages and customs, old rivalries, and even
hatreds still stand between many tribes. The unity among them has sometimes
been forced out of desperation, mutual agony, or pride. These differences were
laid aside...on the common ground of oppression.[15]

The Native Indian ethnicity has developed under the dual forces of the
"larger group" defining them as "Indian" and consequently Natives making the choice to unify under the umbrella of oppression. Our own school
curriculum on North American history conveniently ignores the very real
"foreign" aggression that forced this circumstance of identity transformation. Stephen Cornell describes Pan-Indianism as an "Indian consciousness" and asserts that Indians are increasingly thinking of themselves in
terms of a whole rather than the individual tribe.[16] With this comes an
increased Pan-Indian political involvement in which Natives are increasingly thinking in terms of what is best for the entire Indian "race" instead
of what is good for one particular tribe. In effect, once there are too few of
you to demand recognition for your individuality, group or personal, you
try to take control of even the stereotypes that have been placed upon you.
    The fundamentalist elements of the (Middle) East are increasingly rec-
ognizing that their common problems are forcing them, sooner or later, to
act as one, and the West is more than primed to see even the majority moderate in one all-encompassing broad stroke. When we hear the phrase
"over a billion Muslims," is it meant to elicit a response of respect for a
religion that has influenced a vast mosaic of cultures and people, or does
it conjure up images of a monolithic horde of dangerous evil and violent
"Ayrab" types, plotting to destroy liberty and democracy just...because?
What dangers lie in wait for the indigenous of the East and the immigrant
Easterners in the West? If it hasn't happened already, how long before

Pakistan or Afghanistan becomes associated with the Middle East, along with Iranians as Arabs as this same kind of Pan–Middle Eastern entity, and how many teachers are actively trying to understand this developing situation?

Being associated with this Pan-terrorist-Arabism identity in North America must be a source of torment for children, as the images in the media regarding their ethnic identity are continuously being imposed upon them in the most unpleasant light. As Shaheen notes, this is not a recent phenomenon.[17] I always thought it amusing that perhaps the first organized attempt at mass slander and humiliation of the people of the East was the croissant, meant for symbolic consumption of Islam by the Christians during the Crusades. Mass consumption of the East has become a lot more slick and high-tech in modern times, but in the end the message still seems to be the same.

Some readers may be thinking, "I just treat everyone as Canadian (or American), and all this isn't applicable to me," but is this always the case? (Marilyn Cochran-Smith gives an excellent narrative account of the struggles of "unlearning racism in teacher education."[18]) The notion that we are all just "Canadians" or "Americans" is a lovely sentiment and I would truly be happy if this were the case, but the reality is that those who exist outside of the white power blocks[19] simply don't have this luxury. Neil Bissoondath describes how visible minorities *can't* simply say, "I'm Canadian" or "I'm American." He writes, "One never really gets used to the conversation. It will go something like this: 'What nationality are you?' 'Canadian.' 'No, I mean, what nationality are you *really?*' "[20] The end result is a feeling that you are just a shade away from being truly Canadian or American.

Just as the larger Canadian and American identity sometimes feels to be a conditional acceptance, one must also deal with the added pressures of having no individuality. On a social level (although some may argue this point at a state level as well), you are excluded from your North American country based on perceived ethnic membership but are forced into an association with your ethnicity—and usually the most heinous aspects of it.

In difficult times, few people have the fortitude of teachers like Jane Elliot, who was so enraged by the portrayal of African Americans on the news during the era surrounding the assassination of Dr. Martin Luther King Jr. that she felt that her profession demanded she do something about it. In her famous classroom "brown eyed–blue eyed" lesson, as depicted in the documentary "A Class Divided" (which should be required viewing for all educators), she demonstrates how easily children fall back in school when they are targeted by discrimination and stereotyping. In this lesson children were hierarchically divided based on differing eye color in an effort to highlight the absurdity of racism in U.S. society.[21]

One of the factors that drove Elliot to create this experiment was the reporting on the civil rights movement, particularly when journalists and interviewers asked African Americans what "they" were going to do now that "their" leader had been shot and how "they" were going to handle all the hostility that was building up in "their" people. Much is the same for this newly created "Pan-Arab" group, as we are continuously asked to personally feel and express some kind of shame for the events of September 11. Somehow, over 500,000 people in Canada and seven million people of Eastern descent are being asked to feel shame for the acts of 19 people, while at the same time the average power block member of North America rebukes the idea of shame for its conquest of North America. If it hasn't happened already, we are quickly losing our individuality and autonomy as humans. Some would argue that we are even losing the title of human as well. This effort to stereotype and dehumanize is a dishonor that, to a great extent, lies at the feet of the mass media.

The effort to dehumanize and stereotype a people has long been used by some groups to justify domination over others. Linda Tuhiwai Smith cited A. Memmi in her analysis of the dehumanizing campaigns against indigenous people, stating, "The use of zoological terms to describe primitive people was one form of dehumanization. 'How often do we read in the newspaper about the death or murder of a Native man, and in the same paper about the victimization of a female Native, as though we were a species of sub-human animal life?...A female horse, a female Native, but everyone else gets to be called a man or a woman.' "[22] The attempt to do the same thing to people of the East is just as apparent. There is a manner of describing Eastern people on television as unable to control their emotions or behaviors, almost in the same way people warn you that Rottweiler dogs are genetically predisposed to be aggressive. Even the way in which public figures state that "these people over there" only understand force, much in the same way my old next-door neighbor would say that the only way his Rottweiler would listen to him is when he "gave him a good swat on his nose." Think about how much was made of the 9/11 hijacker Mohammed Atta's roots in Islam and synonymous Arabness as opposed to, let's say, Adolf Hitler or Timothy McVeigh's roots in Christianity and whiteness. Ask yourself why members of some groups are allowed to swiftly dissociate themselves religiously and ideologically from these sorts of undesirables but others are not. Part of the problem is that there is little to no representation of academics and professionals from or of the East to enlighten and explain within the media.

Recently, Said wrote on this subject "that Orientalist learning itself was premised on the silence of the native...presenting that unfortunate creature as an undeveloped, deficient, and uncivilized being who couldn't represent himself."[23] Said observes that some forms of representation regarding certain ethnic or racial groups from Occidental researchers are now considered inappropriate and that it is no longer "fashionable or even acceptable to pontificate about the Oriental's (i.e., the Muslim's, or the Indian's, or the Japanese's) 'mentality.' "[24] In our post-9/11 world, for anyone who derives from "the East," "the Arab world," or the "Muslim world," it is easy to see how media experts about these people are usually not of these people, and when they are, there is always the presupposition that they are somehow not objective due to their indigenousness. How I wonder: Do these experts and the research they have presumably done to gain the title of "expert" benefit the people they have studied? Before embarking on his examination of Native issues in Canada, Alan Cairns wrote, "We are all informed and shaped by our individual past experiences—informed and shaped, but of course, not controlled. For an academic, each new intellectual venture is simultaneously a continuity and departure."[25] Moving outside of the realm of academia, statistics, and numbers, think in practical and real terms: how many of the "experts" that you receive your information from are actually of Middle Eastern descent? Think of your own personal community. Would you accept complete domination of representation and expertise from those who did not belong to your community?

In discussing with a student teacher an upcoming lesson she had to plan for her sixth-grade social studies unit on current issues in the news, I asked her how she was going to prepare for the subject matter. She threw her arms in the air in exasperation, sighed loudly, and expressed that she barely had time to watch the news, let alone run to the library and do research. Teaching is a time-consuming profession, and we are in the unfortunate position of having to count on the integrity of the news media and news-type television and radio talk shows, most of which seem to be neglecting the educational aspect of reporting. For instance, CNN's Larry King missed an excellent "teachable moment" while interviewing the three medical students I mentioned at the beginning of this chapter when he didn't follow up and explain the diversity of the Middle East. In an attempt to demonstrate that their accuser's statements had no credibility, two of the students, Ayman Gheith and Kambiz Butt, argued that Arabic was not their common language, so therefore, how could she have heard them all communicating in Arabic?

Butt: We don't even understand or speak Arabic.

Gheith: So how does that work into how well she heard?

King: So then, all right, he's reading into you that you're not fessing up now because it looks bad for you.[26]

I'm not sure what King's reasons were for not pursuing this teachable moment, but he definitely added to the miseducation of his viewers by implying that they were not "fessing up." Even another reputable television personality, Oprah Winfrey, added to the dehumanization of the Arabs when during a June 16th, 1998, homage to actor Harrison Ford she said, "My favorite scene of all time is where you shoot that Arab." Oprah chuckled, then emulated in part the shoot-'em-up.[27] In a sense Oprah, completely unintentionally, I believe, validated that we can say certain things about certain ethnic groups. Think about whether you would think it acceptable if she said "Jew" or "black" instead of Arab. Try it; say it out loud and ask yourself if you felt comfortable saying it. I tried this in class, and the only two groups of students who did not cringe while saying it were Arabs (in that Pan-Arab sense) and Native Indians. What should we expect when government leaders like George W. Bush are not admonished in the same way Trent Lott was over his segregation comments in December 2002? I find it odd that no one mentioned George W. Bush's January 2002 reference to people of Pakistan as "Pakis," either at the time he said it or later in regard to Lott's comments. It almost appears as if the media and the citizens of North America felt that this comment was OK. But it was not OK. We should have all felt revulsion at his choice of words.

As educators, we would like to think that we would have marched beside Martin Luther King, fasted in support of Mahatma Gandhi; spent time in jail in solidarity with Nelson Mandela, stopped a Canadian or American government official from stealing a Native child from the warm embrace of her parents' arms to the cruelty of residential schooling, or even simply protested during World War II against the removal of Japanese Canadians and Americans to internment camps. However, the truth is that very, very few of us ever have the foresight or the courage to take even the most basic of stands. Hindsight makes us wiser, more compassionate, and braver, and we sleep easier when we assure ourselves that we would have been different if only we had been there. Movies are filled with these types of images, making us feel better through imagined characters, scenarios, and histories, such as powerful images of white FBI agents secretly beating up racist KKK members in *Mississippi Burning*, or a white American soldier aiding, living, and fighting with Native Indians during America's expansion into the west in *Dances with Wolves*, that comfort us in retrospect.

When I discussed the cruel reality of Native Indian residential schooling with my multiculturalism class within the Department of Education at McGill University, all of the students, the majority of whom were young, white women, were outraged over the incidents and were unanimous in their assurance that had they been there, they would have done something. But when the realities of the final residential school's closure dating in the relatively recent 1980s and current issues regarding Native people were made apparent to them, you could feel their embarrassment as they realized there was still much to be done in our own backyard and the ensuing shame as they quietly admitted to themselves that they would all return to their comfortable, middle-class homes not having done or planning to do anything.

In Ushma Shah's narrative of her student teaching experience shortly after the Persian Gulf War, she describes one of the conscious efforts she made to veer from the mandatory curriculum she was provided with, to the "worthwhile" educating she felt her profession demanded. In one of her examples, she discusses how a prepackaged fifth-grade unit developed by the school board on Islam was filled with aspects of the religion and people that mainly focused on a "history of acquiring land through war—a misconception that meshes nicely with media misrepresentations of Muslims."[28] Despite the relative powerlessness of her role as a student teacher, Shah made the conscious and professional choice that she was going to reject the role of "teacher as a puppet"[29] and educate her students on aspects of Islam that were more informed. In doing this, Shah followed in the footsteps of risk takers like Jane Elliot. These teachers took the risk, took the time to educate themselves and not simply regurgitate what was being fed to them through the media; simply, they chose to be accountable yet autonomous professionals. This is the challenge.

I began this chapter in the unorthodox manner of presenting an actual event that appeared to be a joke. So, in keeping with this theme, I would like to end with an actual joke that I worry will be somewhat prophetic. To contextualize it, this joke was told to me by a friend who is white and had no intention to offend:

Three men were sitting at a table in a restaurant: an Arab, a Native Indian, and a Texan (when I was told this joke, it wasn't specified that he was white, but of course we're supposed to assume that if it doesn't have a hyphen, as in Arab-American, then a Texan's whiteness is a given). The Native American is visibly upset; his head is down on the table and he's sobbing into his folded arms. The Arab, showing concern, pats him on the back and says, "My friend, what's wrong?" The Native Indian half lifts his head off the table and weeps, "At one time my people were many and now they are so few!" "Please, my friend," the Arab says in a consoling manner, "Do not be sad. Listen, at one time my people were few and now they are many!" With this news, the Native American's spirit instantly brightens, and he sits upright in his chair, looking the Arab straight in the eyes with a smile on his face. Listening to the conversation, the Texan slowly rocks back in his chair, then says to the Arab, "That's only because we haven't played cowboys and Arabs yet."

Let us hope that the future has something better in store.

Chapter 6

The United States and Israel: Double Standards, Favoritism, and Unconditional Support

Mordechai Gordon

Those who did not want him as minister of defense will get him as prime minister!

—*Slogan that originated in 1982 about Ariel Sharon*

I first heard this slogan, I believe, in the summer of 1982, after Israel had invaded Lebanon, toward the end of my three-year tenure as a paratrooper in the Israeli army. My service in the Israeli Defense Force included fighting in the 1982 war in Lebanon and being stationed very close to the Sabra and Shatila camps in which the massacre of hundreds of Palestinians took place, the acts for which Ariel Sharon, then minister of defense, was forced to resign. Twenty or so years ago, when this slogan was first coined, many people like myself easily dismissed it as being far-fetched and even absurd. Today, the bitter irony of this prediction has become a horrible reality for many Israelis who, just a few years ago, believed that peace was within sight and for millions of Palestinians who dreamed of finally being liberated after decades of Israeli occupation. But I am getting ahead of myself.

In this essay I will attempt to make sense of the relationship between the United States and Israel over the last 35 years. As its title indicates, I will argue that this relationship is characterized by double standards, favoritism, and unconditional support. If one compares this relationship to the United States' treatment of the Arab countries in general and the Palestinians in particular, it is difficult to deny these blunt conclusions. Relying on the works of Noam Chomsky, Edward Said, and other progressive critics, I will examine the United States' policy toward Israel and

the Palestinians since 1967 in terms of three points of contention. In the first section, I look at the question of terrorism and how it has been manipulated by the mainstream media in the United States. Such distorted coverage neglects the larger issue of "state terrorism" and has been used to justify Israel's occupation of millions of people in the West Bank and Gaza for over three decades. The next section analyzes how Israel, with the support of the Unites States, has consistently striven to deny the Palestinians the basic political right of self-determination and thwarted their attempts to create an independent state. Finally, in the last part I show how major U.S. politicians and media have traditionally displayed an attitude of apologetics toward Israel and racism toward the Palestinians.

Who Is a Terrorist?

One issue that rarely receives any serious consideration from the mainstream media or leading intellectuals in the United States is the question of who is a terrorist. Regarding the Middle East, it is commonplace to find that Arab suicide bombers (representing organizations such as Hamas, Islamic Jihad, and Hizbollah) who target Jewish Israelis are labeled as terrorists whereas Israeli soldiers who assassinate suspected Palestinian leaders are said to be engaged in "targeted killings." Moreover, when Israeli soldiers go into Arab villages or refugee camps looking for suspected terrorists and kill innocent civilians, including women and children, they are merely retaliating or acting in defense of Israel, according to the mainstream media in the United States. In the same way, Jewish settlers in the West Bank who murder innocent Palestinian citizens are considered a few hotheaded extremists who are reacting to Arab terrorism.

Noam Chomsky has carefully documented numerous examples of Israeli crimes against Palestinians since the 1967 occupation of the West Bank and Gaza and argues that these crimes should be considered as nothing less than atrocities and systematic terror. He notes that during the first intifada (Palestinian uprising) of the late 1980s the endless humiliation and repression of Palestinians reached the level of "regular pogroms" in which Israeli soldiers would "break into houses, smash furniture, break bones, and beat teenagers to death after dragging them from their homes."[1] During the same time, settler violence was conducted with virtual impunity, and the defense ministry sanctioned collective punishments, deportation, and systematic torture.

Yet, as Chomsky demonstrates, the mainstream media in the United States did a remarkable job of minimizing their coverage of Israeli terror while at the same time went out of their way to defend Israel's actions. For example, during one of the peak periods of the intifada in which beatings, killings, gassing, and collective punishment of Palestinians were conducted on a daily basis, the editors of the *New York Times* described Israel as "this tiny nation, symbol of human decency." A few years earlier, the editors of the *Washington Post* referred to Israel as "a country that cares for human life."[2] Other leading commentators in the United States such as Elie Wiesel assured the American public that the atrocities committed by Israeli soldiers and settlers against Palestinians were nothing more than "regrettable exceptions." Wiesel's apologetic view was typical of many American Jews who refused to criticize the oppression of the Palestinians, contending that "only those in power [in Israel] are in a position to know."[3] One wonders how such an argument would be received in the United States if the issue was the oppression of Jews in the former Soviet Union or the Nazi atrocities during the Second World War.

In the summer of 1989, I had the unfortunate experience of personally witnessing the oppression of Palestinians when I was called for reserve duty in the Israeli army to serve in the West Bank city of Hebron. Unwilling to participate in the policing of civilians (as my battalion was ordered to do), I reached an agreement with the commanding officers that enabled me to work only in the kitchen of our base. Still, I had a chance to learn about the reasons for the Israeli occupation of Hebron as well as its devastating results. To begin with, it became evident from the very outset that our mission had nothing to do with the defense of Israel and everything to do with protecting a few hundred fanatic settlers who insisted on maintaining a presence in the middle of a city of close to a hundred thousand Arab residents. Among these settlers were members of a Jewish militia who were convicted of murdering Arabs and members of other extreme factions. The daily duties of our battalion consisted of providing a shield for the settlers, policing the streets, rounding up Palestinian suspects, dispersing riots, and enforcing collective punishment (e.g., curfews were imposed on the local Arab residents when stones were thrown at our soldiers). I personally witnessed how suspects were rounded up, handcuffed, blindfolded, and forced to sit for hours in the torching summer sun waiting to be interrogated. Other men were pulled out of their homes and forced to paint over graffiti on the walls of their houses or to pull down a Palestinian flag that was hanging from a telephone pole. Humiliation, detention without trial of teenagers and young men, and beatings were part of the daily routine.

This personal narrative as well as the numerous examples cited by Chomsky clearly demonstrate that there is a policy of double standards regarding the United States' relation toward Israel in which the latter is not held accountable by its "big brother" in the West for atrocities committed against Palestinians. We should recall that during the time of the first intifada, Arafat was heavily criticized by the mainstream media in the United States and was denied entrance to this country by the Reagan and Bush administrations for failing to unequivocally renounce terrorism and to publicly acknowledge Israel's right to exist. As an Israeli Jew who feels a deep connection to the state of Israel, I am troubled by such double standards. I fear that Sharon and other Israeli leaders can exploit the anti-Arab rhetoric in the mainstream media to further their aggressive political ends.

Of course, this double standards policy does not apply only to Israel and should be understood as part of a much broader attempt by the United States to obliterate its own as well as its allies' responsibility for terrorism and aggression. Chomsky explains this principle very well:

The guiding principle is clear and straightforward: *their* terror is terror, and the flimsiest evidence suffices to denounce it and to exact retribution upon civilian bystanders who happen to be in the way; *our* terror, even if far more extreme, is merely statecraft, and therefore does not enter into the discussion of the plague of the modern age.[4]

Moreover, the concept of terrorism itself is defined in such a way as to serve the interests of those in power. The common use of the word terrorist refers to "a member of a clandestine or expatriate organization aiming to coerce an established government by acts of violence against it or its subjects."[5] In other words, terrorism is normally used to signify the violent actions of an individual or a group against the people or property of a sovereign state (i.e., against the people in power). However, this description disregards a much more significant form of terrorism, namely, state terrorism, which can be defined as "terrorizing the whole population through systematic actions carried out by forces of the state."[6] Such terrorism is an essential part of a government designed to protect the needs of the privileged and is aimed at eliminating any significant opposition among the subjugated people. Writing in 1996, Edward Said argued that Israel, while claiming to be making peace with the Palestinians, continued to intervene in Palestinian life, using its military to assassinate leaders, destroy homes, shut down schools, and arrest or deport anyone it deemed a threat to its security. Said goes on to note,

It is simply extraordinary and without precedent that Israel's history, its record— from the fact that it introduced terrorism against civilians to the Middle East, that it is a state built on conquest, that it invaded surrounding countries, bombed and destroyed at will, to the fact that it currently occupies Lebanese, Syrian and Palestinian territory against international law—is simply never cited, never subjected to scrutiny in the U.S. media or in official discourse never addressed as playing any role at all in provoking "Islamic terror."[7]

Based on the distinction between the conventional use of the word terrorism and state terrorism, I think that one can make a pretty strong case that since 1948, and certainly since 1967, Israel's acts of state terror against the Palestinians have been far more severe than all the acts of terror committed by Arabs against Israelis. Consider, if you will, Israel's 1982 invasion of Lebanon in which thousands of people were killed (most of whom were innocent civilians), with many more injured and maimed, thousands displaced from their homes, and hundreds of people tortured by the Israeli army or by members of the secret service. Or consider the aforementioned Israeli occupation of the West Bank and Gaza, which has resulted in thousands of Palestinian deaths; many more deported; thousands detained without trial; confiscation of land; and in general, the daily humiliation, intimidation, and terrorizing of an entire population. Such actions should be considered criminal, much like the acts of Arab suicide bombers in Jerusalem, Tel-Aviv, and Netanyah. In making such comparisons, I do not mean to diminish in any way the suffering and pain of Israelis who have lost loved ones to acts of terror. In my view, any act of terror (i.e., an act of violence that targets innocent civilians), whether "conventional" or state terror, is both immoral and counterproductive. Yet, following Cornel West, I maintain that an honest and progressive morality has to be able to say loud and clear that "a baby in Iraq and a baby in Guatemala, and a baby in Tel-Aviv and a baby on the West Bank, and a baby in Oakland and a baby in Chicago all have exactly the same value!"[8]

A progressive morality that confronts the issue of terrorism will have to not only avoid selectivity and double standards but also view this issue historically, that is, attempt to make sense of the root causes and the historical, social, and cultural contexts of terrorism. From this perspective, it is clear that President George W. Bush's so-called war on terrorism is a wholesale attempt to obliterate history, and indeed the entire political, social, and cultural context that brought about the September 11 attack on the United States. For Bush, there were no reasons for this attack, despite decades of American aggression in the Middle East and the exploitation of the natural resources of many Arab countries.

Such effacing of history and the social context is equally true of how Israeli leaders like Sharon and Netanyahu view the problem of Arab terror against Israel. These leaders have argued continuously that Arab terrorism is aimed solely at the murder of innocent Jewish civilians and the destruction of the state of Israel, as though ending the 35 years of Israeli occupation and oppression of over two million Palestinians has nothing to do with Arab violence against Israel. This kind of argument is designed to demonize one's enemy while absolving oneself of any responsibility for the crimes being committed. Again, Edward Said is very instructive on this point:

For the main thing is to isolate your enemy from time, from causality, from prior action, and thereby portray him or her as ontologically and gratuitously interested in wreaking havoc for its own sake. Thus if you can show that Libyans, Moslems,

Palestinians and Arabs, generally speaking, have no reality except that which tau-tologically confirms their terrorist essence as Libyans, Moslems, Palestinians and Arabs, you can go on to attack them and their terrorist states generally, and avoid all questions about your own behavior or about your share in their present fate.[9]

Palestinian Self-Determination and Statehood

During the recent wave of violence in the Middle East, which is proba-bly the worst since the 1982 Israeli invasion of Lebanon, until the 2003 "road map to peace" there was little discussion of reconciliation between the Palestinians and the Israelis. And the road map at this writing looks dead in the water. The voices, on both sides, calling for revenge, sepa-ration, and even annihilation of the other are becoming louder and louder. In this climate of increasing desperation and senseless killings, it is very difficult not only to discern the voices of reason and moderation, but also to understand why the peace process, culminating in the July 2000 summit between Barak and Arafat, ultimately failed. According to the mainstream media in the United States, Arafat was the major culprit for this failure, balking in the face of a unique opportunity to reach a historic peace agree-ment. Barak, on the other hand, was hailed as courageous and generally given much praise as the Israeli leader who was willing to offer the Pales-tinians more than any previous leader.

However, a close examination of the 2000 peace proposal reveals that it failed to resolve virtually all the major obstacles for peace since the 1967 Israeli occupation of the West Bank and Gaza. Thus problems such as Israeli settlements and the status of Jerusalem, as well as the rights of the millions of Palestinian refugees to return to their homeland, were never seriously addressed. According to the Palestinian position, the 2000 Camp David peace proposal amounted to a phony state, with partial Palestinian sovereignty, because Israel would be able to retain control of the borders, security, water, and other strategic assets.

The Israeli rejection of Palestinian sovereignty and statehood has a long history that spans the policies of both the "moderate" Labor administra-tions and the right-wing Likud governments. For example, during the Likud administration of the late 1980s and early 1990s, Israel and the United States offered the Palestinians "autonomy" over their own cities and towns. Danny Rubinstein, a respected journalist for the liberal Israeli daily *Haaretz*, wrote that autonomy in this context referred to "autonomy as in a POW camp, where the prisoners are 'autonomous' to cook their meals without interference and to organize cultural events."[10] He noted that this proposal granted the Palestinians essentially what they already had: control over local services. During the same time, the Labor party's position, while acknowledging the fact that Israel would not be able to hold on to the densely populated Arab areas, called for Jordanian control of these areas and rejected the idea of an independent Palestinian state. The people of the territories overwhelmingly rejected both of these options, but this fact was not given much weight, and the civil and human rights of millions of Palestinians never became a serious issue for the ruling parties in Israel.

Indeed, not so long ago, during the peace negotiations of the late 1980s, the Israeli government, backed by the United States, denied the Palestinians the basic right to select their own representatives for the peace talks. Regarding this fact, Chomsky noted that "the United States and Israel have adopted a position comparable to the refusal in 1947 to allow Jews to be represented by the Zionist organizations in the negotiations of that time, a position that would have been regarded as a reversion to Nazism had it been put forth."[11] It should also be remembered that for many years Israel had a parliamentary law prohibiting any citizen from meeting with members of the PLO because it was considered a "terrorist organization," as though Israeli leaders past and present did not belong to terrorist groups (Begin and Shamir, to mention only two). More recently, in the spring of 2002, Israel was once again attempting to deny the Palestinians the basic right of self-determination by holding Arafat hostage in Ramallah; killing many of his guards; denying him food, water, and electricity; and "encouraging" him to leave the country with no possibility of return. All this went on while the United States hardly mustered an objection, and it continues to fund Israel more than any other country in the world and supply it with the latest weapons.

For the past three decades, Israeli governments have, with few exceptions, not only rejected the idea that Arafat and the PLO can be partners in the peace negotiations but also propagated the lie that the Palestinian leadership is not interested in peace. Given such propaganda, it is not surprising that many Israeli citizens still cling to the old belief that what the Arabs really want is to "seize control of all of Israel and throw the Jews into the sea," despite numerous Palestinian statements about peace and reconciliation. As a peace activist in Israel during the first intifada of the late 1980s and early 1990s, I had the opportunity to meet with many Palestinian people from the West Bank and Gaza. In these meetings I heard Palestinians from all walks of life state over and over how tired they were of struggle and war. They insisted that all they really wanted were basically two things: an independent state that was economically viable and peace with Israel.

Indeed, a close examination of history leaves no doubt that the belief that the Palestinian leaders do not want peace with Israel is really disingenuous. In fact, Chomsky has documented that even prior to the peace agreement between Israel and Egypt, in January 1976, Egypt, Syria, and Jordan, supported by the PLO, advanced a UN resolution that called for a two-state diplomatic settlement in terms of the international consensus, with territorial and security guarantees. On the rights of Israel, the proposal of the Arab "confrontation states" and the PLO reiterated the wording of UN Resolution 242, calling for "appropriate arrangements...to guarantee...the sovereignty, territorial integrity and political independence of all states in the area and their right to live in peace with secure and recognizable boundaries."[12]

The 1976 proposal was only the first of many endorsements by the PLO and major Arab countries of UN Resolution 242 (and later 338). The Saudi peace initiative proposed in February 2002 was only one of numerous attempts by the Palestinian leadership to reach a settlement with Israel based on UN resolutions and the international consensus. Ibrahim Abu-Lughod summarizes the evolution of the position held by many Palestinians on reaching a peace agreement with Israel over the last 35 years:

There is no question today that the Palestinians have recognized the reality of a Jewish people's presence in Palestine—illegal as it might be construed. And accordingly the Palestinian call for the establishment of a non-confessional democratic State in the whole of Palestine—its feasibility notwithstanding—signaled that the Jewish presence in Palestine was irreversible and therefore had to be accommodated.[13]

In order to take the pressure off of Israel and the United States for rejecting the PLO and Arab peace initiatives, it has been necessary to expunge from the historical record major events such as the 1976 UN resolution, mentioned above, that guaranteed "the sovereignty, territorial integrity and political independence of all states in the area."[14] Numerous other cases of Israeli and U.S. opposition to an equitable resolution of the Middle East conflict have been suppressed and, therefore, did not receive the stamp of "official history." Also significant is the fact that the mainstream media in the United States have never really challenged the Israeli and U.S. rejection of various peace proposals by the PLO and others. Consider, for instance, the April 1981 Soviet peace plan, endorsed by the Palestinian National Council, that contained two basic principles: (1) the right of the Palestinians to achieve self-determination in an independent state; and (2) the guarantee of security and sovereignty for all states in the region, including Israel. The fact that the Soviet plan was not taken seriously by the administration as well as the media in the United States, as an initiative that could help advance a peace agreement, calls into question the United States' commitment to a just and peaceful resolution of this conflict. Consistent with the U.S. and Israeli opposition to a fair and humane resolution to the Middle East conflict is the doctrine that Sadat's 1977 Camp David agreement with Begin is an exception to the Arab rejection of peace, regardless of all the existing evidence that contradicts this doctrine.

Thus, a careful and honest examination of history clearly shows that Israel and the United States, rather than the Palestinians, have put forth the most obstacles to reaching a peace settlement in the Middle East since 1967. Ironically, however, it has been the Palestinians and Arafat, in particular, who have received the most blame in the U.S. media for this failure, a practice that is sometimes referred to as "blaming the victim." For instance, Thomas Friedman of the *New York Times* wrote in 1988 that Arafat "has to face the choice of either going down in history as the Palestinian leader who recognized Israel in return for only, at best, a majority of the West Bank or shouldering full responsibility for the Palestinians' continuing to get nothing at all."[15] These are the only two options that, according to Friedman, should be considered because they represent the alternatives proposed by Israel and the United States for a resolution of the conflict. It follows from Friedman's analysis that the Palestinians should just accept the less than 22 percent of historic Palestine that Israel is willing to offer it on which to build a "pseudo-state," with no territorial integrity, natural resources, or possibility for economic independence.

Racism versus Apologetics

Friedman's statement about Arafat, quoted previously, betrays a subtle racism, one that has historically dominated many of the discussions of the Israeli-Palestinian conflict in the United States. He and other leading American commentators have uncritically embraced the assumption "that the indigenous population does not have the human and national rights that we naturally accord to the Jewish immigrants who largely displaced them."[16] As illustrated above, Israel has consistently denied the Palestinians not only the right to self-determination and statehood, but also the more basic human rights like freedom of movement and expression and the right to get medical treatment. Also, prevalent among leading commentators is the false notion that the Palestinians are essentially aggressive in nature and do not have a movement comparable to Israel's Peace Now and other leftist organizations that struggle for a just and peaceful resolution of the conflict. For instance, *New Republic* editor Martin Peretz writes about a "crazed Arab" who is "intoxicated by language, cannot discern between fantasy and reality, abhors compromise, always blames others for his predicament and in the end lances the painful boil of his frustrations in a pointless, though momentarily gratifying, act of bloodlust."[17] Such racist assumptions are rarely perceived, let alone challenged, in the mainstream media in the United States, notwithstanding the existence of abundant evidence to the contrary.

Edward Said draws an interesting parallel between the relationship of whites and blacks in the United States and that of Israelis and Palestinians in Israel. Said argues that the white majority in the United States treats the blacks as a permanent underclass that can be maintained in a state of exploitation and dehumanization. "By the same token," he continues, "Israelis can exist inside Israel, drive their cars, water their lawns, fill their pools, go to their schools and universities without having in any way to think of Palestinians except as a nuisance to be tolerated."[18] Said correctly points out that few Israelis are concerned with the daily oppression of the Palestinians even though they are the same people who build their houses, clean their streets, and serve as waiters and cooks in their restaurants. Just as the average American does not spend a great deal of time thinking about the oppression that defines African American life, so do most Israelis not lose any sleep over the awful plight of the Palestinians and Israel's role in bringing about this situation.

At times the racism against Arabs among politicians and reporters in the United States is not subtle at all. Consider, if you will, statements such as the one made by former president Bill Clinton and secretary of state Madeleine Albright that "there is no equivalent between bombs and bulldozers." Again, Said is very insightful about this statement, insisting that they need to explain to a recently evicted Palestinian family or Palestinians under curfew or Palestinians whose houses have been destroyed or whose young men and women languish in Israeli jails or who are strip-searched by Israeli soldiers or driven out of Jerusalem so that Russian Jews can be settled in their homes or who are killed in massacres or deprived of any right to resist Israeli occupation policies, what *is* the equivalent of an Israeli-American bulldozer in such a context. There is a simple racist premise underpinning the "peace process" and subsequent rhetorical ambushes set in its name that Palestinian and Arab lives aren't worth as much as Israeli Jewish lives.[19]

To better understand the subtle and blatant racism that characterizes the depiction of Arabs and Palestinians in the American media, we need to juxtapose this coverage to the way in which Israel is represented in the United States. I have already mentioned that major newspapers such as the *New York Times* and the *Washington Post* have chosen to praise or apologize for Israel's "benign" occupation while ignoring the daily humiliation, torture, and collective punishment of the Palestinian people. Also significant is the fact that the mainstream media in the United States downplayed Israel's 1982 invasion of Lebanon and the devastation that this war caused. For example, the *London Times* reported that Israeli death squads were operating in southern Lebanon after the 1982 invasion. Yet, U.S. editors were not very interested in this story, most likely because "it was a matter of indifference that Arabs were being murdered and their villages destroyed by a Western state armed and supported by the United States."[20]

In addition, Chomsky has documented how the media in the United States have been relatively uninterested in Israel's nuclear threat "even after ample evidence appeared on Israel's nuclear forces and its testing of a nuclear-capable missile with range sufficient to 'reach the Soviet

Union.' "[21] This lack of interest on behalf of major U.S. media came at a time when Leonard Spector from the Carnegie Foundation published a study on nuclear proliferation that identified Israel as the most advanced of eight emerging nuclear powers. Commenting on the coverage of this study, Chomsky points to the *Times* article headlined "Nuclear Arms Races in Third World Feared," which mentioned Israel only once, namely, in a positive light as helping to reduce the danger of proliferation by bombing Iraq's nuclear reactor in 1981.

My claim is, therefore, that there is a huge discrepancy between the way in which Palestinians are depicted in the mainstream media in the United States and how Israeli Jews are portrayed. Regarding the latter, it is common to hear the comment that those who do not live in Israel and suffer its problems do not have a right to criticize its policies (e.g., its oppression of millions of Palestinians). Yet, the same argument is never used to excuse the actions of Palestinian suicide bombers on the grounds that those who do not live in the refugee camps should not condemn these desperate acts. There is also an overwhelming agreement among intellectuals, politicians, and media personnel that nothing can be compared to the Jewish Holocaust, as though the genocide of the Kurds and Armenians were mere minor historical events. This double standard leads to a mentality that considers Jews as "perpetual victims," despite that Israel is far more powerful than any country in the Middle East, that it is the only country in the area with nuclear weapons, and that it has been oppressing the Palestinians for at least 35 years now.

Regarding this "perpetual victim" mentality, it has been my personal experience that anyone who dares to question the Israeli occupation of the West Bank and Gaza and the oppression of the Palestinian people in the context of the Holocaust is immediately labeled anti-Semitic or a "hater of Israel"—that is, any comparison between the subjugation of the Palestinians and the Nazi atrocities against Jews is considered taboo. Even more dangerous is the fact that for many Israeli and American Jews the Holocaust is used as a justification for crimes committed by Israel. Thus, in mainstream political and intellectual debates in Israel and the United States, one is not likely to hear the Holocaust mentioned as a moral basis for condemning Israel's occupation of the Palestinians or even as a reason to struggle for peace in the Middle East. The point is that the suffering of Jews in the Holocaust has been used not only to eclipse the suffering of the Palestinians but also to gain a privileged moral position that is beyond reproach.

Conclusion

It is not an exaggeration to say that the years more or less since Sharon became prime minister of Israel have been some of the worst in the century-old conflict between Jews and Palestinians in the Middle East. Anyone who doubts this statement should just count the dead and injured on both sides. Yet even if we ignore the massive killing, maiming, and destruction, one cannot deny that Israel and the Palestinians are further today from reaching a peace agreement than they were at any time during the last decade. Neither can one refute the notion that the level of fear, hatred, and mistrust on both sides is much higher now than at any time in recent history.

In assessing the role of the United States in bringing about this horrific state of affairs, it is important to keep in mind the three main points this essay has analyzed. First, in the aftermath of the September 11 attack on the United States and President Bush's "war on terrorism," it is clear that the efforts on the part of Israel to demonize Arafat and to brand him as one of the world's leading terrorists have intensified. Indeed, both Israeli and U.S. leaders now consider Arafat personally responsible for all Palestinian suicide attacks against Israeli civilians even though he has condemned these attacks, and despite the fact that he was confined to his house in Ramallah for a month during some of the worst suicide bombings. Such demonizing is not unlike the way in which bin Laden was portrayed in the United States. It shifts the focus away from the state terror that Israel has been conducting in the occupied territories, much like the demonizing of bin Laden was aimed in part at taking attention away from U.S. attacks against civilians in Afghanistan.

Second, during the Oslo peace process there was at least some movement on the part of Israel toward recognizing Palestinian self-determination and statehood. However, in the last year and a half, Israel has reoccupied major parts of the West Bank and Gaza, undermined the political credibility of Arafat, and continued to reject the idea of a Palestinian state along the 1967 borders. Although the United States may say it supports a Palestinian state, in reality its leaders have done nothing as Israel has continued to confiscate Palestinian land and build more settlements. By doing nothing about Israeli colonialism and by continuing to fund Israel at increasing levels, the United States is tacitly supporting these unjust and inhumane policies.

Finally, the tendency, as I described, by U.S. media and politicians to defend and apologize for Israel's crimes while strongly attacking Palestinian violence is at best favoritism, and at worst plain racism. Given this favoritism and the unconditional support that characterizes the United States' relationship with Israel, it is not surprising at all that many Arab leaders and people are angry at the United States. And given the many years of U.S. opposition to, hostility to, and even racism toward the Palestinians, as well as the fact that American F-16s, Apache helicopters, and bulldozers are being used to destroy Palestinian houses and kill its citizens, it should not come as a big shock that the United States has become a target of Arab terrorism.

The road map to peace in Israel and Palestine proposed by the United States, the UN, the European Union, and Russia in April 2003 is another example of America's lack of empathy with the Palestinians' plight. The plan demanded that the Palestinians immediately cease their armed resistance against Israeli occupation while asking little from the Israelis. At the apex of his declaration-of-victory-in-Iraq bravado, President George W. Bush described the road map for peace as a starting point for the development of both a state of Israel and a Palestinian state. The plan required that the Palestinian Authority be restructured, the cessation of all Palestinian violence against the Israelis, and the construction of a Palestinian government acceptable to both Israel and the quartet who offered the plan. Israel was required to move in a humanitarian direction by easing restrictions on the Palestinians. The details of such an easing of restrictions were not specified. Conspicuously omitted from the plan was the 347-mile-long "separation wall" being built in the West Bank of Israel. The road map allowed for the continued construction of the 20-foot-high, 10-foot-thick fence complete with moats, electric wiring, and trenches. What is worse is that all along the wall Palestinian land has been confiscated, and 300,000 Palestinians will be separated from their homes and land.

The timing of President Bush's campaign for the road map in late April 2003 coincided with his administration's need for a modicum of calm in the Middle East after the disruptive invasion of Iraq. The Muslim peoples of the region were highly agitated by the war, and Bush and his advisors sensed the time was right for peacemaking gestures—gestures he had studiously avoided in Israel and Palestine for the first two years of his presidency. Always the unilateralist, Bush dismissed the UN, the European Union, and Russia and pushed the United States forward as the major player in the negotiations. Pushing the rhetoric of U.S. supremacy to a new level, Bush informed Israeli and Palestinian leaders that he was on a "mission from God"[22] to make peace between the Israelis and Palestinians. Over the summer of 2003 Bush and his representatives were caught up in the minutiae of the process while the work of Palestinian suicide terrorists and the Israeli government's response to them tore the negotiations apart. By September 2003 the process was presumed dead by most of the nations of the world. The only way that a lasting solution will ever be developed in the region is for a truly international group to display sympathy for the plight of both Israelis and Palestinians. In such a context an international group of peacekeepers stationed throughout Israel and Palestine with a powerful international court behind them to arbitrate disputes between the parties and execute legal action will be necessary.

Chapter 7

The Great European Denial: The Misrepresentation of the Moors in Western Education

Haroon Kharem

Sitting in an undergraduate history course on the history of the Middle East, I listened as a well-known professor in Middle Eastern history began a conversation stating that the Ethiopian people and the Moors who had invaded Spain were not black Africans but white North Africans. He continued his dialogue, asserting that Ethiopians and the Moors were not Africans or of the so-called Negroid race. This well-known professor, who was supposed to be an expert on the history of East Africa (renamed the Middle East by Western journalists), was not ready for the response he received from a small group of five black students in his class of about 60 students. As we entered into a debate with the professor, we asked how he explained the fact that Ethiopians and the Moors were dark skinned, like other Africans and African Americans, and yet could not be black or African. Also, we asked why those same people would be categorized as black or African when they entered the United States. We never received an answer. As the debate continued, the professor became increasingly agitated and with anger told us to leave the classroom.

As I look back on that day, we were all mad not because we were asked to leave the classroom, but because of the racist ideology of the professor who could not see his Eurocentrism. I also remember the discussion that took place as we sat in the library questioning why it is so important for Eurocentric scholars to continue to disparage Africans and people of African descent, claiming that we as a people have never produced any civilization or cultural norms worth studying. I saw that race was and still is the pivotal point of the debate: How could some black Africans conquer the Iberian Peninsula, defeat so-called superior white human beings, and control all the conquered territories until 1492? More central to the debate is this: How could inferior black Africans bring to Europe the knowledge that would awaken the world to what we now call modernity? The very thought of Islamic people bringing Europe out of the Dark Ages does not portray the Christian European mind as superior in the traditional way Western education teaches its students.

We discussed how the United States constructs race, which socially identifies and shapes categories to define whether an individual is white. I find it insidious that from 1790 until the Immigration and Nationality Act of 1952, this so-called democratic nation maintained a racial prerequisite for naturalization and citizenship that allowed and restricted people through racially constructed laws. The United States hides behind the slogan that democracy is still an experiment while at the same time purposefully maintaining and restructuring laws and public policy that are highly discriminating and racial. We also discussed how this professor still used the term Negro as he claimed that Ethiopians and Moors were not Africans or Negroid racial stock. We considered that *Negro,* the word allegedly used to define dark-pigmented people from sub-Saharan Africa, was coined by the Portuguese somewhere around 1441 when they were raiding the West African coastline for slaves. Richard B. Moore, in *The Name "Negro" Its Origin and Evil Use,*[1] maintains that Gomez Eannes de Azurara first used the word *Negro* to describe sub-Saharan Africans in 1453 in the *Chronicle of the Discovery and Conquest of Guinea.*[2] Azurara describes how the Portuguese slaver Dinnis Fernandes Diaz (referred to in Western history as an explorer) called North Africa the land of the Moors and Guinea the land of the blacks. The Arabs called the kingdom of Mali *Bilad es Sudan,* or the land of the blacks, while referring to the people of Mali as the Moors.

Eurocentric scholars have devoted much time and energy to prove that the Moors were not black Africans. Yet there is a wealth of scholarship from the Arabs themselves and recent researchers that refutes the Eurocentric paradigm and states that people with dark or black pigmentation were always referred to as Moors, Sudanese, or Ethiopians.[3] The word *Negro* was never used to describe Africans until the advent of the Portuguese raids for slaves up and down the West African coast in the 1440s. The early raids led to the Atlantic slave trade and the creation of an ideology that positioned black peoples outside the boundaries of the human race, inferior to whites. I remember my fellow black students and me sitting down in the African American studies department library referring to the problematic ideological framework that the history professor defended, no matter how insensitive his pedagogy came across to African American students. We also talked about how in the United States one could be classified as white even though that person may be dark skinned but living apart from the so-called black race.

Although many anthropologists, biologists, and other scholars have come to the conclusion that race is a socially constructed dogma designed for the purpose of maintaining white supremacy, I find very little pedagogy in U.S. classrooms refuting society's persisting belief in black inferiority. In my observations of schools, what I do see are the ways educators teach around the subject, never forthrightly confronting the issue or addressing the topic of race. While there are some teachers and various other educators who confront the issue of race candidly, many others hand out readings on race but avoid the topic in the classroom, feeling that they have fulfilled their duty to address the issues of race and class. As I look back and think about my history professor's Eurocentric pedagogy—although I had ample proof that the Moors were black Africans—the experience made me research and solidify my knowledge concerning just who the Moors were and develop a clear understanding of why that professor was so wedded to his defense of his position. There was no discussion needed: Sub-Saharan Africans never—nor could they ever have—invaded Europe or made any contributions to what the West calls civilization.

In the year 710 c.e. a force of 100 cavalry and 400 footmen under the military leadership of Tarif ibn Ziyad, a young Islamic Berber, crossed over to the Iberian Peninsula and made a successful reconnaissance of Southern Spain. Tarif, the son of Zar'a ibn Abi Maurdrik, was part of a generation of young Islamic Berbers who were well-read in the military thinking of the Arab generals Hassan ibn al-Numan and Musa ibn Nusayr, who had just conquered Northwest Africa. One year later Tarif led another force of some 12,000 Berbers, crossed the strait, and disembarked near the place that bears his name, Dajabal Tarik (Tarik's mountain), and what the West today calls Gibraltar. Tarif defeated a Visigoth army six times larger than his own under the command of Roderick, king of the Visigoths, at a small river near the Cape of Trafalgar, which afterward gave Tarif command of the Iberian Peninsula. Musa ibn Nusayr joined Tarif with an army of 18,000 Berbers and within three months had conquered the entire peninsula north of the Ebro River as far as the Pyrenees and annexed the territory of the Basque. The Islamic armies would later be stopped in France at what is known as the Battle of Tours in 732 c.e., a battle that Western scholars believe saved Europe from the Islamic infidels. Most history textbooks on Western civilization do not include anything on the Moors' conquest of Spain, but they do include the victory of Charles Martel and his Franks over the Arabs at the battle of Tours.

The Moors ruled Spain from 711 to 1492 and brought a sophisticated culture that instigated a scientific as well as a cultural revolution. Since modern Eurocentric historians could not erase this period of Islamic culture and power completely from the history books, they resorted to maintaining that the Moors were white Arabs. However, primary sources from Arab scholars themselves, like Ibn Husayn, reveal that the Berber soldiers under Tarif were "Sudanese"—an Arabic word that describes people who are black. Other Arab writers, like ibn Hayyans and ibn al-Athir (1160–1234), both wrote that Tarif's army was of Sudanese origin.[4] According to Titus Burckhardt's work, *Moorish Culture in Spain,* the word *Moor* comes from the Latin term *Mauri,* which means "black or dark" complexion.[5] On the other hand, European scholars like H.T. Norris continue to deny that the Berbers who conquered Spain were dark skinned and therefore support the racist assumptions that Africans could not have been part of the Moorish invasion of Spain. In his work *The Berbers in Arabic Literature* Norris writes that "it is improbable that they were Nubian or Ethiopians."[6]

Race-conscious European historians have also denied that the Moors controlled Sicily for over a hundred years and mingled and intermarried with the local population. Western textbooks generally delete the fact that between 827 and 937 Islamic armies of mostly Sudanese Berbers invaded Sicily and took control of the island. Indeed, blacks were so common in the city of Palermo that Ibn Hawkal, an Arab geographer from Baghdad in the tenth century, referred to Palermo's city gate as *Bab es Soudan,* or gate of the blacks. Pope Leo III was confused about their racial identity, calling them at different times Moors, Agareni, and Saracens.[7] Even Rome itself was not safe from the Moors who landed at the mouth of the Tiber River in 846 C.E. and sacked the basilica of Peter and occupied forts only a hundred miles from the city of Rome. Pope John VII pleaded with the Moorish armies not to lay siege to Rome and agreed to pay a yearly tribute of 25,000 marks of silver for the "Saracens" to retreat.[8]

Western history, of course, claims that Europe brought civilization to the "dark continent" of Africa. Most Western historians would agree that the first civilized Europeans were the Greeks, who created the knowledge they later passed on to the Romans. According to scholars such as Martin Bernal in *Black Athena: The Afroasiatic Roots of Classical Civilization* and George G.M. James in *Stolen Legacy: The Greeks Were Not the Authors of Greek Philosophy, but the People of North Africa, Commonly Called the Egyptians,* the Eurocentric historical paradigm is wrong.[9] These authors suggest that Greek civilization was profoundly influenced by Afroasiatic civilizations and that this knowledge was (and to a great extent still is) deliberately obscured by unbridled Eurocentric racism. Such a perspective has consistently refused to acknowledge that the Greeks always recognized the Afroasiatic roots of their civilization and culture. Bernal and James, along with other scholars, suggest that the Africans from the Nile Valley freely gave the Greeks their knowledge. The Greeks in turn transmitted it to the Romans, who lost it, thereby bringing on the five hundred years of Dark Ages.

Many Eurocentric historians portray the Dark Ages as an exceptionally barbaric period of human existence. This notion, however, is an ethnocentric one that arises from historians who claim that Europe was the only civilized part of the world. The Dark Ages were dark for Europe, but not all human civilization was thrown into this period of turmoil and savage brutality brought about by a supposedly superior civilized region of the world. In fact, at the time when European rulers were preoccupied with religious tyranny, wars among themselves, keeping the masses in utter poverty, burning witches, and disemboweling heretics, the Moors brought Islamic civilization and culture to Europe and essentially ended the Dark Ages. Thus, it can be argued that the Muslims actually helped civilize the barbaric ways of Christian Europe.

Contrary to the history given by modern Eurocentric scholarship, Europeans recognized and utilized the scientific thought of the Moors and other Muslim scholars and even studied under them. While most educated Europeans believed that the black plague, or black death, was from the hand of God, the Moorish physician ibn Khatib asserted that the plague was caused by "tiny contagions." Sanitation was a priority for the Islamic Moors; city planners and public health officials understood that health standards could be achieved only when citizens—rich and poor alike—were educated and held responsible for their own personal hygiene. It must be stressed that the Christian Church taught the masses that bathing and personal hygiene were not important ingredients for good health and the prevention of diseases. The Church banned public baths and preached that daily baths were sinful, and after the Reconquista plagues and syphilis ran rampant throughout the Spanish countryside, as they had already run throughout the rest of Europe.[10]

Islamic culture at its best was welcomed by the Europeans in Iberia. Jews and Christians alike preferred the Moors to the greedy Gothic rulers. Religious tolerance was more acceptable under the Islamic rulers, although Jews and Christians could not build new temples for worship and were required to pay a special tax. In most cases, however, they practiced their religion without persecution.[11] Islamic scholars were well versed in the ancient Egyptian philosophers and sciences and the works of the Greek philosophers who had studied in Egypt and translated these works into Arabic. These were the documents that were translated into Latin after the Reconquista and rediscovered by European scholars in the Renaissance. Islamic scholars took advantage of their access to the writings of the Ethiopians, Egyptians, Phoenicians, Greeks, Indians, and Chinese and used them to create new paradigms of knowledge. These new paradigms enabled the Muslims to make profound progress in the areas of mathematics, theoretical and applied sciences, medicine, astronomy, navigation, and new concepts of geography. This knowledge had a compelling effect upon European civilization. Islamic scholars who associated with Nestorian and Jacobite Christians and educated Jewish scholars translated many of the Greek scientific works into Arabic and later into Latin.[12]

Moorish Spain became the center of intellectual activity, as Arabic became the language used by scholars throughout Europe, Asia, and Africa. Islamic universities in Spain such as Toledo, Seville, Cordova, and Granada became meccas of learning and attracted students of the wealthy from Europe, Africa, and Asia. Europeans relied on Moorish physicians to cure them of various ailments. Even after the Reconquista, Christian rulers continued to rely upon Moorish scholars to assist with their expertise and knowledge.[13] The remarkable achievements of the Moors and other Islamic scholars in Spain in general are acknowledged by all historians of repute; for example, George Sarton's encyclopedic treatise, *Introduction to the History of Science*,[14] which is considered a definitive work on the subject, convincingly accentuates this fact: From the second half of the eighth century to the end of the eleventh century, Arabic was the scientific, progressive language of mankind. It will suffice here to evoke a few glorious names without contemporary equivalents in the West: Jabir ibn Hayyan, al-Kindi, al-Khwarizmi, al Farghani, al-Razi, Thabit ibn Qurra, al-Battani, Hunain ibn Ishaq, al-Farabi, Ibrahim ibn Sinan, al-Masudi, al-Tabari, Abul-Wafa, Ali ibn Abbas, Abul-Qasim, Ibn al-Jazzar, al-Biruni, Ibn Sina, Ibn Yunus, al-Karkhi, Ibn al-Haytham, Ali ibn Isa, al-Ghazalli, al-Zarqali, Omar Khayyam! "If anyone tells you that the Middle Ages were scientifically sterile, just quote these men to him, all of whom flourished within a relatively short period, between 750 and 1100."[15]

Eurocentic scholars have never acknowledged that the Renaissance was a direct result of the Moorish Muslim scholars who brought their knowledge to Spain. During the Middle or Dark Ages, Islamic scholars who were of both Arab and African origin were leading the world in the sciences, mathematics, literature, and medicine. Most Western historians claim that Islamic scholars only preserved the writings of the Greeks and essentially deny that such scholars *created* any forms of knowledge. In his essay in the prestigious scientific journal *Nature*, "What Is Wrong with Muslim Science," Francis Ghiles writes in contrast to this Eurocentric interpretation:

At its peak about one thousand years ago, the Muslim world made a remarkable contribution to science, notably mathematics and medicine. Baghdad in its heyday and southern Spain built universities to which thousands flocked. Rulers surrounded themselves with scientists and artists. A spirit of freedom allowed Jews, Christians, and Muslim to work side by side. Today all this is but a memory.[16]

It is important to note that paying tribute to Islamic scientific achievements during Europe's Dark Ages is entirely a twentieth-century phenomenon. One does not find anything resembling this in the literature of the eighteenth and nineteenth centuries because until the West gained military and economic world supremacy, Islam in the Christian mind represented the principal military and moral threat to Christianity. The Church could not tolerate losing thousands of people, its land, and the wealth it was still accumulating to a more liberal religion like Islam. Therefore, Christian theologians, in order to explain the spread of Islam, developed a self-protective theoretical framework designed to demonstrate that Islamic success was the product of violence, lasciviousness, and ungodly deceit. This was a useful framework at the time when European racism, protocapitalist imperialism, and colonialism were asserting themselves. In this context, not only did the "white man's burden" become easier to bear, but also military conquest could assume the form of a moral imperative. Conquered peoples could be portrayed as barbarians in need of civilization who were ignorant of scientific and artistic understanding. Hence a prohibition emerged against scholarship that might lay such assumptions open to question.

Also, the eighteenth and nineteenth centuries were dominated by an enslavement such as the world had never experienced. This European colonialism, slavery, and racism demanded an ideology that justified such inhumane actions. The extent and depth to which Western scholars created an epistemology of racism that constructed and framed the actions of this era have had a long-lasting effect on what today is perceived as the truth about culture and race. Eurocentric scholars portrayed the eleventh-century Almoravids—the nomadic dark-skinned Tuaregs of Mali,[17] who had conquered most of North Africa and West Africa including the Soninke kingdom of Ghana—as religious extremists. At the same time they presented the Crusaders as heroes and pious soldiers of the Christian God. The empire of the Moors stretched across the western half of Algeria through Morocco and all of Ghana and from the Atlantic coast of Portugal stretching east past the Pyrenees to the Rhone Valley in France.

Why would European scholars produce knowledge that either erased the fact that black Africans had invaded and controlled Spain until 1492 or produce a history that the Moors were not black Africans but white or light-skinned Africans? Many of us believe the answer is obvious: to promote that dark-skinned Muslim Africans controlled or even created the Islamic empire of Spain would undermine the belief that Africans were ignorant children, savage and uncivilized and meant only to be slaves. Today, students in the United States read about the classical Greco-Roman literature that had been collected and translated from Greek into Arabic. Curricula mandate that they read and study the works of Michelangelo and others who had an impact on the Renaissance that took place in Europe. Yet these same students do not learn that behind this era of knowledge and progress in Europe was the scientific enlightenment of the Arab and African Islamic scholars. Western science is built upon the foundation of the influence of the Moors who controlled the Iberian Peninsula, renamed al-Andalus by the Moors and Arab armies.

Most American secondary and even college students do not learn that the Islamic commercial techniques were superior to the European standards. They are unaware that trade routes for goods always went through the hands of the Islamic rulers, thus causing much contempt for them among European monarchs. African gold from the kingdoms of Ghana and Mali, along with ivory, slaves, and other goods as well as the spices of China, India, and other parts of Asia, were under the control of the Islamic rulers and commercial traders. The exported spices, sugar, oranges, peaches, silks, and other goods were coveted by the Europeans and soon found their way into many European castles. Resentment, however, on the part of the European rulers who saw large monetary value in removing Islamic control of the trade routes would later lead to the advent of capitalism and European colonialism. Students in the United States have not been encouraged to study advanced Islamic banking systems with their early use of checks and credit. The same students do not know that the European colonists in the Americas modeled their large sugar plantations on those established centuries earlier by the Muslims in the Mediterranean lands.[18]

American students are not made aware that Islamic libraries were superior in quality and quantity and more numerous than the libraries of Europe. The love of learning and books was indigenous to the cultures in Asia and Africa. Enormous libraries were built in cities like Baghdad, Damascus, Cairo, Cordova, Toledo, Seville, and Granada, and smaller libraries were maintained in tiny Muslim towns and villages. In following the great ancient libraries in Babylon and Pharaonic Egypt, libraries were called "houses of wisdom," "houses of knowledge," or "treasuries of wisdom." One of the most famous was financed by al-Mamun (the son of the great Caliph, Harun al-Rashid), administered by Persians who were known for their bibliographical expertise. Mosques also held collections of books, and Islamic rulers displayed their respect for libraries by paying librarians decent wages and employing numerous translators and calligraphers.[19]

Young Americans are not taught that Spain and Portugal were the first to benefit from the Moorish Islamic culture and knowledge that made European global expansion possible. The men whom the West calls the great explorers and the rest of the world refers to as enslavers and invaders could not have sailed anywhere without the navigational knowledge that the Islamic Moors brought with them to the Iberian peninsula. Prince Henry the Navigator, da Gama, Columbus, Cabot, Cabral, Magellan, and many others benefited from the charts, navigational skills, and tools that were brought to Europe by the Moors. Without the work of many Islamic scholars who brought together and created new ways of seeing from the works of the ancient Egyptians, Indians, Chinese, and Greeks; examined them; and created new knowledge, the European

Renaissance might not have happened as we know it. The universities at Seville, Toledo, and Cordova attracted students from all over Europe, Africa, and Asia and gave birth to the ideas that Prince Henry would use to initiate what would be Western imperialism throughout the world.[20]

Whatever we may say about the creation of knowledge, the Islamic culture, and the scientific advancements that the Moors brought to the Iberian Peninsula, they changed the world dramatically. That the contributions of the Moors to European civilization have been largely ignored, hidden, and denied is an act of historical and epistemological violence that continues to shape European consciousness in the twenty-first century. Moorish influence reached not only throughout the European continent but also all the way to the British Isles, as evidenced by the coats of arms of many English families.[21] The efforts of scholars to disprove that the Moors were black, downplay the humanity of their conquest and administration of the Iberian Peninsula, dismiss their control of the Mediterranean, and erase the Islamic enlightenment that brought Europe out of the Dark Ages constitute a disservice to Western education. Indeed, such efforts also reflect a racist ideology that distorts relations between the West and the Islam world to this day.

Chapter 8

Schooled to Order: Education and the Making of Modern Egypt

Yusef J. Progler

"They opened fire with cannons and bombs on the houses and quarters, aiming specially at the mosque, firing at it with those bombs. They also fired at suspected places bordering the mosque, such as the market. And they trod in the mosque with their shoes, carrying swords and rifles. Then they scattered in its courtyard and its main praying area and tied their horses to the prayer niche. They ravaged the students' quarters and ponds, smashing the lamps and chandeliers and breaking up the bookcases of the students and the scribes. They plundered whatever they found in the mosque, such as furnishings, vessels, bowls, deposits, and hidden things from closets and cupboards. They treated the books and Qur'anic volumes as trash, throwing them on the ground, stamping on them with their feet and shoes. Furthermore they soiled the mosque, blowing their spit in it, and urinating and defecating in it. They guzzled wine and smashed the bottles in the central court and other parts. And whoever they happened to meet in the mosque they stripped. They chanced upon someone in one of the student residences and slaughtered him."[1]

This is how Abdul Rahman Jabarti described the attack by Napoleon's troops on al-Azhar University in Cairo during the French invasion and occupation of Egypt in 1798 C.E. Jabarti, a Muslim scholar, wrote a chronicle of the occupation. The incident is significant for a number of reasons not apparent in the text. Mosques can be rebuilt, and people are born to replace those who are slaughtered. But the task of creating a lasting colonial order required more than bombs and barbarities: it needed a plan that would alter the foundations of the society. One of the overt goals of the French occupation was to attempt a disruption of British communication with the Eastern wing of its empire, but it was also about the French "mission to civilize" North Africa. Napoleon presented his adventure as being in the best interests of Egypt and claimed to be the liberator of the Arabs from the Turks. But Jabarti, and many others, denounced the occupation, and the French soon realized that the strongest resistance to their grand designs would come from pious Muslims. With their attack on al-Azhar and other centers of Islamic learning, the French initiated an effort to destroy or subvert the Islamic base of society in the region, a task that involved reorienting people away from the Muslim style of education.

A few decades later, in 1845, a French military officer in Algeria boldly proclaimed, "In effect the essential thing is to gather into groups this people which is everywhere and nowhere; the essential thing is to make them something we can seize hold of. When we have them in our hands, we will then be able to do many things which are quite impossible for us today and which will perhaps allow us to capture their minds after we have captured their bodies." In this case, having been thwarted by traditional Islamic resistance in the Algerian hinterland, as elsewhere, the French realized that they needed a strategy, part of which required the rounding up and enumeration of the people they sought to control. Modern schooling served this purpose well. Soon, selected Algerians were being schooled the French way, where they could be easily "seized hold of" and rewarded with positions of nominal authority in the emerging French colonial order.

The thinking in French intellectual circles seems to have been that, eventually, the roots of Islamic culture, the main threat to their designs in the region, would have to be ripped out and replanted, and education was an important site for this operation. As the French author Fenelon noted in his novel *Telemaque* in 1867, "We, the masters, should seize on our subjects in their early youth. We shall change the tastes and habits of the whole people. We shall build up again from the very foundations and teach the people to live a frugal, innocent, busy life after the pattern of our laws." The novel was more than conjecture or fantasy. To many, it was also a blueprint. Since it was not enough to kill the Islamic scholars and subvert the students away from Islam, the colonizers needed to root out Islam from among ordinary people, who retained a strong faith. The way to do this was through schooling. Accordingly, schools were pressed into service of the colonial state, to "change the tastes and habits of the whole people."

In 1893, only a few generations after Napoleon's invasion of Egypt, the colonization of selected segments of the Muslim populace in North Africa was nearly complete. By then convinced that West was best, the editor of an Egyptian academic journal, lamenting the supposed "backwardness" of his people, wrote, "It is we who have placed ourselves in this position. There is one thing that unites us all in the Orient: our past greatness and our present backwardness." But these were not original thoughts; he wrote those words only after consulting with his masters, a group of

French Orientalists who at the time were developing hierarchical theories of human development, putting white Christians on top, as was the fashion in the social Darwinism that had emerged in the nineteenth century.

Dazzled by Western military power and technocratic order, many Muslims did not realize that they were participating in their own colonization, and that they were legitimizing a colonial order in their own societies. One of the most influential French Orientalists among Egyptian intellectuals and rulers was Gustav Le Bon. His work on the "psychological laws of the evolution of peoples" helped form the nationalist ideas of modernist Muslim scholars like Muhammad Abduh. Abduh, along with other Egyptian nationalists, used the now-discredited racialist theories of Le Bon, as well as the work of other French social scientists like Emile Durkheim, to formulate a vision of what has been called "modern Islam," in complete conformity with then current Western theories of science and society. While the time-bound theories of Le Bon and Durkheim came to be viewed critically in the West, their legacy lived on in the East, and reformist Muslim thinking along the lines of people like Abduh survived in the Muslim world.

In 1910, American president Theodore Roosevelt visited Egypt to deliver an address at the newly opened National University in Cairo. Roosevelt, also an avid reader of Le Bon, insisted that the Egyptian people were "not sufficiently evolved" to deserve any form of self-government, his arrogance blinding him to the century of colonization that produced the modern confusion of Islamic identity in the Arab Muslim world. And, after nearly a century of adjusting Arab Muslim culture toward the West, the Western colonials still viewed Islam as a potential threat to their designs in the region. To the extent that local rulers were dependent on the West, they, too, supported further adjustments. But Islam still remained one of the key stumbling blocks to colonial designs. A systematic attack on Islam had begun nearly a century earlier, soon after Napoleon's invasion, when an Egyptian national, Hasan al-Attar, was sent to study in Napoleon's Institut d'Egypte in Paris. Later a scholar at al-Azhar university, he taught the modernist reformer Tahtawi, who was instrumental in Westernizing Egyptian schools and translating the works of French social scientists. Tahtawi's work, in turn, influenced a new generation of modernist-minded Muslims associated with al-Azhar, including Abduh, who became its chief scholar. Soon, another student at the newly adjusted al-Azhar, Mustafa Abd al-Raziq, whose father was associated with Abduh, later studied at the feet of the French sociologist Emile Durkheim in the Sorbonne. Upon returning to Egypt, Abd al-Raziq taught Western philosophy at the Egyptian University, and, in 1945, he became the rector of al-Azhar.

The university at al-Azhar, like many other centers of Muslim learning, had ceased to be a place of resistance to colonization, emerging instead as a quietist, legitimizing force of the colonial order. Beginning with cannons and proceeding through canons, Western colonial powers worked to neutralize places like al-Azhar, a process nearly completed during the twentieth century. Once the indigenous centers of resistance to Western imperialism, many schools and educational institutions became part of the colonial order. The case of al-Azhar illustrates a two-pronged Western methodology for its attempt to order the Islamic world in its own image: marginalize or destroy the traditional Islamic foundations, while building a new set of West-directed foundations, including the main pillar of an unquestioned reliance on the Western sciences and ways of understanding the world, a key feature of which is a formalized concept of sociopolitical order.

Muslim Education in Medieval Cairo

To appreciate the impact of the colonization of Muslim life in Egypt, it may be useful to glance at what Muslim education looked like prior to Napoleon's invasion. Studies of education in the Muslim world by Western scholars are often limited to higher religious education in major metropolises, focusing on the "medieval period," the thirteenth to sixteenth centuries C.E. In this context, the concept of "Islamic education" is misleading, since it refers primarily to the training of scholars (*'ulama*), without paying attention to such areas as vocational training, medical and architectural studies, the arts, or farming and animal husbandry. Presumably, Muslims did study such things, but modern Western studies of Muslim history do not seem to consider them within the broad rubric of "education." Some scholars, however, are aware of the inherent tensions of such a narrow approach: "Judges and professors were *'ulama* but so were members of social, occupational, and cultural groups who might not rely primarily on education or legal activities for a livelihood."[2] This tension was particularly pronounced in Cairo during the medieval period, although many works fail to address it and focus instead on religious education, rendering other forms of education rather mysterious, amounting to a separation of Islam from society. Nevertheless, such works provide a glimpse of Muslim educational life.

An important factor in traditional Islamic education was its informality: "The variety of men and women—sultans and emirs, scholar and bureaucrats, the wives and daughters of the same—who undertook the construction of schools of higher religious and legal education guaranteed that those schools would not be uniform. On the most obvious level, for example, religious institutions might be established by individuals of widely differing financial means."[3] Consequently, "the schools that were established varied considerably in physical size, in the preference that they allotted to one particular rite, in their commitment to Sufi devotions as well as rigorous academic work, and above all in the value of their endowments (and the income they generated) and the quality of education they offered."[4] One aspect of the informality of education is apparent in the student-teacher relationship. Before institutionalization, teachers were not salaried, but made or inherited their livelihoods independently of their scholarship. There were also no diplomas or degrees; instead, students received an *ijaza*, an informal recommendation from the scholar to teach the knowledge he or she has learned. Only in an institutional setting, either when introduced partially under the Mamluks, or in toto during the colonial period, were these informal and personal authorities replaced by a system of formal and hierarchical qualifications.

The Islamic approach to educating religious scholars, though utilizing books, primarily emphasized oral sources and transmissions. Thus, a book is a valid medium of study only in so far as it has been learned by way of a living authority. This involved, among other things, students essentially writing their own books, based on recitations by the teacher and developed through discussions with the teacher. The oral mode of learning and inquiry is embedded in the Arabic language itself, with its triconsonantal root system brought to life by what is literally called the movement (*harakat*) of vowels. The precise meaning of words in such a language can be ascertained only by listening to them being spoken; written texts, therefore, are secondary. In fact, some medieval Muslim scholars considered it scandalous to base one's education solely on books. This is illustrated by the informal study sessions that students engaged in when the teacher left. These study sessions involved reading out loud in order to embed the meaning of the words in the hearts of the learners. This points to another key component of education at the time: the primacy of memorization. After a core of fundamental materials were memorized and could be easily reproduced, students would then be encouraged to develop "the ability to use critically the materials memorized and apply them to particular academic and legal problems." By way of such training, "Muslim scholars produced rigorous critiques of both ancient and contemporary writers, and academic exchange, at least at the higher levels of the study of jurisprudence, often revolved around the organized disputation of controversial questions."[5]

But even with the strong and vibrant legacy of informality in Islamic education, it would be unfair to say that institutionalized formal education came only with Western colonization. The Mamluk regime had already begun some institutionalization of religious education in Cairo, by creating a network of institutions, many of which were endowed by the government. This was partly in the name of ideological hegemony, since al-Azhar was established as a Shiite center of learning, and the Mamluks sought to bring it more into the Sunni ideological sphere. Endowments were "dispensed to the educated classes, and to other sectors of the urban community, as stipends and payments in kind to support the work of passing on the vast corpus of traditional learning from one generation to the next." However, "the spread of such institutions never resulted in any formalization of the educational process," and that informality "guaranteed its vigor, and imparted a measure of openness missing from Western institutions of higher learning until a comparatively recent period."[6] Even so, more than one hundred religious institutions were established during the Mamluk period, ranging from large *madrasas*, built on the model of the one in al-Fustat established by Salah al-Din al-Ayyubi in 1170, to small *madrasas* attached to private homes, mosques, and the Sufi orders.

One controversial by-product of the Mamluk attempt at the institutionalization of religious education was the emergence of professional scholars, and of people in general who began to make their living from teaching religion. However, this did not create as many problems as it did in the West: "Indeed, the Medieval Islamic world generally avoided that radical division of intellectual and commercial labor that has at times impoverished both the academy and the corporation in the West...Islam had never known a sharp social divide between men of religious learning and men of commerce."[7] However, the professionalization of teaching created some problems, and the sultan had to occasionally intervene between teachers vying for the financial rewards of institutionalized education, while some fathers bequeathed their academic positions to their sons. Another unfortunate aspect of the early institutionalization of formal education was that it tended to marginalize women. While the predominantly informal nature of education in Islamic Cairo still had many places where women could study, they could not study or teach in the newly endowed institutions, even though they could endow and administer them. Even so, it is important to remember that "in practice *madrasas* were by no means monastic in character. Islam, by and large, had always rejected celibacy as a permanent lifestyle."[8] Nowhere in the Islamic world does one find the celibacy and exclusion of women from academia, which, as one historian has put it, made Western institutions of higher learning a "world without women."[9] As the Islamic sources suggest, it is incumbent upon both men and women to know their religion, even though the modes of learning may differ. Beyond the childhood Qur'anic schools, which accepted young boys and girls, women could pursue their Islamic learning in a variety of informal settings, including their homes. In fact, the homes of many prominent Muslim women became centers of learning for other women.

One public arena in which women were highly visible was in the area of *hadith*, the recitation of sayings and traditions of the Prophet Muhammad, upon whom be peace, and the deeds of his companions and family. As Berkey suggests, "No less a scholar than Jalal al-Din Suyuti (d. 1505 c.e.)

relied heavily on women as his sources for *hadith*." Many women achieved high regard in their knowledge and transmission of *hadith*, but this "should not obscure from us the fundamental difference between the character of education they received and that accorded to men," a difference that often resulted in "the absence of women from endowed positions in schools of higher learning and from judicial posts." In the institutionalized, formal system of education begun by the Mamluks, this "gender barrier affected the core of the relationship between teacher and student as it was known in medieval Islam." Still, scholars "openly relied on many women for secure and persuasive chains of authority," and "the social horizons of Islamic education were very wide indeed."[10]

Despite the creeping institutionalization, the Mamluk centers of learning did not cater only to an elite class of intellectuals. Many local people worked as functionaries in the *madrasas,* as prayer callers; assistants to Friday prayer leaders; readers of poetry in praise of the Prophet; or as language teachers, writing teachers, and scribes. These services also entitled them to study with some of the most prominent scholars of the day. Even so, there was some tension, highlighted in a treatise by Ibn al-Hajj (d. 1336), who chastised the learned elite of the day for dressing ostentatiously and alienating ordinary people from higher learning. But, as Berkey suggests, this proclivity was not as widespread as some Orientalists have presumed.[11] On the contrary, "The contemporary sources leave little trace of any of the structural antagonism that set 'town' against 'gown' in late Medieval Europe." Most schools also kept numerous people on staff who recited Qur'an, and, during certain times of the year, recited *hadith* from a number of well-known compilations: "The prominence of organized groups of Qur'an readers at virtually every school may suggest that one of the principal reasons why the academic and nonacademic spheres mixed so harmoniously was that these were more than mere institutions of education. They were also centers of public worship." So while there was some exclusion of ordinary people, the practice was not widespread. In fact, the recitation of *hadith* was a widely acceptable community activity involving men and women from all walks of life, and "the transmission of this important field of Muslim learning took place in a very open world, one that drew no distinct boundaries between instruction and devotion, and in which large and disparate groups of Muslims could and did participate."[12]

In general, therefore, "Muslim society in the later Middle Ages was far less segmented and divided than we might otherwise have thought," and "education acted as a leveler." Muslims studied the Islamic knowledge and wisdom as spoken words, "because their very pronunciation contained a reservoir of enormous power, capable, as we have seen, of defeating the Mongol armies and warding off the dreaded plague. One studied these texts because they provided a convenient and recognized model on which to pattern one's own life. To transmit them, to Mamluks, women, and common people, as well as to full-time students, was to transmit a body of information valuable to each and every Muslim." It is into this dynamic milieu of knowledge production and transmission that the Western colonial powers stepped with Napoleon's arrival in Egypt in 1798.

Schools as Mechanisms for Normalizing Judgment

During the seventeenth and eighteenth centuries in Western Europe, a particular mode of schooling emerged containing within it the mechanisms that on the surface seem to sunder cultural, ecological, and spiritual unities. But this sort of fragmentation can also be seen as a way of creating an entirely new and redirected system, just as pervasive as that which it replaces. Along these lines, Foucault places schooling in the same category as prisons and other "total institutions." The notion of a "total institution" brings to mind the work of the psychologist and sociologist Erving Goffman, who wrote about asylums, prisons, boarding schools, and army training camps. Goffman defined a total institution as "a place of residence and work where a large number of like-situated individuals, cut off from the wider society for an appreciable period of time, together lead an enclosed, formally administered round of life."[13] As a total institution, Foucault sees schooling to be a "sort of apparatus of uninterrupted examination that duplicated along its entire length the operation of teaching."[14] Therefore, school buildings are "mechanisms for training" characterized by interlocking procedures that come together as "teaching proper, the acquisition of knowledge by the very practice of the pedagogical activity, and a reciprocal, hierarchized observation. A relation of surveillance, defined and regulated, is inscribed at the heart of the practice of teaching, not as an additional or adjacent part, but as a mechanism that is inherent to it and which increases its efficiency."[15]

One outcome of total disciplinary institutions is what Foucault calls "normalizing judgment."[16] Today, normalization paves the way for reintegrating people into pseudo-unities, as in consumer culture and identity politics, or, in the case I will illustrate below, subjecthood within a colonial order. The key issue is that normalization creates something new:

Like surveillance and with it, normalization becomes one of the great instruments of power at the end of the classical age. For the marks that once indicated status, privilege and affiliation were increasingly replaced—or at least supplemented— by a whole range of degrees of normality indicating membership of a homogeneous social body but also playing a part in classification, hierarchization and the distribution of rank. In a sense, the power of normalization imposes homogeneity;

but it individualizes by making it possible to measure gaps, to determine levels, to fix specialties and to render the differences useful by fitting them one to another.[17]

Foucault is instructive on how Western schooling circumscribes thinking while maintaining a sense of individuality, and how this training is infused with the subtle mechanisms of power. In his discussion on the "means of correct training," Foucault describes European culture during the seventeenth and eighteenth centuries—the beginning of the modern period of colonization—as possessing "a technique for constituting individuals as correlative elements of power and knowledge." He continues:

The individual is no doubt the fictitious atom on an "ideological" representation of society; but he is also a reality fabricated by this specific technology of power that I have called "discipline." We must cease once and for all to describe the effects of power in negative terms: it "excludes," it "represses," it "censors," it "abstracts," it "masks," it "conceals." In fact, power produces; it produces reality; it produces domains of objects and rituals of truth. The individual and the knowledge that may be gained of him belong to this production.[18]

Education is a normalizing mechanism, and the development of colonial education was a tool of European imperialism in its quest to order the world in its own image. This process began at home but was soon carried forth to the colonies.

Order and Disorder in the Western Perception of Egypt

Foucault's focus on France and northern Europe "has tended to obscure the colonizing nature of disciplinary power," according to Mitchell:

Yet the panopticon, the model institution whose geometric order and generalized surveillance serve as a motif for this kind of power, was a colonial invention. The panoptic principle was devised on Europe's colonial frontier with the Ottoman Empire, and examples of the panopticon were built for the most part not in northern Europe, but in places like colonial India. The same can be said for the monitorial method of schooling, also discussed by Foucault, whose mode of improving and disciplining a population...came to be considered the model political process to accompany the capitalist transformation of Egypt.[19]

Edward Said understood this when he said of Napoleon's invasion of Egypt, "What would happen as a continuing legacy of the common Occidental mission to the Orient...would be the creation of new projects, new visions, new enterprises combining additional parts of the old Orient with the conquering European spirit."[20] According to Said, Napoleon's invasion of Egypt was motivated by three things: (1) his military successes up to that point "left him no other place to turn for additional glory than the East"; (2) he had a long fascination with the Orient, particularly with Alexander's conquest, and thus "the idea of reconquering Egypt as a new Alexander proposed itself to him, allied with the additional benefit of acquiring a new Islamic colony at England's expense"; (3) he knew it well, especially textually, and "Egypt was a project that acquired reality in his mind, and later in his preparations for its conquest, through experiences that belong to the realm of ideas and myths culled from texts, not empirical reality."[21]

Despite what appears to be a fascination with Islam, Napoleon gleaned much of his learning from the Islamophobic Orientalist Volney, who warned that anyone attempting to colonize the East would be faced with a three-front war, against the British, against the Ottoman Empire, and against the local Muslim population. In his planning and in consultation with a team of Orientalists, Napoleon "used Egyptian enmity towards the Mamelukes and appeals to the revolutionary idea of equal opportunity for all to wage a uniquely benign and selective war against Islam."[22] Since his military force was too small to impose itself on all of Egypt, he opted for co-optation, beginning with the religious scholars at al-Azhar, the ancient teaching mosque in Cairo. Though not a complete success, he was able to gain the support of several leading scholars to interpret the Qur'an in favor of French colonial intervention. This approach was successful enough for Napoleon to instruct his officers to work through co-opted religious scholars, and compliant local leaders in general, in a French form of the British-perfected method of indirect rule.

All this was necessary because Egypt was central to the European colonizing drive, and the prize was not in geopolitics alone:

Because Egypt was saturated with meaning for the arts, sciences, and government, its role was to be the stage on which actions of a world-historical importance would take place. By taking Egypt, then, a modern power would naturally demonstrate its strength and justify history; Egypt's own destiny was to be annexed, to Europe preferably.[23]

After the Suez Canal opened to international fanfare later in the nineteenth century, an observer remarked that it was especially valuable "for bringing more closely together the countries of the West and the East, and thus uniting the civilizations of different epochs."[24] Thus, to the West, Egypt was frozen in its past, to be resurrected and laid open by the European gaze. This imagined unity of East and West, old and new, would be brought about by the "imposition of the power of modern technology and intellectual will."[25]

But such an ambitious prospectus required much preparation, much thought. The redoubtable Orient needed "first to be known, then invaded and possessed, then re-created by scholars, soldiers, and judges who disinterred forgotten languages, histories, races, and cultures in order to posit them—beyond the modern Oriental's ken—as the true classical Orient that could be used to judge and rule the modern Orient."[26] But even with all these elements, French colonization of the Muslim world had elements of colonial adventures in other parts of the world. One main tactic in this standard colonial model was to find an authoritarian and ambitious headman to deal with, and implement colonial rule through him. These factors help us to avoid the misleading but persistent dichotomies of Western academic analysis: East and West, Us and Them, Christendom and Islam, North and South.

Although many discussions of local collaboration with European colonization discuss it in terms of "reform," the term has connotations of improving, making better. To most people who lived through the period, and who are living in systems inherited from the colonial period, there is little to see as improvement. Colonization fragmented local Muslim societies, as it did in other areas, and created in their place something new and often completely inappropriate to local conditions; it brought lands and peoples out of traditional economic and social sways and integrated them directly into the emerging capitalist, technicalist, secularist Western order. For this reason, it is more appropriate to use "disrupt" and "redirect" rather than reform. This is especially useful for a study of schooling, which was a major site of colonization. Modern schooling became a tool of disruption and redirection in the Muslim world, and its use was inextricably bound up with the local ruler's entanglement in the Western system of order, especially in the dimensions of commerce and war.

The Mechanization of War in the West

The European drive for domination over Mediterranean trade initiates a long cooperation between merchants and princes, and a growing interdependence of commerce and war. Even the late Crusades can be seen as an early effort of mass mobilization designed by European barons to take over trade in the Mediterranean. At the time, the entire system was geared up for that but got sidetracked with interstate fighting. However, once they had conquered Cyprus, formerly inhabited by Eastern Christians, Jews, and Muslims who were either enslaved, driven off, or eliminated, crusading knights turned the island into a vast sugar plantation. This took place in the thirteenth and fourteenth centuries but provided a model for later colonial plantations in the Caribbean. The growing intersection between princes and merchants was an alliance of convenience to consolidate control over Mediterranean trade. Naval research was supported by Italian merchants, resulting in the militarization of commerce; Italian merchant vessels became the first gunboats. This is the beginning of a centuries-long arms race that would entangle most European states and eventually their colonies. In short, despite military power seeming to be amoral, it has fueled the growth of Western civilization, and the birth of modernity takes place in the intersection of commerce and war.[27]

Beginning in the fifteenth century, rationalism replaced Christianity as the religion of the West. This was aided by the European rediscovery of Greek sources, which Muslims had known about for centuries. But Muslims didn't develop these sources the way Europeans did. While Christianity and Islam were both largely about morality, Christian Europe shifted to pure rationalism in the space of less than a century, abandoning morality in favor of rationality. Any dabblings with rationalism in the Muslim world remained tempered by a strong sense of its relationship to Islamic morality. In the West, science in the service of rationalism became an absolute end in it itself, with an exclusive adherence to the reductionist, experimental method and a growing dependency on advanced technology, hence a dependency on commercial interests, military interests, or both. Rationalism also gets bound up with enumeration, first of money but then quickly encompassing anything else that can be counted, in a new way of looking at the world that required it to be ordered and quantified.[28]

While this is not the place to trace the origins of this legacy in any great detail, one outcome of the legacy is a highly rationalized war machine. This rationalization was coupled with a strong will to kill, even an ease with killing, for which William McNeill offers a possible explanation:

Habits of bloodshed were deep-seated, perennially fed by the fact that Europeans raised both pigs and cattle in considerable numbers but had to slaughter all but a small breeding stock each autumn for lack of sufficient winter fodder. Other agricultural regimes, e.g. among the rice-growing farmers of China and India, did not involve annual slaughter of large animals. By contrast, Europeans living north of the Alps learned to take bloodshed as a normal part of the routine of the year. This may have had a good deal to do with their remarkable readiness to shed human blood and thinking nothing of it.[29]

Europeans continued to develop sophisticated ways to carry out violence, systematically and often with great efficiency. In contrast, according to McNeill,

the Moslem world failed to take full advantage of the new technical possibilities opened by the diffusion of Chinese skills in the wake of the Mongol unification of Eurasia. To be sure, the Ottoman Turks used improvements in cannon design to capture Constantinople in 1453; but the craftsmen who cast the cannon for Mohammed the Conqueror were Hungarian. Even as early as the mid-fifteenth century it appears to be true that gun founders of Latin Christendom had achieved a technical lead over cannon makers in other parts of the civilized world, including China.[30]

Soon, Europe proceeded to "recklessly…commercialize war more effectively and enthusiastically than any other population on earth."[31]. By the time that Napoleon invaded Egypt, the French military had become one of the most powerful and disciplined armies in Europe. The commercialization and rationalization of war directly corresponds with a strict systematization of schooling and continued into the twentieth century, with the birth of the warfare state, in which educational institutions and commercial interests continue to play a central role.[32] For now, however, it is important to consider the impact of its eighteenth- and nineteenth-century variant on the Muslim world and return to the French invasion of Egypt, focusing on the cooperation of local rulers in building a West-directed order.

Bad Subjects in the Construction of Colonial Order

Colonization comes in many shapes and forms. A colonial order is most pervasive and stubborn when it permeates the intellectual life of a people, and it is most effective when it remains undetected or obfuscated to the colonized peoples. To construct order in this way, the colonizer first needs to create disorder. The resulting colonial (dis)order is self-perpetuating and it is maintained through forms of schooling that introduce and gradually normalize the colonizer's culture. Modern schooling establishes and institutionalizes a normative system that empowers the colonial order and circumscribes the paths of resistance. Revealing such systems can help to outline the parameters for a possible dialogue on the role of schooling and education in the continuing subjugation of Muslims to the West.

In this context, much can be learned from the struggles of other peoples whose lives embody resistance to the various colonial orders, especially those peoples who are framing their resistance in ways that operate outside the conventional norms and patterns. For instance, the struggles of Native Americans are relevant and instructive. Native American scholars and activists Yvonne Dion-Buffalo and John Mohawk believe that colonized peoples have three choices when confronted with a systematized Western discourse and its accompanying power dynamics:

They can become "good subjects" of the discourse, accepting the rules of law and morals without much question, they can be "bad subjects" arguing that they have been subjected to alien rules but always revolting within the precepts of those rules, or they can be non-subjects, acting and thinking around discourses far removed from and unintelligible to the West.[33]

While good subjects and bad subjects "tend to impose the West's social conditions of domination and hierarchy which they learned from the colonizers upon their own poor and downtrodden," nonsubjects of the West "will increasingly support alternative and non-Western discourses of reality that legitimate entirely unfamiliar stories and versions about how the world works."[34] This model provides a useful heuristic for understanding cognate issues in the Muslim world, especially for a study of modern schooling as a tool of colonization. But while schooling has often been an integral instrument of colonization, it can also, paradoxically, be turned to as a form of defense or resistance to colonization. The diffuse, fragmenting, and atomizing effect of modern schooling in the West and its colonial sphere obscures natural interconnections and interrelationships, so that forms of resistance can work at constructing and strengthening colonization.

To Western historians, Napoleon's invasion and occupation of Egypt in 1798 is an insignificant footnote; for Muslims, it is a major turning point in history. This event marks the beginning of the modern era in the Muslim world. Although other Muslim states, notably the Ottoman Empire, had exchanges with Western Europe in previous centuries, Egypt is the first region to bear the full weight of Western modernity. One of the key figures in this process is Muhammad Ali Pasha, who to this day is both revered and disdained by Arab and Western historians for introducing a Western technocratic order into the Islamic world. A military officer of Albanian descent whom the Ottomans sent to repel the French occupation, Muhammad Ali took advantage of the ensuing instability to entrench himself as the ruler of Egypt, and he "set out to establish an efficient and Westernizing despotism with foreign (mainly French) technical aid."[35] Muhammad Ali claimed absolute authority, after massacring the Mamluk military brigades and co-opting some of the religious authorities. He also confiscated all land assets for himself, including the reserved lands (waqf) administered by al-Azhar University in Cairo and regional mosques and religious schools. By so doing, he became the "sole farmer" of Egypt, and his authority "subsequently came to be shared and exercised among a new land owning class, with the ruling family as the largest single landowner, together with European creditors and commercial interests."[36]

Impressed with French and British military and industrial technical supremacy and convinced of their utility for his own power struggle, Muhammad Ali embarked on a campaign of reordering traditional Muslim culture in Egypt. But the ensuing disruptions to local life were met with wide-ranging popular resistance, especially in the villages, and also from mosques and Islamic scholars in both urban and rural areas. Farmers and peasants deserted their lands, and some people slated for military service even mutilated themselves to avoid conscription.[37] When the traditional village mosque schools were forced by the emerging military/commercial state into acting as feeder institutions for military conscription, "Many parents preferred to deny their children a traditional education rather than make them eligible for enrollment in the colleges which were rightly regarded as sources of manpower for the hated military."[38] This in turn may have contributed to illiteracy, paving the way for further cultural disruptions later in the nineteenth century, intended to *eliminate* illiteracy. Conventional modernist Arab nationalist historians,[39] who generally celebrate such disruptions of Islamic culture, give the impression that illiteracy was a perennial problem in the Muslim Arab world, overlooking the possibility that it may have been a temporary and recent phenomenon brought about by colonization and forced military conscription.

Along with cannons and muskets, Napoleon brought the first Arabic printing press to Egypt in 1798, after stealing it from the Vatican.[40] He arrived with an army of linguists, Orientalists, and archaeologists, and one of the first uses of the printing press in Egypt was to mass-produce a leaflet dictating the terms of the French occupation. After the French occupation, Muhammad Ali used it to set up his own press, and the first book was an Italian-Arabic dictionary,[41] which allowed access to Italian naval schools and consultants. Italian had become a lingua franca in the Levant by that time, though it was soon superseded by French.[42] Proclaiming himself "Lord of Egypt," Muhammad Ali ambitiously sought the advice of European technocrats and experts in various fields. He also "began sending missions of students to Italy as early as 1809, particularly to Leghorn, Milan, Florence and Rome, in order to study military science, ship-building, printing and engineering."[43]

One student who was sent by Muhammad Ali to Paris to study engineering brought back a fateful gift from Auguste Comte—a copy of his work on positivism.[44] Within a few years, a host of French intellectual works, at first those by Comte and Voltaire and later including social scientists like Le Bon and Durkheim, were being translated into Arabic, not by Europeans but by members of the emerging and newly bilingual Westernized ruling class and its functionaries. Translations of European works soon began to fill Egyptian libraries, and some of these works would come to have a profound impact on the ordering of social and intellectual life in Egypt. During these formative stages in the early nineteenth century, the Saint-Simonists, proponents of megatechnic development who occupy "a peculiar place in the history of both capitalist and anti-capitalist development,"[45] worked with Muhammad Ali. The Saint-Simonists conceived of the Suez Canal and other megatechnic projects, with the full support of Muhammad Ali. Their worldview also helped in laying the foundation for modern schooling in Egypt, which played a role in ordering the emerging modern state, as well as resistance to it. The Saint-Simonists and the French social scientists deserve special attention due to the direct and indirect impact their ideas and activities had on creating a West-directed order in Egypt.

Social Science as Civil Religion

The Saint-Simonists were a "sect...of speculative technological adventurers" acting as "chief propagandists of the kind of industrialization
which needed heavy and long-range investment."[46] They "never ceased
their search for an enlightened despot who might carry out their proposals, and for some time believed they had found him" in Muhammad Ali.[47]
After Muhammad Ali's consolidation of power in Egypt,

European leftwingers in the 1820s and 30s hailed this enlightened autocrat, and
put their services at his disposal, when reaction in their own countries looked too
dispiriting. The extraordinary sect of the Saint-Simonians, equally suspended
between the advocacy of socialism and of industrial development by investment
bankers and engineers, temporarily gave him their collective aid and prepared his
plans of economic development. They thus also laid the foundation for the Suez
Canal...and the fatal dependence of Egyptian rulers on vast loans negotiated by
competing groups of European swindlers, which turned Egypt into a center of
imperialist rivalry and anti-imperialist rebellion later on...the young men fired by
Saint-Simon became the planners of Suez canals, of titanic railway networks linking all parts of the globe, of Faustian finance.[48]

Beginning in the 1820s, after he had a firm grip on power and control of
substantial military forces, Muhammad Ali attracted the attention of the
Saint-Simonists, "believers in the new religion of 'social science' who had
traveled to Cairo in the 1830s to begin from within Egypt their project for
industrialization of the earth,"[49] and who "greatly assisted in his adminis-
trative, educational, and economic projects."[50]

Ideologically, the Saint-Simonists were dedicated to the reconciliation of
seemingly conflicting schools of thought in eighteenth-century France,
those of Maistre and Voltaire. Isaiah Berlin traces the origins of modern
Western totalitarian systems to this synthesis:

[P]olar opposites as they are, they both belong to the tough-minded tradition in
classical French thought...the quality of mind is often exceedingly similar...Nei-
ther...is guilty of any degree of softness, vagueness or self-indulgence of either
intellect or feeling, nor do they tolerate it in others. They stand for the dry light
against the flickering flame, they are implacably opposed to all that is turbid,
misty, gushing, impressionistic...They are ruthlessly deflationary writers, contemptuous, sardonic, genuinely heartless and, at times, genuinely cynical...The
tendency to cast a glance upon the social scene so chilly as to cause a sudden
shock, to deflate and dehydrate, to use ruthless political and historical analysis as
a deliberate technique of shock treatment, has entered into modern political systems.[51]

Voltaire was hostile to all religious thought and any display of sentiment, while Maistre, a historicist and pragmatist, had a low estimate of

human nature and the capacity of humans to be good. Like Hobbes, Maistre believed that a strong centralized government was needed to repress weak-natured humans and allow an enlightened elite to rule; he had no faith in humanitarian efforts. Looking at the Saint-Simonist fusion of these two schools of thought, Isaiah Berlin suggests that "we begin to approach the strong strain of nihilism in all modern totalitarianism." He continues:

Voltaire can be made to strip away all liberal delusions, and Maistre to provide the nostrum by which the bleak, bare world which results is to be administered...The Saint-Simonians were not perhaps being so paradoxical after all; and their founder's admiration for Maistre, which seemed so odd to the liberals and social-ists whom Saint-Simon inspired, is founded on a genuine affinity. The content of Orwell's celebrated nightmare (as well as the actual systems which inspired it) is directly related to the visions of both Maistre and Saint-Simon.[52]

By the beginning of the nineteenth century, Saint-Simon had already "foretold the revolutionary role to be played by the union of applied sci-ence, finance and industrial organisation."[53] This would also require the replacement of traditional religion with a new secular religion—national-ism. People like Saint-Simon's disciple and private secretary Auguste Comte, along with the Orientalist Gustav Le Bon, are especially important for having developed this latter aspect. Comte envisioned a "species of secular religion, organised by an authoritarian church dedicated to rational, but not liberal or democratic, ideals."[54] In Egypt, it was Muham-mad Ali's "Westernization, not his people's aspirations, [that] laid the foundations for later nationalism," primarily because he "was in the main paths of Westernization,"[55] that is, Mediterranean trade routes, the once-prized goal of the Crusades.

The full blossoming of this new outlook would have grisly repercus-sions in its European birthplace, which would far outstrip the already long and sordid history of European mass murder, both in the name of commerce and for its own sake. Berlin again:

The transformation in our own century of political and social movements into monolithic bodies, imposing a total discipline upon their followers, exercised by a secular priesthood claiming absolute authority, both spiritual and lay, in the name of unique scientific knowledge of the nature of men and things, has in fact occurred, and on a vaster scale than even the most fanatical systematiser seems to have imagined.[56]

Hobsbawm, who notes that prior to 1848 the Saint-Simonists were them-selves not set on socialism or capitalism as the best system to implement their gargantuan plans, also makes the connection between their thought and the emerging nineteenth-century Western worldview:

Saint-Simon himself is best regarded as a prolongation of the "enlightenment." It is significant that the young Marx, trained in the German (i.e. primarily romantic) tradition, became a Marxist only when he combined with the French socialist critique and the wholly non-romantic theory of English political economy.[57]

By 1844, Marx noticed that the Saint-Simonists had declared that "industrial labor as such is the essence, and now also aspires to the exclusive role of the industrialists and the improvement of the workers' condition."[58] And in 1878 Engels said of Saint-Simon:

[S]cience and industry was to lead and command...the bankers especially were to be called upon to direct the whole of social production by the regulation of credit...But what Saint-Simon especially lays stress upon is...the lot of the class that is the most numerous and the most poor...Saint-Simon lays down the proposition that "all men ought to work"...what is here already very plainly expressed is the idea of the future conversion of political rule over men into an administration of things and a direction of processes of production—that is to say, the "abolition of the state"...almost all the ideas of later Socialists that are not strictly economic are found in him in embryo.[59]

Many historians underestimate the impact of Saint-Simonist ideology on the development of Western civilization and on the Westernization of the colonies. This tendency has also prevented Arab nationalist historians from seeing the clear links. For example, Hourani, who generally applauds the disruption and redirection of Muslim society in Egypt as necessary progress toward modern achievements in transport and commerce, at the same time underestimates the impact and breadth of the Saint-Simonist direction of Muhammad Ali:

[H]e may have been influenced by the followers of Saint-Simon who spent some years in Egypt in the 1830's, working as doctors, engineers, and teachers, and helping him to design and execute the first great modern work of irrigation in Egypt, the barrages on the Nile...Saint-Simon's vision of a model society directed by a priesthood of scientists, and with the system of scientific truth taking the place of the religious systems which had broken down, is not likely to have appealed to him, even had it been explained in familiar terms; but the exaltation of industrial development and the planned economy was in line with his own interests.[60]

Many of the Egyptian schools opened during Muhammad Ali's reign were directed by Saint-Simonists. A girls' school opened in 1834 by Saint-Simonist Mlle. Suzanne Voilquin taught French language, midwifery, and basic medicine. From 1835, the artillery school at Tura was directed by Bruneau, a Saint-Simonist and graduate of the Paris Polytechnique, while the School of Mines came under the charge of Lambert, another Saint-Simonist, who was later to direct the School of Mineralogy.[61]

Soon thereafter, the several small schools were absorbed into the new School of Engineering, which was organized by a number of Saint-Simonists. A main project of this new school was planning the Suez Canal:

The main avowed objective of the Saint Simonites was the industrial and cultural development of Egypt and the opening of the Suez Canal. The project of encouraging engineering studies in Egypt, while providing employment for a number of Frenchmen and giving a good opening for the growth of French culture, certainly seemed sincere, and, although it bore fruit in the long run, yet the tradition of the Egyptian engineering service has never been sufficiently strong to remain independent of European experts. In fact, it has rarely become a part of the traditional system in technical branches of the Egyptian service that serious enterprises are always undertaken by Europeans.[62]

In realizing the dream of the Suez Canal in 1869, the Saint-Simonist technocrat de Lesseps "had melted away the Orient's geographical identity by (almost literally) dragging the Orient into the West and finally dispelling the threat of Islam," as Edward Said put it.[63] And,

[d]espite its immemorial pedigree of failures, its outrageous cost, its astounding ambitions for altering the way Europe would handle the Orient, the canal was worth the effort. It was a project uniquely able to override the objections of those who were consulted and, in improving the Orient as a whole, to do what scheming Egyptians, perfidious Chinese, and half-naked Indians could never have done for themselves.[64]

In a plan to reorganize the army and military schools suggested by a Polish general in 1834, Saint-Simonists supported colonial subjects like Sulaiman Bey and Adham Effendi, both of whom had been "attracted by the ideas of that group." During this period,

the Saint-Simonists were in great favor; there were over fifty of them in Egypt, several of whom were employed as doctors, engineers and teachers, and there was great hope of a further demand for Frenchmen after the completion of the reorganization which Sulaiman was undertaking in connection with the educational system and which he was considered to be the director.[65]

The Saint-Simonists recommended forming a "commission of inspection" that was to be independent of all other ministerial bodies and would evaluate all schools—military and otherwise—and that included Sulaiman Bey, Adham Effendi, General Seguera, and a number of Saint-Simonists. Another member was Mukhtar Bey, a close friend of Muhammad Ali who had been sent to France on one of the education missions and who was a "favorite" of the Saint-Simonists, although he was also said to be of "bad character."[66]

However, all parties in this phase of creating order were not united and there were a number of "intrigues" involving several members of the commission, which "were the combined machinations of the Saint-Simonites and the ex-mission students against three officials who were not of their way of thinking...they sought to create a situation by their intrigues whereby they might bring about the elimination of these officials for their own advantage and advancement."[67] By 1836, the mission students and the Saint-Simonists had "taken over the control of the schools." However, soon thereafter, the direct presence of the group seems to have dwindled, and although some returned to France, many remained in the service of Muhammad Ali, who had an especially strong interest in the new Egyptian engineering services. In 1837 this came under control of Mukhtar Bey, a Saint-Simonist protégé. While Muhammad Ali gradually attempted to replace more Saint-Simonists with his own people, there is little evidence that he questioned the underlying assumptions of their policies. This and a plague in Cairo caused an exodus of many Europeans.[68]

One early product to emerge from the Saint-Simonist-directed schools was Rifa'at Tahtawi, Egypt's "first considerable political thinker."[69] This quote is instructive in Hourani's definition as a Western-trained subject as the first "thinker" in Egypt, ignoring nearly a millennium of Islamic scholarship at places like the al-Azhar University. One of Tahtawi's lasting contributions was to redefine what it meant to be a scholar, which in the Islamic world meant religious scholar, to mean someone who is versed in the European sciences; these new scholars were to become Saint-Simon's and Comte's priesthood of positivist scientists. The traditional teachers at al-Azhar in Cairo, like most ordinary Muslims through their local mosques, as Hourani sees it, "did not accept the new sciences which were necessary for the welfare of the nation."[70] While this is not the place to trace all the details of the local resistance, the makings of an initial Islamic response to the early stages of this incursion can be found in Jabarti's 1798 chronicle of the Napoleonic invasion and occupation.[71]

By the early 1840s, attendance at the various technical schools was in decline, coinciding with a reduction in government support for schools, illustrating the direct connection between schooling and the military-commercial state in Egypt. Perron, a Saint-Simonist, wrote to France, blaming

the European coalition for having obliged Muhammad Ali to withdraw from Syria and to cease hostilities, thus putting him in the position of reducing his army and, consequently, the number of men required for the schools; Perron seems to have had an idea of the meaning of civilisation quite as confused as that of his Turkish and Egyptian friends for he maintains that this action on the part of the European powers did great harm to civilisation in Europe.[72]

In any case, despite their important early influence, the Saint-Simonists were not the only European advisors working in Egypt. Others would also have profound impact on the future of Egypt.

Schools in the Colonial Military Order

European military men often worked with Muhammad Ali and subsequent rulers to develop Egypt's Westernized army. A Spanish military man, Col. Seguera, organized an artillery school in 1831, which taught French and Italian.[73] By 1836, there were over 3,000 European advisors in Egypt, mostly in military and technical fields. This number grew to 80,000 by 1872 and would exceed 200,000 by the turn of the century.[74]

In a particularly fateful case of long-lasting Western entanglement, a French textile engineer, Louis Alexis Jumel, introduced American-style long-staple cotton into Egypt in the early nineteenth century. By the mid-1820s, Egyptian cotton fields were supplying to British textile mills raw cotton that was of comparable quality to the American varieties,[75] thus giving Britain an alternate and more reliable source of raw materials in the wake of the American Civil War. Cotton quickly supplanted the varied Egyptian agricultural ecology, and by World War I it accounted for over 90 percent of Egypt's exports. Cotton transformed Egypt "from a country which formed one of the hubs in the commerce of the Ottoman world and beyond, and which produced and exported its own food and its own textiles...into a country whose economy was dominated by the production of a single commodity, raw cotton, for the global textile industry of Europe."[76]

Marshall Hodgson also saw the far-reaching implications of Egypt's nearly sudden shift to cotton monoculture:

The old staple wheat was replaced with a non-edible and market fluctuating crop, and eventually Egypt had to import much of its food on terms dictated by the modern international price system...The net result (not unlike what happened in Bengal) was great wealth and power and even legalistic security in the ruling circles, in a close, if dependent, relationship with European interests.[77]

Meanwhile, Muhammad Ali's military schools were "based on the confinement of the students and a regime of surveillance and constraint" and "administered by French and Egyptian military engineers and scholars, many of whom had been trained at the Ecole Polytechnique in Paris, including several disciples of Saint-Simon and of his secretary Auguste Comte."[78] The new school system quickly supplanted many of the traditional centers of learning, causing the Orientalist traveler E. W. Lane to remark in the 1830s:

Learning was in a much more flourishing state in Cairo before the entrance of the French army than it has been of late years. It suffered severely from this invasion; not through direct oppression, but in consequence of the panic which this event occasioned, and the troubles by which it was followed.[79]

What kind of educational system was in place before this disruption? Some elements of medieval informal education in Cairo were surveyed above. In addition to that, Mitchell summarizes three components of traditional education in Egypt, which was relatively consistent from al-Azhar University in urban Cairo to small rural mosques and other places of village learning:

First, learning occurred within the practice of the particular profession or craft to be learnt, and was not separated out as "schooling." The law was one such profession, centered upon the mosque; other professions and crafts were studied in their own locations, in similar ways. Second, within the profession learning was not a relationship that separated practitioners into two distinct groups, students and teachers. The relation of teacher and student could be found between almost any two or more members of the occupation group (though of course the more senior practitioners might distinguish themselves from the rest in several ways, including the way in which they gave instruction). Third, present at almost every point in the practices of a craft, learning did not require overt acts of organization, but found its sequence in the logic of the practices themselves.[80]

In such educational settings, the method was dialectical, "one of argumentation and dispute, not lecturing. The individual was to be deferent where appropriate, but never passive."[81] As a modern autocrat, Muhammad Ali was concerned with training a technocratic elite that would help shore up his power and establish order; there was no room for debate or consultation.

By the 1840s, Muhammad Ali seems to have realized that traditional village learning and Islamic education constituted a threat to this power. Faced with local rebellion, and since the specialized French technical schooling could not be extended to everyone, local technocrats became interested in British factory schooling to use as a tool for enumerating and controlling the masses. This also corresponds with a general distancing from French influences, which continued until the 1880s, when a deeply in debt Egyptian successor to Muhammad Ali became unhappy with French terms to buy shares in the Suez Canal and turned to the British. By the 1840s, Muhammad Ali's sons and successors further entrenched modern schooling, but while the early schools were intended to "produce an army and the particular technicians associated with it," the new schools were to "produce the individual citizen" of the newly ordered state.[82] Muhammad Ali had already begun sending students to England to study the Lancaster factory school method, and these students were instrumental in bringing the Lancaster system to Egypt in the 1840s, coinciding with an increasing British imperial presence in Egypt in the second half of the nineteenth century.

A primary component of the Lancaster method was to redistribute authority with a system of monitors, thus diffusing disciplinary power throughout the school, "implicating every individual in a system of order."[83] By 1847, school supervisors laid plans to establish the new schools throughout the country, forming a new network of "national schools." As Szyliowicz notes,

teaching involved the inculcation of feelings of obedience and discipline and the memorization of curricula drawn up in Cairo. Discipline and obedience were the very characteristics the British desired in the Egyptians who entered the administration since the overwhelming majority were restricted to routine clerical tasks. Nor were the few Egyptians who did achieve responsible positions expected to display any initiative and leadership.[84]

While the Lancaster schools were attempting to train obedient citizens for the emerging Egyptian state, the ruling circle came to be dominated by graduates of the military school in Paris run by the French Ministry of War, where "a significant proportion of the future educators and administrators who from the 1860s were to attempt to construct a new system of disciplinary power in Egypt."[85] One of the first things they did was to legislate a three-tier school system. The primary level was intended to provide literacy, while the secondary level, in the words of European-trained administrator Rifa'a al-Tahtawi, "civilises the community."[86] Higher education continued to be reserved for the ruling class.

In short, colonial schools in Egypt served two basic functions: (1) to provide well-trained armies for policing Western investments, which also entailed training a strong ruling class and an obedient populace, and (2) to systematically undermine and replace local culture with a Western-derived system of political and economic order. In both cases, successful colonization depended on a local ruling class that directed the process and provided a semblance of native legitimacy, and who at the same time believed in the supremacy of Western science and technics.

By the time of the Urabi nationalist revolt in 1881, Egyptian resistance had come to be expressed within the framework of European terms. One of the demands of the revolt was to provide schooling—British and French style—for all members of Egyptian society, not just the technocrats who were running the country and policing foreign investments. The new nationalists seized power partly in the name of "national education," and one of the first official acts of the new leader, Ahmed Urabi, was to lay the foundation stone for a new school, after giving a speech asserting the "usefulness and necessity of a good education."[87] The revolt, however, was short-lived. Alarmed at the danger to resources and investments, European commercial interests agreed to let the British navy move into Egypt and restore order. British warships destroyed Alexandria in 1882, occupied the country, and installed a more compliant ruler. However, more importantly, national aspirations would continue to be framed almost entirely in terms of Western assumptions, "turning the colonisers' methods of instruction and discipline into the means of organized opposition."[88] Even the highest religious authority of Egypt, Muhammad Abduh, would seek the wisdom of the French Orientalist Gustav Le Bon.

Abduh's view of a reformed Islam, as a system of social discipline and instruction with which an intellectual and political elite would organize the country's "political education" and thus assure its stability and its evolution, was indebted to his reading of Le Bon and other French social scientists; indeed, when he visited France he paid a call on Le Bon.[89]

Abduh called for redirecting al-Azhar, making changes that would affect the millennium-old teaching mosque up until the present.[90] Abduh also called for the revision of Islamic law to conform with the new technical knowledge coming from Europe, which he, along with his mentor Jamaluddin al-Afghani, mistakenly saw as the sum total of all human knowledge. By the mid-twentieth century, the colonization of al-Azhar had been completed to the point that the newly appointed rector was a student of Durkheim at the Sorbonne.[91] As canons began to supplement cannons in the Western drive for world domination, redirecting Islamic law for political and economic expediency would become a technique that came to be used throughout the nineteenth century and into the twentieth.[92] Western colonizers utilized this technique with great effect on Muslim peoples. This colonial order was implemented in the guise of modern schooling, and its legacy remains today.

The Shadows of Colonization in Modern Muslim Education

The basic infrastructure for social order in parts of the Muslim world was in place by the end of the nineteenth century. We could trace the details of interminable education "reforms" since then, but most are basically adjusting a system that at its foundation is a colonizing order. The impact of this order is felt to this day throughout the Muslim world, though the intellectual and economic entanglements have shifted away from Europe and closer to the United States, especially since the Second World War. This problem is particularly pronounced in the Arab world, as Edward Said described it in the late 1970s:

[U]niversities in the Arab world are generally run according to some pattern inherited from, or once directly imposed by, a former colonial power. New circumstances make the curricular actualities almost grotesque; classes populated with hundreds of students, badly trained, overworked, and underpaid faculty, political appointments, the almost total absence of advanced research and of research facilities, and most important, the lack of a single decent library in the entire region...the few promising students who manage to make it through the system are encouraged to come to the United States to continue their advanced work...the patronage system in scholarship, business, and research makes the United States a virtual hegemonic commander of affairs...the Arab and Islamic world remains a second-order power in terms of the production of culture, knowledge, and scholarship.[93]

Though, as Said suggests, American hegemony pervades the Muslim world in the postwar period, French intellectual sway also continued into the twentieth century; in midcentury Sayyid Qutb and other modern Muslim intellectuals turned to the work of French philosophers like Alexis Carrel. But during the twentieth century, there was a gradual shift in the use of European thinking: rather than accepting it as a total system of thought to be implemented, modern Islamic thinkers and activists like Sayyid Qutb in Egypt or Ali Shariati in Iran (who met Franz Fanon while studying in France) began to use a Western discourse against itself, in some cases as part of a larger project of rediscovering and implementing a framework of thought and life grounded in Islam, while simultaneously dismantling the colonial-derived system.

What can be discerned here are the beginnings of an attempt to dismantle colonial rules with colonial tools, or, as it was put by activists for black liberation in America, "tear down the master's house with the master's tools." But, as Audre Lorde insightfully reminded us, "The master's tools can never tear down the master's house." Colonial systems often die slowly, and they also transmogrify, demanding constant vigilance. So, while Egyptian revolutionary leader Gamal Abdel Nasser was resurrecting de Lessups, the nineteenth-century Saint-Simonist, in his nationalization of the Suez Canal and his building of the gargantuan Aswan High Dam in the late 1950s and early 1960s (the latter project would surely have made Saint-Simon smile), his military police hunted down Islamic activists, throwing them into dungeons and marching them to the gallows, in the name of Egyptian nationalism and dreams of social order through Western technics. In 1966, two years after Malcolm X visited Egypt in search of Third World support for black liberation in America, the Nasserists in Egypt executed the great Islamic thinker and social activist Sayyid Qutb, as the ghost of Saint-Simon struggled to maintain order along the Nile, a multiple irony of subjugation made possible in the halls of modern schooling.

Chapter 9

The New Bogeyman under the Bed: Image Formation of Islam in the Western School Curriculum and Media

Ibrahim Abukhattala

For the great enemy of truth is very often not the lie—deliberate, continued and dishonest—but the myth—persistent, persuasive and unrealistic. Too often, we hold fast to the clichés of our forbears.
—*President John F. Kennedy, July 1962*

Introduction

Western media reinforce to the public the message that Islam has replaced communism as the new enemy. This propaganda intends to stir up crusade-like sentiments in the minds of Western nations and encourages them to adopt policies projecting Western domination over Islam, incites prejudices and racial discrimination against Muslim communities and minorities, and promotes the clash of civilization theory. Approximately 1.2 billion Muslims all over the world are suffering because they are being collectively charged with the offenses, or the alleged offenses, of a few who invoke Islam to sanctify terrorism against Westerners.

Because Westerners who watch the news regularly are bombarded with news, views, and information about Arabs and Muslims, it is important to ask what ideas, impressions, and notions the Westerners receive from the media about Arabs and Islam. We all know that today there are many Westerners for whom Islam can be reduced to three ideas: backwardness, terrorism, and polygamy. How and why are these misconceptions established? This chapter is concerned with the origins and forms of the images of Arabs and Muslims in the West, and more particularly, with the cultural portrayals of Islam, Muslims, and Arabs, with emphasis on the misconceptions and negative pictures provided by Western writers, media, and school textbooks. I also question the use of a number of incorrect and misleading terms that are widely used in the West to refer to Islam and Muslims. The chapter concludes with recommendations and emphasizes a crying need to portray Islam and Muslims in at least a balanced manner.

My Muslim birth and education, and my having been nurtured by Western education for a considerable number of years, have made a deep impression on me and give me a modest claim to exchange these thoughts with you. My intention is to make an appeal to the well-known Western tradition of justice and democracy for a mutual understanding, recognition, and respect. My ultimate desire is to attempt to bridge the gap, to eliminate misunderstanding, and to enhance communication between Muslim and Western individuals in a world growing ever more interdependent. My understanding of this issue is a result of many experiences, including my life in Canada as a graduate student, researcher, and lecturer. I have been able to experience firsthand the influence that the media, in all of their different forms, can have on forming public opinion. Also, my exposure to research conducted in the domains of anthropology, sociology, and education has helped me come face-to-face with these issues and to be able to stress the crucial role education can and should play in helping to create recognition of the legitimacy of Islam as a religion and a civilization.

Arab Muslims on Television and in the Movies

Although blatant racist attitudes are intolerable toward any group (e.g., blacks, Chinese, Native Indians), they are still accepted when directed against Arabs and Muslims. Arabs in the Western milieu experience misunderstanding, prejudice, and even hatred from some non-Arabs, although usually not in its violent form.[1] Lamb writes that "probably no ethnic or religious group has been so constantly and massively disparaged in the media as the Arab over the past two decades. Being Arab is a liability everywhere but in the Arab homelands, for virtually everywhere else the Arab is stereotyped in negative terms."[2] Arab Muslims have been subjected to misrepresentations of their culture and religion by mass media and books. While formal education has created many of the misconceptions about Arabs that abound in the West, many more misconceptions come from the informal education provided by the media and popular culture, such as movies, television, radio, newspapers, comic books, and advertisements.

Film and television function as both art and entertainment. They are also sources of information. Screen images provide information and help shape values. Intentionally or unintentionally, images have the power to "teach people whom to fear, whom to hate, and whom to love."[3] The media have such a strong power over people's views that at times it seems like only the media can break what they create. Negative images of Arabs have been formed largely in response to media coverage of events in the Middle East countries and of the recent tragic terrorism in the rest of the world.[4]

In her book *Price of Honor*, Goodwin reports that "...in the West today, it is fashionable to designate all Muslims as the new pariah: terrorists, fundamentalists, fanatics. They have filled the bogeyman niche under the bed where communists used to lurk....There is a perceived oil well in every backyard, a stretch Mercedes and a camel in every garage, a klashinkove machine gun in every closet, and a harem in every home."[5] Yet, these notions are as false as saying that blacks are lazy, Jews are greedy, Italians are members of the Mafia, Hispanics are dirty, or Americans are child abusers.

The creation of negative images, as Suleiman states, has made young Arabs in Western societies "feel ashamed of their ancestors and their former homeland. As a result, some have avoided reference to their Arab heritage, for instance, often describing themselves in terms of geographic region from which they came or the religious sect to which they belong."[6] These kinds of unfavorable conditions have been extensively described and documented. For example, Sergent, Woods, and Sedacek's investigation of the attitudes of American college students toward Arab Muslims revealed strong negative attitudes and prejudice toward followers of this faith.[7]

These attacks on Islam as a culture and people have made many Westerners strongly believe that their own code of behavior is the only legitimate code of behavior in the world. For example, for many it is quite normal and natural to see two people indulging in some kind of amorous physical contact in public places, for they are obviously practicing their inherent human rights. By contrast, for a Muslim to wear Islamic dress or to pray in a public park is a scene that many regard as most embarrassing, uncivilized, and even insulting. Apparently, in Western eyes Muslims engaging in these activities are just manifesting their backwardness and practicing their superstition.

Muslims Are Backward and Uncivilized

The Western image of the Arab is a fictional one. Literature and popular humor often show Arabs as nomadic Bedouins. According to Richardson, many North Americans regard Arabs as primitive and opposed to all forms of progress.[8] An important theme to impress, though, is that underlying that deliberate distortion is an equalization between the notion of Westernization and the notion of modernization. People in the Western media, unfortunately, seem unable or unwilling to comprehend that Arabs and Muslims have never rejected technology or development. In fact, they may have rejected Western behavior that conflicts with their cultural and religious teachings. This rejection of Western values is not unique to Arabs. Other peoples, such as the Chinese, have also rejected some Western ways of behavior that conflict with their beliefs. Perhaps some Westerners may reject some typically Western behaviors that they consider in conflict with their own values. However, it seems that differences in values between the Western and the Islamic worlds provide fertile ground for negative stereotyping.

It is very rare for Western media to show how Islam created a brilliant civilization in different parts of the world for more than a thousand years. Islamic culture at its height was far superior to that of Western Europe, and many of its contributions were vital to the European Renaissance. Hundreds of English words we use today are a sign of this legacy (e.g., algebra, alcohol, alkali, almanac, alchemy, cipher, arsenal, logarithm, admiral, check, syrup).

It was the inclusive approach and the love of learning encouraged by Islam that enabled Muslims to make their remarkable contributions to all fields of knowledge: science and sociology, arts and music, philosophy and medicine. During the days of the Islamic empire (570–1400), the culture at large adopted certain aspects of the great civilizations that were influential at the time, namely the Greek, Roman, and Persian empires. Using this as a departure point, the Islamic civilization witnessed great intellectual, cultural, scientific, and artistic achievements that became the building blocks for much of the world's culture. To name just a few achievements and personalities: the Muslims invented and developed algebra; they also invented the notion of zero, which changed mathematics forever. The philosopher Ibn Khaldoun is credited for inventing sociology even before Jean-Jacques Rousseau, and the philosopher Averroes (ibn Rushd) sought the meaning of existence and provided Europe with its great understanding of Aristotle.[9] Unfortunately, many Westerners are not aware of these contributions to human civilization.

Muslims Are Terrorists and Want to Destroy the West

Another type of portrayal Arab Muslims have received in movies is by far the most common among many negative stereotypes: the depiction of Islam as a warlike religion and, consequently, Arabs and Muslims as terrorists. In his seminal book *Reel Bad Arabs* Jack Shaheen, a well-known scholar in this area, has investigated extensively and historically the images of Arabs and Muslims in the Western film industry.[10] His findings are troubling. In his review of nearly one thousand movies, Shaheen documents that most of these movies totally distort the images of the Arabs and Muslims and never show them in their authentic reality. What is so shockingly misleading about many of these movies is that they portray, with absolutely no justification, *all* Arabs and Muslims as being at war with the West. Think of all those "Arab Muslims" and how they were shown innately "inhumane" in films such as *True Lies* (1994), *Terror Squad* (1988), *Executive Decision* (1996), *The Siege* (1998), *The Voyage of Terror* (1990), *Indiana Jones and the Last Crusade* (1989), and many others.

Even though the Middle East is home to fewer terrorist incidents than Latin America and Europe, it is still regarded as the region where terrorism is rooted. Hollywood and, it seems, all of the media are stuck in a vicious cycle. For example, if a filmmaker wants to write a movie about terrorism, there is an automatic identification of terrorists with Arab Muslims because that is the most prevalent notion of Islam in Western societies. When the movie is eventually produced and Muslims are portrayed as the terrorists, the stereotype is created, reinforced, and maintained.

This distorted image in films becomes more alarming when it is emphasized by highly regarded Westerners in the church or in the press. The recent Islamophobic speeches spewed by Jerry Falwell and other evangelists such as Franklin Graham and Pat Robertson, who, unfortunately, view Islam from a very narrow religious bigotry, provide just one example. After the September 11 tragedy, Ann Coulter, in some eyes a respected American columnist, firmly states that "not all Muslims may be terrorists, but all terrorists are Muslims—at least all terrorists capable of assembling a murderous plot against America...We should invade their countries, kill their leaders and convert them to Christianity."[11] This is a blatant lie intended to evoke and justify antagonism and racism against all Muslims. I would say that anyone who tries to make such a link and attempts to smear innocent people with no relation to terrorism is aiming to suit a specific political agenda and to promote religious hatred. Coulter and other writers of that ilk remind us of the "yellow journalism" that backed the institutional racism practiced against other groups (e.g., Japanese, Jews) in North America in the 1900s.

It seems that these journalists ignore the fact that there are many terrorist groups all around the world, and certainly not all of them are Muslim! The Tamil Tigers in Sri Lanka, the Basque separatists in Spain, the Shining Path in Peru, the Red Army faction in Germany, the National Liberation army in Columbia—the list goes on. Moreover, according to a recent U.S. State Department report, *Patterns of Global Terrorism*, issued earlier this year, 272 terrorist events occurred in Europe, 92 in Latin America, and 45 in the Middle East. Sixty-two anti-U.S. attacks occurred in Latin America last year, 21 in Europe and 6 in the Middle East.[12]

Why do the media rarely feature these groups as terrorists? What about the Irish Republican Army in Ireland? Is it because they are Catholic Christians that the Irish cannot be referred to as terrorists? I think they should be if we employ the same standard of generalization the media use with 1.2 billion Muslims. There is no moral justification for terrorism regardless of the ethnic or religious background of the perpetrator or the victim. Also, when right-wing Christians in the United States bomb abortion clinics, they are not called "Christian terrorists." When two U.S. army veterans, Timothy McVeigh and Terry Nichols, were indicted for the 1995 Oklahoma City bombing, the media did not report them as Christians. Why was that? In reporting the unspeakable crimes and ethnic destruction committed by Serbs in the former Yugoslavia against Bosnian Muslims, Western correspondents did not refer to them as "Orthodox Christian terrorists." One just wonders why. If we are to denounce violence, should we not denounce it at all levels, including violence enacted by states against civilian populations in a systematic way? Many questions remain vaguely unanswered. Do media authors realize that linking Islam to terrorism and violence is as absurd as associating Hitler with Christianity?

Muslims as Presented to Western Children

Television has been influencing the impressionable minds of young children throughout the world for years. The number of hours of television that children watch, because it is commonly used as a babysitter, is staggering, and the effects are alarming as children believe what they see on TV as a form of reality. It is no wonder, then, that they grow up with false "defining characteristics" of Arabs and Muslims. Television is not solely to be blamed for this tragedy, however; movies play a big part in it, too. Here I do not mean the PG-13 or R-rated movies parents try to make sure their children do not sneak home and watch. Our concern is the movies parents willingly buy and sit their children in front of day after day. It is "The Wonderful World of Disney." It is my opinion that Disney promotes cultural and racial stereotypes of Arabs and Muslims just as much as, if not more than, our average television shows.

Many recent children's movies have distorted the images of Arabs and Muslims (e.g., *Aladdin, Father of the Bride II,* and many others). In these movies, the "typical" Arab stereotype is taken to the extreme. These types of movies show no authenticity of the Arabic culture, no elements of the true Arab culture or personality. No child can gain any real understanding of Arabs or Muslims by watching them.

A perfect example of this caricature-type movie is *Father of the Bride II* (1995), which portrays Arabs as less human than Westerners. This movie presents a fabricated image of an Arabic family living in America, one that stereotypes Arab men as grossly rich, abusive, hot-tempered control freaks and the women as voiceless, submissive, and weak. This movie ridicules even the Arabic language by making it sound like humorous gibberish.

What is more disturbing about these kinds of movies is that their usual audience is young children who, without firsthand knowledge or instruction, would not know that most Arabs do not speak or act the way they are portrayed in the movies. How do you expect them to realize that what they see in the movies does not represent real Arab people, but is just a twisted American version of what Americans believe, or rather want, an Arab to be? Movies that children watch for enjoyment and pleasure rather than instruction unfortunately leave a deeper imprint on a fresh, impressionable mind than does an unexciting textbook. I end this section with a statement from Sister Mary de Lourdes: "Every bigot was once a child free of prejudice." These words are something to think about and perhaps to act upon.

Misleading and Inaccurate Terminology Describing Islam and Muslims

Television news reporters and movie producers, out of either ignorance or lack of concern for authenticity, are guilty of employing inaccurate Islamic terminology, which negatively affects Westerners' opinions. For example, they misuse the Islamic term *jihad* to mean a holy war. In fact, it does not. The truth is that, according to Islamic teachings, it is unholy to instigate or start war. The Arabic word *jihad* means struggling or striving and applies to any effort exerted by anyone (e.g., student, employee, politician). The greater jihad is the ongoing struggle within one's own soul to be a better person. The Arabic word for war is *kital* or *harb*. Perhaps this terminology confusion is a reflection of the Christian use of the term *Holy War* to refer to the Crusades of a thousand years ago.

Another wrong term used by news anchors is *fundamentalism*, which has absolutely no equivalence in a religious sense in the Arabic language. It is an English term that refers to certain Protestant Christians who take the meaning of the Bible literally.[13] The term evokes the idea of a return to the fundamentals of the faith and conveys a sense of waging war for these fundamentals. In the Islamic world, even modernists believe in a return to Islamic principles because to them Islam has never conflicted with modernism. This is particularly true where Muslim women are concerned:

many Islamic movements consider women as the symbolic and substantive key to the Islamic revival. The point here is that those who follow, or want to follow, Islamic orthodoxy are not automatically fanatics or fundamentalists. Therefore, "revivalists" and "progressives" are more accurate and meaningful terms. This, of course, does not deny the existence of some organizations that use or have used Islam to sanction a desire for or a continuation of political power.

Also, Western writers and news anchors use the terms *Arab* and *Muslim* interchangeably, although they are not necessarily the same: not every Muslim is Arab, nor is every Arab Muslim. In fact, Arabs comprise less than 15 percent of the whole population of the Islamic world, and considerable numbers of Arabs are Jews or Christians. The largest Muslim country in the world is Indonesia, with around 95 million non-Arab Muslims. Furthermore, Iran is not, as commonly thought in the West, an Arabic country. Iranians are Persians and they speak Farsi, an Indo-European tongue closely related to several European languages.

Another misconception about Islam that the media lead many Westerners to believe has to do with the word *Allah*. The media show Muslims worshiping a different God than Christians and Jews. This is completely false, and the media's intention in using it, I think, is just to show viewers and readers that Islam is an alien religion and Muslims are pagans. The reality proves otherwise: Islam is also a monotheistic faith and Muslims believe in the same God for Jews and Christians. It is important to note that *Allah* is the same word that Arabic-speaking Christians and Jews use for God. In the Arabic Bible, the word *Allah* is used where *God* is used in English versions. To say *Allah* is just some Arabian God is as laughable as saying French people worship a different God called *Dieu*.

It is unfortunate that we have to go into details on such seemingly minor issues, but so many falsehoods have been heaped upon Islam that it is important to try to break down the barriers of falsehood in literature that tries to make Islam look like something strange and foreign to Westerners. No, the media have never been innocent: they always have a hidden message for the public. Terminology is a highly effective device for influencing opinions.

It is really sad to see that although Islam is one of the three great monotheistic religions and the fastest-growing religion in the world, many Westerners know little about its teachings, its holy days, or its commonalties with Christianity and Judaism. In an influential paper presented at the Oxford Center for Islamic Studies, Britain's Prince Charles insightfully discusses this point:

It is odd, in many ways, that misunderstanding between Islam and the West persists, for what binds our two world together is much more powerful than what divides us. Muslims, Christians and Jews all are "[P]eoples of the Book." Islam and

Christianity share a common monotheistic vision: a belief in one divine God, in the transience of our earthly life, in our accountability for our actions, and in the assurance of life to come. We share many key values in common: respect for knowledge, justice, compassion towards the poor and underprivileged, the importance of family life, and respect for parents. "Honor thy father and thy mother" is a Quranic precept too. Our history has been closely bound up together."[14]

Muslim Women and the Media

How Islam regards woman is one topic that is both inaccurately and badly exploited and represented by the media. The combination of misinformation and lack of depth of knowledge about the role and position of women in Islam contributes to fostering the notion that Islam puts women firmly in a second-class position.

The status that Western women have reached in today's society was not achieved due to the kindness of men. We all know that it was only in 1964 when equal rights legislation was extended to include women. I think this has been accomplished through a long struggle and sacrifice on the part of women, and has come at a time when Western societies need women's economic contribution. In the case of Islam, this consideration to women's status was decreed. This was, however, not because of the threat or pressure of women and their organizations but rather because of the principle of equality in Islamic ideology. Many Qur'anic verses give indication that Islam shatters all notions of women as subhuman. One chapter, *sura*, is completely dedicated to Mary (Miriam in Arabic). Moreover, there are more verses in the Qur'an devoted to matters related to women as individuals, in the family, and as members of society than all other social issues combined. I think that these gender dimensions of the Qur'an were radical concepts, especially in light of the then deeply entrenched patriarchy of seventh-century Arabia—a society where burying female infants alive was a very common practice because of the disappointment, shame, and disgrace associated with having daughters instead of sons.

I believe it is misleading and unfair that the media analyze the codes of Islam regarding women on the basis of the actions of some Muslims at a certain time or place. If some Muslims abuse women's rights, this injustice should not be attributed to Islam. This mistreatment is regrettably culture specific and does not stem from the teachings of this religion. Patriarchal customs are still powerful in most Muslim societies. The diversity of the ethnic and cultural backgrounds of the 56 Islamic countries spread around the globe is reflected in the broad range of Muslim viewpoints. In fact, as with Christianity and Judaism, there is no single way Islam is observed. There are Muslims in virtually every country on the globe, and their interpretations of the Qur'an are as varied as the cultures in which they live, often influenced by their histories and political and cultural environments (e.g., the situation of Muslim women in Afghanistan differs from that of Muslim women in Canada). The media, unfortunately, deny the true diversity and complexity of 1.2 billion Muslims.

It is essential, however, that Westerners not judge the liberation and advancement of women in the Islamic world by Western standards, because these criteria reflect nothing but Western values. The Western definition of liberated women is different from the one recognized by Muslim women in Islamic society. For example, the cultural imposition of wearing Islamic dress is to many Westerners a sign of women's backwardness. The media portray Islamic *hijab* as outdated and oppressive. For these ethnocentric Westerners, full entry in the public domains and other indicators of liberation are reflected in Western styles of dress. Do Muslim women really need to dress in skimpy clothing and use their sexual charm to get them to higher grounds? Should they wear scandalous clothing that is very provocative to be seen as liberated? Do Muslim women lack sophistication because they do not walk around topless? Do women want men to ignore their personalities and minds and be attentive only to their appearance and physical attributes? Does the relatively recent military and economic superiority of the West qualify to set absolute values for Muslim women?

I would argue that a yes answer to any of these questions is obviously very degrading and demeaning to women because it shows them as brainless creatures. It reinforces the notion that nothing defines an ideal woman except how beautiful, sexy, skinny, and tall she is. Clothing fashions and social patterns that reduce a woman to a sex object and exploit her as such are not acceptable to Islam. Modesty is a virtue that Islam demands of Muslim men and women. A Muslim woman who wears *hijab* is making a statement about her cultural identity. She conceals her sexuality but allows her femininity to be brought out. Unfortunately, for some ethnocentric Westerners, wearing *hijab* is a sign of backwardness and oppression, whereas joining a nudist club is a matter of personal freedom.

What the media fail to reveal to the public is that the history of Islam is rich with women of great achievement in all walks of life, beginning as early as the spread of Islam in the seventh century, and that those women scholars vastly contributed to the Islamic civilization. One good example is Aisha, the wife of the Prophet. She was a great scholar and thinker from whom the prophet said we should learn "half our religion." She was referred to as an advisor to the early Muslim jurists. The first martyr in Islam was Somaia, a devout Muslim woman who was assassinated by an anti-Islam Meccan clique in the early days of Islam. The first person who converted to Islam was Khadija, an aristocratic beauty of substantial wealth who proposed to Muhammad as she was his employer before Islam and was impressed by his honesty and charisma. During their 25 years of harmonious and monogamous marriage, which ended only when she died, she was his strongest supporter, confidante, and councilor. There were other influential Muslim women—Hind, Al-Khansa, and Khaula, to name just a few. These women displayed traits that a modern-day feminist would recognize. Even now, there are many successful Muslim women who significantly contribute to their societies, but nevertheless, it seems the media are very selective about what they want to present. What they show to viewers is the exception and not the rule. One need only look at the relatively large number of Muslim females enrolled in universities to see how the picture is not as bleak as the media want us to believe.

The media have made the Western public believe that Islam is the ultimate symbol of the subordination of women. To understand how firm this belief is, it is enough to mention that the minister of education in France, the land of Voltaire, recently ordered the expulsion of all young Muslim women wearing *hijab* from French schools. Also, according to Wayland, in September 1994, three girls were threatened to be expelled from a high school in Montreal, Canada, because they insisted on wearing Muslim head scarves.[15] Canada's positive record of human rights and commitment to democracy and freedom of religious expression will prevent such discriminatory incidents if the rationale behind *hijab* is accurately presented by the media.

It is quite ironic that at a time when the hostile Western media are persistent in their attempts to defame and ridicule Islam and to portray Muslim women as oppressed, abused, and worthless, police report ever-rising statistics for rape, teenage pregnancies, murder, and domestic violence against women in Western societies. How, then, can Western societies justify their accusations against Islam's treatment of women?

Distorted Images of Muslims and Islam in Western School Textbooks

Certainly the perceptions North Americans have of Arabic cultures and Islam are not derived only from the mass media. Indeed, Western children, at a very early age, are often given a negative image of Arab Muslims. School textbooks play a vital and distinctive role in influencing students' social images and interactions.[16] Textbooks provide formal means of learning about other cultures. Images of other cultures that students receive from their textbooks are symbolic representations, and students usually do not attempt to look further for alternative realities. Because texts used for education are fraught with misconceptions about other nations, Westerners could learn early on to form negative stereotypes, images, and value judgments of "others" during their school years.

Some studies conducted in the last two decades have examined representations of Arabs and Muslims in textbooks in North America and Europe.

Burke reviewed several college textbooks used in the teaching of world religions in religion departments in Britain and investigated the manners in which images of Muhammad, the Qur'an, Muslims, and Islam were presented. His findings indicate that these textbooks are "extremely dubious...based on accounts which were factually misleading and in some cases inaccurate."[17] For example, in one of these texts, "Mohammadism" is used to refer to "Islam." Not only is this usage offensive to Muslims, but it is incorrect as well. Muhammad is not God, and Muslims do not worship him. According to Muslims, Muhammad is just God's messenger. Burke insightfully concludes that "if our study in the classroom aims at an initial understanding of what Islam means to Muslims, then we need texts which present this."[18]

Abu-Absi reviewed the Middle East chapter in an American sixth-grade social studies textbook, *People and Culture,* and examined the manner in which images of Muslim women and their culture, as well as Islam, were presented.[19] According to Abu-Absi, this book contains information on a number of aspects of Islam that is shockingly misleading. For example, according to this textbook, Islam is a primitive and oppressive religion, it humiliates women, it forbids girls to attend school, and it emphasizes a subordinate role for females. After giving the most simplistic explanation for the role of women in Islam, the authors ask the reader, "Would you like to be a woman in the Middle East?"

Kenny reviewed Canadian geography and history textbooks and examined how images of Arabs and their culture, as well as Islam, were presented. In the 70 textbooks used in Canadian schools that he investigated, he found that the coverage of the Middle East is "...narrow, parochial, and Western oriented."[20] The treatment of Islam in the history texts contributed to the perpetuation of fundamental misconceptions about Islam as a religion, culture, and civilization. Many factual errors, questionable assertions, and omissions helped in reinforcing the negative images.

According to Kenny, in these textbooks, Arabs and Muslims are portrayed as primitive and backward. Nomadism is highly visible in the discussions regarding the Arab world, giving the wrong impression that it is the dominant way of life in the area. Even Islamic contributions to world civilization are either briefly discussed or totally overlooked. The authors of these textbooks referred to by Kenny, for reasons known only to themselves, give misleading mental images about the Arabic culture and Islam as a religion.

These distorted pictures of Arabs and Islam provide us with the context for understanding how Western students perceive what the words *Arabs* and *Islam* mean or imply when used in Western classrooms. No doubt this distorted picture greatly influences how Muslims in general perceive themselves in this world and in their host Western societies, where they increasingly comprise a considerable portion of the immigrant population. Muslims are taught to hold tremendous pride in their heritage, in their historical, cultural, religious, and linguistic contributions to the world. They also exhibit increasing pride in their contemporary societies and their capabilities to interact internationally as equals with other nations. Curriculum in most of the Islamic countries is positively inclusive, teaching respect and full recognition to other faiths and their followers. Therefore, it is a great shock for Muslims when they swiftly realize that Westerners have a different view of them and when they do not encounter any mutual recognition, respect, or appreciation of their part in the world and its significance. They ask themselves, "Is all our seemingly rich history a lie?"

School textbooks cannot, and in fact should not, rely on static and oversimplified views prevalent in Western scholarship in interpreting the Islamic world and history. In other words, many Western textbooks present only one perspective. We know that the authors of these books did not create it but inherited it from the European Orientalists. Unfortunately, because authors of these textbooks are not always well informed and the vast majority of teachers have received no formal training in Islam or Arabic culture, the validity of these perspectives goes unquestioned. The following section discusses how and why Orientalists formed, or, more accurately, deformed, the images, culture, and history of Arabs and Muslims.

Orientalists and Their Description of Islam and Muslims

History shows us that this religious propaganda can be traced back to the Crusades, which mark the beginning of a period of direct contact between Muslims and the West. Back then, the Muslim image was distorted by stories of "noble" Crusaders fighting the savage infidels, and idolaters who worshipped "Muhammad" as a god. Up until the end of the eighteenth century, Muslims under the Ottoman Empire were regarded as "less human" by the West, and in fact not much has changed since then. The Arab Muslim still appears as the threatening cultural other. By the beginning of modern imperialism, Muslims became a focal point of Western attention.

The establishment of the colonial European empires created a need for economic expansion. This was achieved through "geographically discovering" and colonizing non-European nations, which had to be sustained by ethical justification.[21] In other words, with the aim of legitimizing the process of colonization, historical and moral justifications were inevitably required in order to impose European culture as the dominant model to be followed. Thus, the destructive myth of "civilizing the uncivilized" was invented. It was said that the purpose of overseas colonization was to "spread the light of faith." In this view the cultural differences between groups were based on biological differences that reflect superiority and inferiority on a graded scale. To illustrate, in a work cited by Ferraro,[22] William McGee, the first president of the American Anthropological Association, shows his extreme ethnocentrism as he states,

Possibly the Anglo-Saxon blood is more potent than that of other races; but it is to be remembered that the Anglo-Saxon language is the simplest, the most perfectly and simply symbolic that the world has ever seen; and that by means of it the Anglo-Saxon saves his vitality for conquest instead of wasting it under the juggernaut of a cumbrous mechanism for conveyance of thought.[23]

This political and military hegemony of the West was accompanied by biased Western cultural studies exclusively focused on "the other."[24] This social reality was constructed by skewed interpretations of the "other cultures' ways" through studies conducted by "Western experts" whose job was to investigate Middle Eastern cultures during the colonization period. These studies necessarily present the Arab as "a deprived creature" to whom must be extended the benefits of European civilization. The result was that in Europe and in North America in particular, the image of Islam and the Arab culture was totally distorted, or simply left out of account altogether. For example, Laffin, in his racist book, states,

Because of the frustration and repressions which follow from the rigidly held sexual mores and prohibitions of his own society, the Arab is dangerous to women of other nationalities...It is impossible for a woman to walk down a public street at night without serious risk...Arab men in groups are constantly on patrol in their own cars, watching for such prey.... In one sense, the Arab concept of cruelty is grotesquely simple: it is better to be unjust, the Arab thinks, than to have other men be cruel to him. It is a variation on the kill or be killed idea.[25]

One in fact gets confused as to whether this "expert" is describing a jungle or a society. This deliberate distortion and defamation have been quite destructive. They have negatively altered the attitudes of many Westerners, psychologically at least, toward everything relating to Arabs and Islam, as if this were yet the age of the Crusades. What appalls me as a researcher is that we still find such texts in respectable university libraries today.

Another example of how this bias works is a book written by Raphael Patai titled *The Arab Mind*.[26] Patai follows an approach emanating from antagonistic attitudes toward the Arabs in the context of power relations and Western domination, or what anthropologists Fanon and Memmi called the colonizer-colonized relationship. As such, it comes as no surprise that in this book not one positive value is mentioned regarding Arabic culture. One would think that sociologists and anthropologists would want to base their views on field research and empirical data. Instead, Patai relies solely on carefully selected Western readings, quotations, and Orientalist scholarship. He indulges in oversimplified generalizations about Arabic culture without even describing the context and the concrete facts that relate to the ideas he is presenting, or, rather, misrepresenting. In other words, such generalizations give a false sense of homogeneity and timelessness to Arabic cultures. The first thing we learn about culture today is that it is not static, not monolithic, and not simple. Anthropologists have long abandoned these ideas as obsolete. Some intellectually dishonest writers such as Patai fail to consider this fact when writing their accounts of Arabic culture.[27] In fact, Patai makes the fatal mistake of examining Arabic culture as if it were monolithic, as if it were a simple thing; the title of his book—*The Arab Mind*—indicates just that. This is a drastically reductionist perspective on culture that Western writers like Patai need to be called on. These pseudo-scholars from the West shamelessly quote Qur'anic verses and cultural sayings out of context and paint a picture of a barbaric religion that seeks death for all.

The West's material successes, which are now centuries old, constitute the rationale behind Westerners' ethnocentrism. This material power of Europe, since it was the prime motivator behind the conquest of the Orient, blinded the West to discovering the Arab Orient as it really is; the West portrayed it as it wished it to be. Many articles and books show how Europe has fashioned its own Orient with its own imagery, its own fantasies, its biased version of history, and its culture that, deliberately or unconsciously, have been falsified. There is plenty of evidence of this in the remarkable books by Edward Said, *Orientalism* and *Covering Islam* (1997), and in *The Arab World* by Barakat, which show how the ethnocentrism of Western writers was one of the venues used to confirm the West's unilateral approach to civilization.[28] In fact, it comes as no surprise that some European intellectuals of the twentieth century found it necessary to deny that they owed their medieval civilization and its Renaissance to other cultures, since they had to invent a necessary ethical-cultural justification for the colonization of that very nation in the nineteenth century.

The social reality of Islam and its history differs dramatically from the picture presented by Orientalists. Many scholars showed that the Orient had been understood, dissected, interpreted, packaged, and presented through Western eyes.[29] Never were the authentic voices of the Muslim people included in any discussion of Islam. As discussed earlier, since the motivation behind any rapprochement with Islam had been economic and military, the perceptions had to fit theories that catered to economic and cultural hegemony. As such, it had to be shown that Muslims were in bad need of the West—that they were uncivilized, perhaps lazy, perhaps of an inferior nature, needing guidance, incapable of rational thinking, incapable of leading an autonomous life, impulsive creatures that were led by their instincts and emotions rather than their minds.[30]

Conclusion and Recommendations

Having briefly shed some light on the image of the Arabs in the West and how these images are created and captured in the literature, I think it is the seriousness of this problem that distinguishes the Arab and Muslim experience from that of other cultures. Different nations have different experiences in their relationships with the West. Perhaps Arabs and Muslims would have more enthusiasm for developing cooperative strategies and meaningful communication with the West if they felt that their culture and religious beliefs were respected.

As we have discussed, it is a favored exercise by the media to associate Islam with violence and terrorism. As documented by many, the image of Muslims, especially as produced by Hollywood, is that of either abuser of women; religious fanatic; Bedouin who is totally incompetent in, or full of hatred toward, the modern world; or primitive who has no language other than grunts and gestures.

It might be ironic for us to speak about tolerance, respect, and recognition in an age when Muslims are so negatively stereotyped that they are associated with intolerance, backwardness, and terrorism. The Muslims, when they built their great empire in Spain, practiced a form of government that was historically one of the most tolerant in history.[31] In fact, Jews, Christians, and Muslims lived together harmoniously for eight hundred years, and many Jews held some of the most important political positions, were doctors to the caliphs, and generated profound philosophical theories. This comes as no surprise given that tolerance is strongly demanded in the Qur'an. One verse reads, "Oh mankind! We created you from a single (pair) of a male and female, and made you into nations and tribes, that ye may know each other (not that ye may despise each other). Verily, the most honored of you in the sight of God is the most righteous of you."[32] The Qur'an also insists, "There is no compulsion in religion."[33]

Another glance at history, however, proves that while Muslims always tolerated and appreciated the existence of Christian communities in their societies, the Christians rarely allowed a Muslim community to live with them. Sad but true. As we can see, there are no more Muslims left in Spain, Sicily, Portugal, or other European countries, although these were all multifaith communities a few centuries ago. Even in the countries where some Muslims still exist, such as Russia, Bulgaria, and the former Yugoslavia,

Muslims are suffering discrimination and are vulnerable every day to ethnic destruction.

True Muslims are peace-loving people. Islam does not permit terrorism. All Westerners must recognize that the face of terror is not the true face of Islam. Islam is a faith that brings comfort to more than a billion people around the world. It is a faith that has made brothers and sisters of every race. It is a faith based on love, not hate. The Qur'an tells that "Whoever kills a soul, unless for a soul, or for corruption done in the land—it is as if he had slain mankind entirely. And whoever saves one, it is as if he had saved mankind entirely."[34] Another verse reads, "Invite to the way of your Lord with wisdom and beautiful preaching."[35] In their history, Muslims distinguishably respected the traditions of war imposed on them: they did not kill civilians, the elderly, women, or children. One good example is the twelfth-century Muslim warrior Saladin, who defeated Richard the Lionhearted and freed Jerusalem from the Crusaders. Although some were guilty of committing crimes against Jews and Muslims, Christians were not prosecuted by Saladin. On the contrary, he allowed them to live in peace with Muslims in this holy city. Many historians titled him "the Champion of Chivalry."[36]

Muslims have no desire to destroy the West. In fact, they admire Western democracy and Western liberalism and justice, which are core notions in Islamic ideology. Many wish Islamic countries would emulate the West in modernization and technological advancement. Not all Muslims see the West as "the Great Satan," something to be shunned altogether. Many would rather live as Muslims in the West than in most of the Muslim countries, because I think the way Muslims are allowed to live in the West is closer to the true Muslim way. Devout Muslims are always offended and shocked to know that the word *Islam,* which means peace, is becoming interchangeable with violence and terrorism against the West.

Education is always and everywhere the basis for social betterment and positive intercultural and interfaith communication and understanding. There is an urgent need to acknowledge that Western civilization is a common heritage of humankind and a world civilization to which many ancient civilizations, including Islam, have made significant contributions. Textbooks should avoid reinforcing the dominance of the white European mainstream. Educators, curriculum developers, policy makers, and authors must have open minds and the courage to question untrue views, for what must be maintained at all times is the truth. This issue will be of specific concern to all of them in that it signals an urgent need for a serious attempt to produce a fair and balanced presentation and understanding of the Arabic culture and Islam. Making them aware of what they take for granted, making the implicit explicit, will increase their level of awareness. Subsequently, their own critical reflection will result in a positive action toward Muslims and toward humankind in general. Their truthful and unbiased books and writings will give Muslims something to hold on to, to help them counterbalance negative stereotyping.

I always remember that, in my early education in Islamic classes, I was taught how the three great Abrahamic religions, Judaism, Christianity, and Islam, share common tenets and pillars and how we share many doctrines. I was taught to believe in Christianity and Judaism and to love Christ and believe in his miracles. I still know by heart many of the Qur'anic verses that honor Christ and refer to him as "Son of Mary," "messenger," "Messiah," "Word of God," and other titles of reverence. I think Muslims know and understand Christianity far more and far better than Westerners know them.

I also realize that it is mere self-deception to forever blame only Western media for negative images of the Islamic world. Certainly, a greater part of the blame should go to the media. Although it is true that film producers and textbook publishers have always felt the freedom to use Muslim stereotypes when there is a noticeable absence of this practice with other ethnic or national groups, this situation also signifies the weakness of Arab and Muslim willingness to challenge that image as it appears. It is time for Muslims also to assume self-responsibility and make themselves available to get their version of the story across to the Western public, and to tell them what the teachings of Islam are all about.

Finally, all I long for is that these comments will provoke fresh thinking on the subject, and I hope readers will be able to take certain responsibilities and remind the Western media, which pride themselves on their ability to uncover and present the facts to the public, that they have an obligation to cover the Muslim situation in a fair and balanced manner. When this happens, the Muslim will appear as neither bogeyman nor angel, but as a fellow human being. I really think that an understanding of Islam is long overdue. Instead of making Islam the problem, let us understand it to make it part of the solution.

Chapter 10

Desert Minstrels: Hollywood's Curriculum of Arabs and Muslims

Shirley R. Steinberg

Media is my pleasure: film, television, radio, and print. We unabashedly have several TVs in the house, and they are always on. We watch movies—on tape, on DVD, on television, and in the theater. I listen to the radio two hours a day while commuting and devour a newspaper when given the time to sit and read. Magazines are a joy...books on tape save me on long trips. Thankfully, the media is my vocation; it is natural for me to play with it, analyze it, and criticize it. After September 11, my pleasure became my pain as I watched each breaking news story, over and over again, on every channel in every venue. I also knew I had to write about what I saw and heard. As I romped through my memories and the construction of my consciousness about Muslims and Arabic-speaking people, I realized how very easy it was to hate Arabs, to hate Muslims. As quickly as those two planes hit the twin towers, the American public was spewing volatile observations about all Arabs, all Muslims.

One of our students from Brooklyn College called on September 13 to say she would not be in class. An observant Muslim, this student wore a modest veil to school. As she attempted to shop on September 12 in her predominantly Muslim part of Flatbush, she was spat upon and called names. She decided that her safety was in danger, and she should not go to school that week. We saw several instances that echoed this student's experience. My partner called the CNN news desk and asked to speak to a researcher. He related the student's story and asked why CNN was not covering the anti-Muslim incidents in Brooklyn during this period. The reporter laughed and told him that they had more important events to cover, and that, indeed, maybe these incidents should happen more often—maybe this student got what she deserved.

How long had I been aware of Muslims? Of Arabs? As a Jew, I guess I have always been aware of our sister religion. In early religion classes I learned that a slave woman, Hagar, had borne Ishmael from Abraham; this lineage became Arabic. The children of Sarah and Abraham became the Jews. Religious mythology followed me throughout my life—stories of how Arabs became dark skinned, versions of nomadic existence, and exotic tales from *The Arabian Nights.* I remember watching many early films with Arabs as grand fighters, usually brandishing swords, fighting the white man. I recall veils, belly dancing, tents, camels, large-toothed men with rifles and dirty robes.

But when did popular culture collide with my religious stories? In 1962, I sat through *Lawrence of Arabia.* It didn't take long to get the point; the rest of the show was tedious. A minor officer from England was sent to visit Prince Faisal and ended up leading an army of Arabic tribes to fight the Turks—he was a hero. Guess that was my earliest media exposure to Arabs.

In 1968 *Time* magazine featured a cover story titled "The Plight of the Arab Refugees." I did a speech in school based on the issue. I couldn't understand why the Arabic countries surrounding Israel would not let their Muslim brothers and sisters in to their homelands. I understood why the Israelis didn't make room; the country was too small and had been given to Jews. My social studies teacher didn't know anything about it.

Then in June 1968, just down the freeway from my school, Robert Kennedy was shot by Sirhan Sirhan, defined in the news as "a man of Jordanian descent." Many readers may remember the dark photos of the swarthy murderer, who quickly disappeared from our news limelight. Many thought all hopes of social equity and freedom died with Bobby that day, at the hand of the Arab.

Four years later, as I was just beginning a new college semester, the news hit that Israeli athletes had been kidnapped by Arab terrorists, a group known as Black September. We were glued to the television as we watched cameras cover the occupied residences; we saw shadowy figures identified as the kidnappers on the phone negotiating with authorities. Then we saw the German police shoot and kill both the terrorists and the athletes on the tarmac of the Munich airport. I flew to Munich once; I assumed the tarmac was still there. No one was able to show me where it was.

I had not visited New York City after the twin towers had been built. When the World Trade Center was bombed in 1993 it was shocking, but very removed from my life. I had never seen the buildings. Few were killed; lots of fancy cars were smashed. The news reported that the bombing was the work of Arabic terrorists. In 1994 we went to New York and scanned the World Trade Center to see where the bomb had hit. We were astounded at how huge the buildings were and how small the bomb damage had been. The buildings were obviously indestructible.

In 1996, I was watching CNN in a hotel in San Francisco when I saw the report that a bomb had destroyed a federal building in Oklahoma City. The first words from the radio, TV, and papers indicated that Arabic terrorist groups had planned the mass attack. Hours later, a white man was in custody. No apology to the previously identified perps. I believe some Arab Americans complained about the erroneous accusation. The news quickly moved on to the unfolding McVeigh story. Upon reflection, I do not recall any attempts by American citizens to spit upon Baptists (McVeigh's religion), attack McVeigh's hometown, or pull over white men around age 30 who resembled the lanky terrorist.

A network break-in to regular programming in 1997 revealed the headline that Princess Diana had been killed in an auto accident along with her boyfriend, Dodi Fayed. Fayed was a Muslim, an Egyptian, whose wealthy father had been denied British citizenship by the Queen; he also owned Harrods of London. Continued tabloid coverage that year claimed that Diana could have been murdered in order to keep her from humiliating the royal family by her relationship with an undesirable man.

By the time the first plane hit in lower Manhattan that Tuesday in September, many Americans' cultural curriculums had been imprinted and validated. That was why it was so easy to hate Arabs and Muslims. Naturally, we would be able to hate terrorists, but McVeigh was a terrorist, and our hatred and outrage was limited only to him, not his entire culture, religion, state, or community. Media literacy being my field of study, it was obvious that I would analyze the cultural pedagogy of Hollywood—how had Muslims and Arabs been depicted in American cinema?

I maintain that if pedagogy involves issues of knowledge production and transmission, the shaping of values, and the construction of subjectivity, then popular culture is the most powerful pedagogical force in contemporary America. The pedagogy of popular culture is ideological, of course, in its production of commonsense assumptions about the world, its influence on our affective lives, and its role in the production of our identities and experiences.[1] Movies help individuals articulate their feelings and moods that ultimate shape their behavior. Audiences employ particular images to help define their own taste, image, style, and identity; indeed, they are students of media and film pedagogy. Audiences often allow popular culture, vis-à-vis films, to speak for them, to provide narrative structures that help them make sense of their lives. This emotional investment by the audience can often be organized in emotional, ideological, or affective alliances with other individuals, texts, and consciousness formations.

Thus, this affect mobilized by the popular culture of film provides viewers with a sense of belonging, an identification with like-minded individ-

uals; this feeling becomes progressively more important in our fragmented society.[2] Keeping in mind the complexity of the effects of film in
popular culture, the affect produced is different in varying historical and
social contexts. With these notions in mind, I went in search of the
assumptions that may have been made in the viewing of films containing
Arab or Muslim characters. I did have a couple of research questions in
mind: Why is it so easy for many North Americans to hate Muslims? Why
are Muslims so easy to fear and blame? With these questions, I hoped the
films I viewed would shed light on some tentative answers, and, more
importantly to my own scholarship, raise more questions.

Selecting my films was difficult—and easy. Difficult because I wanted to
get a large representation of films from which to draw my data. Easy
because few popular films feature content including Arabs or Muslims. I
selected 17 films and watched and rewatched them on television or video-
tape. I selected movies that any modicum of my memory signaled that there
was sufficient depiction of Arabs or Muslims to discuss. I asked others if
they recalled any films that I should be viewing; consequently, these films
were culled out of our combined cultural collective. I did not consult written research to gather my films; I wanted to know what stood out in our
minds as films that depicted Arabs and Islam. (As Ibrahim Abukhattala
mentioned in his chapter in this volume, the book *Reel Arabs* provides an
excellent listing of films throughout history that have Arabic and Islamic
content. My criticism of the book lies in its lack of critical analysis and his-
toricization; however, the book does stand as a good anthology.) I began to
view the films and isolated scenes and dialogue that needed reexamination.
After I had gathered this data, I revisited my notes in order to identify
themes, archetypes, and auteurship in the films. Auteurship is important to
investigate as it allows the viewer or researcher to conclude whether the
author or director is including his or her point of view (self) in the film.

Islam in Contemporary Film

Most of the films I viewed dealt with Muslim Arabs. However, *Not
Without My Daughter* (1990) and *East Is East* (1998) are films about Muslims, not Arabs (those from the Arabian Peninsula). Sally Field's compelling, yet whining performance in *NWMD* (based on a true story of one
woman's experience) deals with an American woman married to an Iranian doctor who deceitfully brings his wife and daughter to his home in
Iran. Sally doesn't want to go: "We can't go to Iran—it's much too violent." Swearing on the Qur'an, Moody, the husband, promises they will be
safe. After the family reaches Iran, Sally is somewhat horrified to be
greeted by a goat slain in their honor. Sally and her spouse attempt cultural analysis: "It just seems so primitive." "Beliefs seem primitive when

they aren't your own." Mother and daughter become prisoners as the husband reverts to ayotollah-generated religious fanaticism. "Islam is the greatest gift I can give," assures Moody. Persian women (in full black burkas) are yammering, scheming, whispering, and occasionally beaten by their husbands or other available men. This is a dark, frightening, and smothering world to the former Sister Bertrille.

Sally's character is starkly white in comparison to the darkness that cinematographically depicts the Muslims in the film. Women peering out of slits in their burkas are routinely belittled, demeaned, and marginalized by their husbands. On a few occasions Sally attempts to bond with women and ask for their help; alas, everyone turns against her, shuns her, or turns her in to her husband. Islam is depicted as unreasonable, and Moody is equally unreasonable as he immediately becomes a tribalized tyrant to his wife and little girl. When Sally reminds Moody of his promise made on the Qur'an and tells a holy man of this breach of faith, she is met with verbal attacks by everyone within earshot. A message is sent to the viewer that Islamic vows on holy books are not kept, and holy men are indeed as evil as everyone else. *NWMD* is based on a true story. Obviously, I am in sympathy with anyone whose child is stolen and who is abused by a spouse. But the film does not center on the marital issues as much as it is an indictment of the entire community in Tehran.

East Is East is a BBC-produced movie and deals with a lower-middle-class Pakistani man who marries a British woman. He insists on being a traditional Muslim, and his wife respects that—as long as her husband doesn't catch the children carrying statues of Jesus during the Easter parade. As the children are proudly marching in the parade, someone warns them that their father is approaching. They toss the religious statues to other people, peel off their costumes, and dash home before their father opens the door. He is obviously stupid for not catching on, and the family continues the ruse, being Muslim to their father, but really being Christians.

Not a bad-looking man, Dad is devastated when his oldest son bails out of his own arranged wedding. He tries to make matches for the other sons, one of whom says, "I'm not marrying a fucking Paki." As a father he is overbearing in his desire to see his children as happy Muslims. He adds insult to injury as he pushes his gift of a watch with Arabic numerals on each child. He has been saving these watches for a special time and ceremoniously presents each of them with a watch. The children explode with anger and disgust at the idea that they would actually wear a watch with "strange symbols." They are angry when he insists they go to a school to learn the Qur'an. After various defeats, now a broken man, he begins to beat his wife and children. Once again, cinematography plays an important role as the camera angles begin to change; as the father gets meaner, his character is filmed from below, highlighting the nostrils of his huge, sweating, bulbous nose as well as his yellowed, crooked teeth. One hour into the film, and he has gone from a princely, kindly father and husband (in both appearance and context) to an evil fool. He frustratingly bemoans that neighbors think he is a barbarian.

Sidekicks to White Men

The rest of the films were about Arabs—those from Arabia (or countries divided from Arabia). With the exception of *Lawrence of Arabia* (1962), all movies were filmed in the West. *LOA* is a dramatic (read: long) saga about a blond, blue-eyed Englishman, T. E. Lawrence, who, caught up in the myth of Arabia and the desert, convinces marauding rival Bedouin bands of "barbarians" to unite in their fight against the equally barbaric Turks. Peter O'Toole's character is a prototype of Sean Connery's and Mel Gibson's heroic adventurers and is accompanied by Omar Sharif, once an enemy but now a converted sidekick. Lawrence's colleagues unapologetically engage in constant disregard for the Arabian peoples they are there to protect:

> "Any time spent in a bed would be a waste—they are a nation of sheepskins."
> "They [the Arabs] are dirty savages."
> "Arabs are a barbarous people."

Angering the British—"Has he gone native?"—Lawrence eventually leaves Arabia, naturally in better condition than he found it: "I did it"; "Arabia is for the Arabs now."

Sharif, as a desert sheik, begins as a proud, brilliant warrior. However, as he is tamed by O'Toole, he becomes his bodyguard and brother-in-arms, and he eventually dies for him. He is reduced in the film from a man of stature to a colonized camel rider. Naturally, he is the example for others to follow. It is obvious to all who watch that the Arabs in tribal form could never survive, and that the British and Lawrence were sent as divine leaders to organize and divide the different groups. Interestingly, even as Lawrence exoticizes the natives, wears their clothing, rides camels, and imitates their lives, he never forgets that he is an Englishman and they are barbarians.

As with Sharif in *LOA,* many of the films introduce a sidekick character for the white male lead. Loyal and faithful to death, the Tonto-ized friend is simpler, devoutly Muslim, full of Islamic platitudes and premonitions, and easily frightened. In both Indiana Jones films set in the Middle East (1981, 1989), Indy is accompanied by his Egyptian pal who fears that Indy's ideas are dangerous and will create anger from Allah. He attempts to convince Indiana that he is not stupid: "Even in this part of the world we are not entirely uncivilized." Endangered at times, this minstrelized sidekick puts his hands in the air, opens his eyes wide, and shouts for safety.

Arabs as Window Dressing

Ironically, films that seem Arabic in context and content have little to do with Arabs. *Casablanca* (1943), *Abbott and Costello Meet the Mummy* (1955), *Arabesque* (1966), *The Jewel of the Nile* (1985), *Ishtar* (1987), *The Mummy* (1998), and *The Mummy Returns* (2001) contain plots directly concerned with Arabic/Islamic themes; actors with dialogue were Western, and depending on the film, extras appeared to be Arabic. Action shots featuring Arabic people were almost exclusively filmed in loud marketplaces. The fez is the accessory of choice for comical extras; no heads left uncovered. The (sword carrying) militaristic extras most often wore *kaffiyehs* (couture Arafat), and several Arabs sported turbans. What struck me about the extras was the "clumping" in which they would always appear. Let me borrow from Joe Kincheloe as he describes the French Fry Guys of McDonaldland: "The most compelling manifestation of conformity in McDonaldland involves the portrayal of the French Fry Guys. As the only group of citizens depicted in the Hamburger Patch, these faceless commoners are numerous but seldom seen."[3]

They intend to look, act, and think pretty much alike. Parent French Fry Guys are indistinguishable from children, and visa versa. They are so much alike that, so far, no individual French Fry Guy has emerged as a personality identifiable from the others. They resemble little mops with legs and eyes and speak in squeaky, high-pitched voices, usually in unison. They always move quickly, scurrying around in fits and starts....[4]

Kincheloe goes on: "As inhabitants of a McDonaldized McWorld, the French Fry Guys are content to remove themselves from the public space, emerging only for brief and frenetic acts of standardized consumption—their only act of personal assertion."[5] In these films, Hollywood's French-frying of Arabs leaves them to stand in clumps, to surround the action, to yell loudly in the background, and to run the market. They are incompetent in keeping their shop areas organized as someone is always running through—knocking the wares down and leaving a fist-flinging *kaffiyeh*-clad merchant screaming from behind.

Messianic White Boys and Nasty, Dirty Arabs

Included in my content/discourse analysis of these films was woven the weft of the white male leader sent to save citizens or artifacts from the unscrupulous. Lawrence and Indiana serve as perfect Arian messiahs to these dark, mysterious Muslims. The word *barbaric* (or *barbarous*, or *barbar-*

ian) was used in each film. *Aladdin* (1996) opens with an overture and opening song that describes the mysterious, dark, barbaric East. Physical characteristics of the Arabs generally show bad teeth, large hooked noses, and unclean tunics, caftans, and headgear that are just a tad too exaggerated. Once again, Aladdin does not run more than five minutes without describing one of the Arabic characters as "pungent." The films I viewed metaphorically included aromavision, as one could vividly smell the camel-shit-smeared, dirt-ridden, sweat-clinging clothing of Muslim characters.

The market scenes imply that Islamic countries center their cities and livelihoods on the marketplace. The Shylockization of these people is obvious in their attempts to barter and cheat consumers. Indeed, once again, in *Aladdin,* the fat, toothless, dirty Arab "businessman" flings out his tablecloth and for-sale sign and indicates that anything can be bought for a price. As I take in his hooked nose and sales pitch, the Semite in his character reminds me vividly that Jews and Arabs share many of the same stereotypes: they lie, cheat, and steal.

Prototyping Hatred

Islamic characters are compared not only to other Semites through an analysis, but also to other marginalized groups. There were many, many visible comparisons to Hollywood depictions and assumptions about African Americans. Many times I was sure that the negrofication of these characters served to show that any hated group can be exchanged with another. Exemplifying this is the language that served to incant slurs to African Americans: *sand nigger* and *dune coon* were among the nastiest I heard in the films.

Negative characteristics of Arabs and Muslims were not compared to those of white people. While Indiana Jones dealt with Nazis in *Raiders of the Lost Ark,* their characters stuck to the traditional expectations of viewers. The Nazis were anal, obsessive (anal-obsessed?), cruel—but clean and human. The characterization of Arabs always had an underlying implication that placed them somewhere between human and animal. In each film, whiteness is the standard against which all Arabs and Muslims are measured. And with the racism that whiteness nurtures, the categories, the lexicon, the otherization all become stenciled from one race and ethnicity to the other. These films bore this out in many instances.

Reading Media Critically

So then, why is it so easy for many North Americans to hate Muslims? Why are Muslims so easy to fear and blame? These questions are so obviously complicated and unanswerable. We have had concrete reasons to deplore the actions of Arabs and Muslims. Terrorism has been tapped as a vehicle to move the causes of many different organizations all over the globe. As a Jew I have always been conflicted as to who has rights over Jerusalem, over the Temple Mount, over Israel. But I know that my research has allowed me to reconsider how my own consciousness has been formed, in large part, by media. If we were able to work with students and parents to learn how to "read" film, the news, the papers, perhaps conversation involving injustice could surround the actions of those who do wrong, not their nationality or religion. I maintain my contention that indeed, popular culture is a curriculum—an overt, influential curriculum that feeds our need to consume entertainment. This Hollywood diet is not innocent; it is constructed on obsession, stereotype, fear, and, most importantly, what sells. I hope we all are able to read the menu.

Filmography

H. Christie, producer, J. Grant, writer, and C. Lamont, director, *Abbott and Costello Meet the Mummy*, United States: Universal Studios, 1955.

S. Daniel and J. Jacks, producers, and S. Sommers, writer/director, *The Mummy*, United States: Universal Studios, 1999.

Disney Studios, producer, *Aladdin*, United States: Disney Studios, 1992.

M. Douglas, producer, M. Rosenthal and L. Konner, writers, and L. Teague, director, *The Jewel of the Nile*, United States: Twentieth Century Fox, 1985.

G. Lucas and H. Kazanjian, producers, L. Kasdan, writer, and S. Spielberg, director, *Indiana Jones and the Raiders of the Lost Ark*, United States: Paramount, 1981.

G. Lucas and F. Marshall, producers, J. Boam, writer, and S. Spielberg, director, *Indiana Jones and the Last Crusade*, United States: Paramount, 1989.

E. May, director, *Ishtar*, United States: Columbia Pictures, 1987.

S. Spiegel and D. Lean, producers, T. E. Lawrence, writer, and D. Lean, director, *Lawrence of Arabia*, United States: Republic Pictures, 1962.

L. Udwin, producer, A. Khan-Din, writer, and D. O'Donnell, director, *East Is East*, United Kingdom: Miramax, 1998.

H. Ufland and M. Ufland, producers, and B. Gilbert, director, *Not Without My Daughter*, United States: Metro-Goldwyn-Mayer, 1990.

H. Wallis, producer, J. Philip and G. Epstein, writers, and M. Curtiz, director, *Casablanca*, United States: Warner Bros., 1943.

Notes

Chapter 1

1. H. Koechler, "After September 11: Clash of Civilizations or Dialogue," http://www.up.edu/ph/forum/2002/Mar02/wept.11.html.

2. Cornell West, *Race Matters* (Boston: Beacon Press, 1993).

3. J. Kincheloe, *Getting Beyond the Facts: Teaching Social Studies/Social Sciences in the Twenty-First Century* (New York: Peter Lang, 2001).

4. Chester Finn's Fordham Foundation's epistle to America's teachers, *September 11: What Our Children Need to Know,* Thomas B. Fordham Foundation, 2002, http://www.edexcellence.net/sept11/september11.pdf.

5. V. Hanson, "Preserving America, Man's Greatest Hope," in *September 11: What Our Children Need to Know*, Thomas B. Fordham Foundation, 2002, http://www.edexcellence.net/sept11/september11.pdf.

6. Z. Sardar, *Orientalism* (Philadelphia: Open University Press, 1999).

7. C. Finn, "Introduction," in *September 11: What Our Children Need to Know*, Thomas B. Fordham Foundation, 2002, http://www.edexcellence.net/sept11/september11.pdf.

8. Finn, "Introduction."

9. B. Hesse and S. Sayyid, "A War Against Politics?" http://opendemocracy.net/forum/document.

10. M. Parenti, *The Terrorism Trap: September 11 and Beyond* (San Francisco: City Lights Books, 2002).

11. K. Weinstein, "Fighting Complacency," in *After September 11: Clash of Civilizations or Dialogue,* Thomas B. Fordham Foundation, 2002, http://www.edexcellence.net/sept11/september11.pdf.

12. M. Ignatieff, "The Burden," *New York Times Magazine,* January 5, 2003, p. 24.

13. J. Agresto, "Lessons of the Preamble," in *September 11: What Our Children Need to Know*, Thomas B. Fordham Foundation, 2002, http://www.edexcellence. net/sept11/september11.pdf.

14. Parenti, *Terrorism Trap*; T. Ali, *The Clash of Fundamentalisms: Crusades, Jihads and Modernity* (New York: Verso, 2002).

15. L. Cheney, "Protecting Our Precious Liberty," in *September 11: What Our Children Need to Know*, Thomas B. Fordham Foundation, 2002, http://www.edex cellence.net/sept11/september11.pdf; Gloria Sesso and John Pyne, "Defining the American Identity," in *After September 11: Clash of Civilizations or Dialogue*, Thomas B. Fordham Foundation, 2002, http://www.edexcellence.net/sept11/septem ber11.pdf.

16. American Council of Trustees and Alumni (ACTA), *Defending Civilization: How Our Universities Are Failing America*, 2001, www.goacta.org/publications/ reports/defciv.pdf.

17. W. Bennett, "Seizing this Teachable Moment," in *September 11: What Our Children Need to Know*, Thomas B. Fordham Foundation, 2002, http://www.edex cellence.net/sept11/september11.pdf.

18. S. Husseini, "A Media Crusade," *Globalspin*, http://www.globalspin.org/ media_crusade.html.

19. A. Gresson, *The Recovery of Race in America* (Minneapolis: University of Minnesota Press, 1995), and *America's Atonement* (New York: Peter Lang, 2003); J. Kincheloe and S. Steinberg, *Changing Multiculturalism* (London: Open University Press, 1997); J. Kincheloe, S. Steinberg, N. Rodriguez, and R. Chennault, *White Reign: Deploying Whiteness in America* (New York: St. Martin's Press, 1998); N. Rodriguez and L. Villaverde, *Dismantling White Privilege* (New York: Peter Lang, 2000).

20. K. Rose and J. Kincheloe, *Art, Culture, and Education: Artful Teaching in a Fractured Landscape* (New York: Peter Lang, 2003).

21. Husseini, "A Media Crusade."

22. For insight into the question, see E. Herman and N. Chomsky, *Manufacturing Consent: The Political Economy of Mass Media* (New York: Pantheon Books, 1988); N. Chomsky, *9-11* (New York: Seven Stories Press, 2001); D. Macedo, *Literacies of Power: What Americans Are Not Allowed to Know* (Boulder, CO: Westview, 1994); D. Kellner, *Media Culture: Cultural Studies, Identity, and Politics between the Modern and Postmodern* (New York: Routledge, 1995); P. McLaren, R. Hammer, S. Reilly, and D. Sholle, *Rethinking Media Literacy: A Critical Pedagogy of Representation* (New York: Peter Lang, 1995).

23. E. Said, *Covering Islam: How the Media and the Experts Determine How We See the Rest of the World* (New York: Pantheon, 1981), p. 164.

24. Sardar, *Orientalism*.

25. Sardar, *Orientalism*, p. 109.

26. Sardar, *Orientalism*.

27. Finn, "Introduction."

28. Ibid.

29. C. Sudetic, "The Betrayal of Basra," *Utne Reader* 110 (2002), pp. 45–49.

30. Agresto, "Lessons of the Preamble."

31. H. Gadamer, *Truth and Method*, translated and edited by G. Barden and J. Cumming (New York: Seabury Press, 1975); G. Madison, *The Hermeneutics of Post-*

modernity: Figures and Themes (Bloomington: University of Indiana Press, 1988); M. van Manen, *Researching Lived Experience* (Albany: State University Press of New York, 1991); Kincheloe, *Getting Beyond the Facts;* B. Thayer-Bacon, *Relational "(E)pistemologies"* (New York: Peter Lang, 2003).

32. Finn, "Introduction."

33. Cheney, "Protecting Our Precious Liberty."

34. ACTA, *Defending Civilization.*

35. Runnymede Trust, "The Nature of Islamaphobia," 1997, http://www.runnymedetrust.org.meb/islamophobia/nature.html.

36. S. Huntington, *The Clash of Civilizations: Remaking of World Order* (New York: Touchstone, 1996).

37. Sardar, *Orientalism;* A. Lueg, "The Perception of Islam in Western Debate," in *The Next Threat: Western Perceptions of Islam,* ed. J. Hippler and A. Lueg (London: Pluto Press, 1995); J. Hippler, "The Islamic Threat and Western Foreign Policy," in *The Next Threat: Western Perceptions of Islam,* ed. J. Hippler and A. Lueg (London: Pluto Press, 1995).

38. B. Lewis, *What Went Wrong? Western Impact and Middle Eastern Response* (New York: Oxford University Press, 2002).

39. Quoted in Husseini, "A Media Crusade."

40. Lueg, "Perception of Islam."

41. Middle East Studies Association (MESA), "Evaluation of Secondary-Level Textbooks for Coverage of Middle East and North Africa," 1994, http://www.umich.edu/~iinet/cmenas/textbooks/reviews/summarya.html.

42. K. Armstrong, "Islam Agonistes: The Arrival of the West," 2002, http://dhushara.com/book/upd3/2002a/histis.htm.

43. Finn, "Introduction."

44. Parenti, *Terrorism Trap.*

45. Hesse and Sayyid, "War Against Politics?"

46. W. Damon, "Teaching Students to Count their Blessings," in *September 11: What Our Children Need to Know,* Thomas B. Fordham Foundation, 2002, http://www.edexcellence.net/sept11/september11.pdf.

Chapter 2

1. Francis Fukuyama, *The End of History* (New York: Penguin, 1992). Fukuyama's 1992 book was an expansion of a 1989 article published in the conservative journal *The National Interest.* The texts generated a tremendous amount of controversy and were seen by some as a new dominant ideology proclaiming the triumph of Western ideals of capitalism and democracy over all opposing ideologies. With a quasi-Hegelian gloss, Fukuyama thus proclaimed the victory of the ideas of neoliberalism and the "end of history," which prompted both skepticism and impassioned critique.

2. Fukuyama, *End of History,* p. 4.

3. Samuel Huntington, *The Clash of Civilizations and the Remaking of World Order* (New York: Touchstone Books, 1996).

4. Chalmers Johnson, *Blowback: The Costs and Consequences of American Empire* (New York: Henry Holt, 2000).

5. The Speeches of President George W. Bush, http://www.vote-smart.org/speech.

6. "You Helped This Happen: Falwell's Controversial Comments Draw Fire," September 14, 2001, www.abcnews.go.com/sections/politics/Dailynews/wtc_falwell010914.html.

7. "Death by Liberal," September 11, 2002, www.newsmax.com/archives/articles/2002/9/10/.

8. Douglas Kellner, *Grand Theft 2000* (Lanham, MD: Rowman and Littlefield, 2001).

9. In an October 5, 2001, *Wall Street Journal* editorial, Rush Limbaugh wrote: "Mr. Clinton can be held culpable for not doing enough when he was commander in chief to combat the terrorists who wound up attacking the World Trade Center and Pentagon." On right-wing attempts to blame Clinton for the terrorist attacks, see John F. Harris, "Conservatives Sound Refrain: It's Clinton's Fault," *Washington Post,* October 7, 2001, A15.

10. Shortly after this and other outbursts, the frothing Coulter was fired from *National Review* when she reacted violently to efforts by the editors to tone down her rhetoric, helping to provide her with martyr status for the U.S. right wing of Talibanites.

11. See the translation of the 1998 *Le Monde* interview where Jimmy Carter's national security advisor, Zbigniew Brzezinski, bragged about how he conceived of arming extremist Islam militants against the Afghan government as a ploy to draw in the Soviet Union more deeply and thus help destroy their system. October 8, 2001, http://www.counterpunch.org/wtcarchive.html.

12. In addition to Johnson, *Blowback,* which I am using to provide a conceptual overview of the September 11 terrorist acts, I am also drawing upon a series of studies of U.S. foreign policy and Afghanistan, including Mary Ann Weaver, "Blowback," *Atlantic Monthly* (May 1996), available at www.theatlantic.com/issues/96may/blowback.htm; a collection of articles contextualizing the events at *The Nation* web site, especially Dilip Hiro, "The Cost of an Afghan 'Victory,'" at www.thenation.com; and articles collected at www.counterpoint.com. I am also grateful to Phil Agre's daily collection of articles on his Red Rock Eater list, collected at http://dlis.gseis.ucla.edu/people/pagre/rre.html.

13. Johnson, *Blowback,* p. 8.

14. See Alexander Cockburn and Jeffrey St. Clair, "Was It Really Worth It, Mrs. Albright? The Price," *Counterpunch,* September 25, 2001; see their archive for useful daily postings on the current crisis, http://www.counterpunch.org/wtcarchive.html.

15. See D. Kellner, "Popular Culture and the Construction of Postmodern Identities," in *Modernity and Identity,* ed. S. Lash and J. Friedman (Cambridge, MA: Basil Blackwell).

16. Mary Ann Weaver, "Blowback," May 1996, The Atlantic Online, www.theAtlantic.com/issues/96may/blowback.htm.

17. In the Southeast Asian press, there are speculations that U.S. policy in Afghanistan under Bush II was designed to stabilize the country under Taliban

rule to enable the UNOCAL corporation to build a gas pipeline across Afghanistan and exploit its potential natural gas and oil resources. Ranjit Devrag writes,

Where the "great game" in Afghanistan was once about czars and commissars seeking access to the warm water ports of the Persian Gulf, today it is about laying oil and gas pipelines to the untapped petroleum reserves of Central Asia. According to testimony before the US House of Representatives in March 1999 by the conservative think tank Heritage Foundation, Azerbaijan, Kazakhstan, Turkmenistan and Uzbekistan together have 15 billion barrels of proven oil reserves. The same countries also have proven gas deposits totaling not less than nine trillion cubic meters. Another study by the Institute for Afghan Studies placed the total worth of oil and gas reserves in the Central Asian republics at around US$3 trillion at last year's prices.

Not only can Afghanistan play a role in hosting pipelines connecting Central Asia to international markets, but the country itself has significant oil and gas deposits. During the Soviets' decade-long occupation of Afghanistan, Moscow estimated Afghanistan's proven and probable natural gas reserves at around five trillion cubic feet and production reached 275 million cubic feet per day in the mid-1970s. But sabotage by anti-Soviet *mujahideen* (freedom fighters) and by rival groups in the civil war that followed Soviet withdrawal in 1989 virtually closed down gas production and ended deals for the supply of gas to several European countries.

Natural gas production and distribution under Afghanistan's Taliban rulers is the responsibility of the Afghan Gas Enterprise which, in 1999, began repair of a pipeline to Mazar-i-Sharif city. Afghanistan's proven and probable oil and condensate reserves were placed at 95 million barrels by the Soviets. So far, attempts to exploit Afghanistan's petroleum reserves or take advantage of its unique geographical location as a crossroads to markets in Europe and South Asia have been thwarted by the continuing civil strife.

In 1998, the California-based UNOCAL, which held 46.5 percent stakes in Central Asia Gas (CentGas), a consortium that planned an ambitious gas pipeline across Afghanistan, withdrew in frustration after several fruitless years. The pipeline was to stretch 1,271km from Turkmenistan's Dauletabad fields to Multan in Pakistan at an estimated cost of $1.9 billion. An additional $600 million would have brought the pipeline to energy-hungry India. (From *OnLine Asia Times*, October 6, 2001, http://atimes.com/global-econ/CJ06Dj01.html.

18. Chip Berlet, "Genocide, Totalitarianism, and Fascism," December 13, 2001, http://csf.colorado.edu/mail/psn/2001/msg01879.html; Robert Antonio, "After Postmodernism: Reactionary Tribalism," *American Journal of Sociology* 106, no. 1 (2000): pp. 40–87.

19. Noam Chomsky, *9-11* (New York: Seven Stories Press, 2001); Ed Herman and Gerry O'Sullivan, *The Terrorism Industry* (New York: Pantheon Books, 1989); Johnson, *Blowback*.

20. *New York Times*, October 7, 2001.

21. George Sorel, *Sorel: Reflections on Violence*, ed. Jeremy Jennings, Raymond Geuss, and Quentin Skinner (Cambridge: Cambridge University Press, 1999).

22. See "Floridians Stockpile Anthrax Antibiotics" and "Bioterrorism Jitters Close Subway Stop, IRS Center," *Los Angles Times*, October 10, 2001, A3.

23. Kellner, *Grand Theft*.

Chapter 3

1. For an interesting summary of diverse fundamentalisms, see, for instance, Haideh Moghissi, *Feminism and Islamic Fundamentalism* (London: Zed Books, 1999),

pp. 64–69; and Nourredine Afaya, *L'Occident dans L'Imaginaire Arabo-Musulman* (Casablanca: Les Editions Toubkal, 1997).

2. See Roger Garaudy, *Intégrismes* (Paris: Pierre Belford, 1990); and Jean-Paul Charnay, *Traumatisme Musulman, entre Charia et Geopolitique*, vol. 1 (Paris: Akfar, 1993).

3. See the writings of such leading figures of Muslim fundamentalism as Mohamed Qutb, *Jahiliyatto al qarn al ishrine* (Cairo: Dar ahourouq, 1991); and Y. Qaradhâwî, *Le Licite and l'illicite en Islam* (Paris: Al-Qalam, 1995).

4. See Mohamed Qutb, *Qadiatu Tahrir al-Mar'a* (The question of woman's liberation) (Riad: Dar al Watan, n.d.).

5. See Franz Fanon, *The Wretched of the Earth* (New York: Grove Press, 1961).

6. Afaya, *L'Occident*; and Dale Eikleman, *The Middle East: an Anthropological Approach* (New Jersey: Prentice Hall, 1989), pp. 23–48.

7. For a comprehensive review and discussion of this literature, see E. Said, *Orientalism: Western Conception of the Orient* (London: Penguin, 1978), and "Orientalism Reconsidered," in *Arab Society: Continuity and Change* (London: Croon Helm), 1985.

8. Fanon, *Wretched*, p. 215.

9. Leila Ahmed. *Women and Gender in Islam: Roots of a Modern Debate* (New Haven: Yale University Press), 1992.

10. See Alison Baker, *Voices of Resistance: Oral Histories of Moroccan Women* (Albany: State University of New York Press, 1998), and *Histoire des Femmes au Maghreb: Réponse à l'Exclusion*. Proceedings of Kenitra Conference, December 4–6, 1997 (Kenitra, Morocco: University Press, 1999). Hereafter referred to as *Histoire des Femmes*.

11. Quoted in Baker, *Voices*, p. 18.

12. Quoted in Baker, *Voices*, p. 18.

13. See Fatima Mernissi, *The Veil and the Male Elite: A Feminist Interpretation of Women's Rights in Islam* (Reading, MA: Addison-Wesley, 1991); and Mounira Charrad, *States and Women's Rights: The Making of Postcolonial Tunisia, Algeria, and Morocco* (Berkeley: University of California Press, 2001).

14. Ahmed, *Women and Gender in Islam*, p. 153.

15. Daniel Rivet, *Le Maghreb à L'épreuve de la Colinisation* (Paris: Hachette, 2002), p. 304.

16. Ahmed, *Women and Gender in Islam*, p. 152.

17. See Moghissi, *Feminism and Islamic Fundamentalism*, p. 15. One of the great philosophers of the Enlightenment, J. J. Rousseau, had this to propose as a cure for female indocility: girls, he suggested, "must be subject, all their lives, to the most constant and severe restraint." The earlier they are "accustome[d]" to "such confinements," the better.

18. Ahmed, *Women and Gender in Islam*, p. 129.

19. Ahmed, *Women and Gender in Islam*, p. 165.

20. The expression is borrowed from scholar of colonial history in North Africa Daniel Rivet, *Le Maghreb à l'Épreuve*, p. 304.

21. Quoted in Houria Alami m'Chchi, *L'Enseignement des Filles a l'Epoque Coloniale: Entre Polimique et Realité*. In *Histoire des Femmes*, p. 235. Translation of this text from the French is by the author.

22. Ibid., p. 236.

23. Ahmed, *Women and Gender in Islam*, p. 137.

24. See Zakia Daoud, *Féminisme et Politique au Maghreb* (Casablanca: Editions Eddif, 1993), p. 241.

25. On the issue of honor, see Soumaya Naamane-Guessous, *Au-dela de Toute Pudeur: La Sexualité Feminine au Maroc*, 7th ed. (Casablanca: Edition Eddif, 1991).

26. M. Lazreg, *Algerian Women in Question* (New York: Routledge, 1994), p. 55.

27. Fanon, *Wretched*.

28. For statistical reports on this, see Daoud, *Féminisme et Politique*, and Rivet, *Le Maghreb à l'Épreuve*, for North African countries; and Ahmed, *Women and Gender in Islam*, and Moghissi, *Feminism and Islamic Fundamentalism*, for Egypt.

29. Rivet, *Le Maghreb à l'Épreuve*, p. 303.

30. For a lengthy discussion of these questions during the Arab-Muslim Nahda, see Afaya, *L'Occident*.

31. For an interesting overview of the ideas of these intellectuals, see Ahmed, *Women and Gender in Islam*, and Afaya, *L'Occident*.

32. Daoud, *Féminisme et Politique*, and *Histoire des Femmes*, especially pp. 197–205.

33. See Daoud, *Féminisme et Politique*, and B. F. Stowasser, *Women in the Qur'an, Traditions, and Interpretation* (Oxford: Oxford University Press, 1994).

34. See Alami, *L'Enseignement des Filles*, p. 239; Daoud, *Féminisme et Politique*, and B. el Alaoui Said, "Représentation des Femmes dans le Discours Réformiste au Maroc," in *Femmes et Islam*, ed. Aicha Belarbi, pp. 31–46 (Casablanca: Editions le Fennec, 1998).

35. JOSSUR, "Forum des Femmes Marocaines," in *Questions Féminine et Role de l'Ijtihad en Islam*, proceedings of conference held February 19–20, 1999 (Rabat: University of Morocco, 2000).

36. See N. Nalini, "Woman, Nation, and Narration in *Midnight's Children*," in *Scattered Hegemonies: Postmodernity and Transnational Feminist Practice*, ed. I. Grewal and C. Kaplan, p. 79 (Minneapolis: University of Minnesota Press, 1994); and Jayawardena Kumari, *Feminism and Nationalism in the Third World* (London: Zed Books, 1986).

37. See Qutb, *Jahiliyatto*, and Qaradhâwî, *Le Licite and l'illicite*.

38. See Fatima Mernissi, *Beyond the Veil: Male-Female Dynamics in Modern Muslim Society* (Indianapolis: Indiana University Press, 1987); and Ait Fatna Sabbah, *Woman in the Muslim Unconscious*, trans. Mary Jo Lakeland (New York: Pergamon Press, 1984).

39. Nearly all Arab-Muslim family laws stipulate that it is men's duty to be the economic "provider" in the family, while it is one of the duties of the wives to be faithful and obedient. Such a distribution of roles attaches an economic dimension to masculinity that, in a way, legitimates control over women. Hence, unemployment and loss of income are experienced as a diminishment of manliness. See Mernissi, *Beyond the Veil*.

40. Stowasser, *Women in the Qur'an*, p. 5.

41. Ibid., p. 103.

42. Influential figures of fundamentalism such as Sayyid Qutb and al-Mawdûdi have all been educated in Euro-American countries and taught Western political, social, and economic theory. See Afaya, *L'Occident*, p. 95.

43. See Leila Hessini, "Wearing the Veil in Contemporary Morocco: Choice and Identity," in *Reconstructing Gender in the Middle East*, ed. Fatma Muge Gocek and

Shiva Balaghi, pp. 40–56 (New York: Columbia University Press, 1994); and Belarbi, ed., *Femmes et Islam.*

44. Moghissi, *Feminism and Islamic Fundamentalism,* p. 45.

Chapter 4

1. Y. Kamalipour, "Windows of Opportunity: Images of Iranians in the U.S. Media," *The Iranian,* 1998, http://www.iranian.com/opinion/aug98/media/.

2. W. Blum, "Making It Safe for the King and Kings," 2001, http://www.thirdworldtraveler.com/blum/iran_kht.html.

3. Y. Bonab, "The Origin and Development of Imperialist Contention in Iran: 1884–1921, Part 1," 2002, http://www.iran-bulletin.org/bonab.html; K. Armstrong, "Islam Agonistes: The Arrival of the West," 2002, http://dhushara.com/book/upd3/2002a/histis.htm.

4. The hajj, the religious pilgrimage to the Sacred Mosque at Mecca, constitutes one of the religious duties of Islam.

5. Armstrong, "Islam Agonistes"; "Iranian History," *Persian Outpost,* 2001, http://www.persianoutpost.com/htdocs/iranhistory.html.

6. The Majlis is an assembly for discussion, a council; the Parliament of any of various North African or Middle Eastern countries.

7. Middle East Studies Association (MESA), "Evaluation of Secondary-Level Textbooks for Coverage of Middle East and North Africa," 1994, http://www.umich.edu/~iinet/cmenas/textbooks/reviews/summarya.html.

8. M. Dankof, "Review of Sandra Mackey, *The Iranians: Persia, Islam, and the Soul of a Nation,*" *The Iranian,* 2002, http://www.iranian.com/books/2002/june/iran/; M. Gasiorowski, "The 1953 Coup d'Etat in Iran," 2001, http://www.geocities.com/athens/olympus/6994/1953coup.htm.

9. Gasiorowski, "1953 Coup"; Dankof, "Review"; Blum, "Making It Safe"; T. Ali, *The Clash of Fundamentalisms: Crusades, Jihads and Modernity* (New York: Verso, 2002).

10. Gasiorowski, "1953 Coup"; M. Byrne, "Twenty Years after the Hostages: Declassified Documents on Iran and the U.S.," 1999, National Security Archive Electronic Briefing Book No. 21, http://www.gwu.edu/~nsarchiv/nasaebb/nsaebb21/index.html; F. Gavin, "Politics, Power, and U.S. Policy in Iran, 1950–1953," 2002, http://www.fas.harvard.edu/~hpcws/gavin.

11. Byrne, "Twenty Years"; Gavin, "Politics"; Gasiorowski, "1953 Coup"; Blum, "Making It Safe"; D. Walsh, "Report Details CIA Role in Overthrow of Iranian Government in 1953," 2000, http://www.wsws.org/articles/2000/april2000/iran-a19.shtml; J. Risen, "U.S. and Iran," 2000, http://www.nytimes.com/library/world/mideast.

12. Risen, "U.S. and Iran."

13. Walsh, "Report Details."

14. Blum, "Making It Safe."

15. Ibid.

16. Risen, "U.S. and Iran."

17. Walsh, "Report Details"; Risen, "U.S. and Iran"; E. Said, *Covering Islam: How the Media and the Experts Determine How We See the Rest of the World* (New York: Pantheon, 1981).

18. Blum, "Making It Safe."

19. K. Bin Sayeed, *Western Dominance and Political Islam: Challenge and Response* (Albany: State University of New York Press, 1995), p. 11.

20. Gavin, "Politics"; Gasiorowski, "1953 Coup."

21. Ali, *Clash of Fundamentalisms.*

22. MESA, "Evaluation."

23. Chester Finn, "Introduction," in *September 11: What Our Children Need to Know,* Thomas B. Fordham Foundation, 2002, http://www.edexcellence.net/sept11/september11.pdf.

24. M. Berenson, "Professors Discuss Islam and U.S. Foreign Policy," http://www.rice.edu/projects/thesher/current/news/story5.html.

25. A. Rabi, "Divergence of Beliefs: Iran in the Aftermath of September 11," *The Iranian,* http://www.iranian.com/opinion/2002/january/iran911/; Gasiorowski, "1953 Coup."

26. Walsh, "Report Details."

27. F. Halliday, "Islam in Danger: Authority, Rushdie and the Struggle for the Migrant Soul," in *The Next Threat: Western Perceptions of Islam,* ed. J. Hippler and A. Lueg (London: Pluto Press, 1995).

28. Dankof, "Review."

29. Chalmers Johnson, "Blowback," 2001, http://www.globalpolicy.org/wtc/analysis/0928blowback.htm.

30. Halliday, "Islam in Danger"; Johnson, "Blowback"; S. Peterson, "In Iran, 'Death to Americans' Is Back," *Christian Science Monitor,* http://www.csmonitor.com/2002/0212/p01s02-wome.html; S. Telhomi, "American Foreign Policy Toward the Muslim World," 2001, http://www.brook.edu/dybdocroot/views/interviews/Telhomi/20010921.htm.

31. P. Atwood, "The Algebra of Terror and Counter Terror," http://www.interventionmag.com/features/article_the_algebra.html; Blum, "Making It Safe"; Bin Sayeed, *Western Dominance*; Persian Outpost, "Iranian History."

32. Ali, *Clash of Fundamentalisms,* p. 128.

33. Dankof, "Review."

34. Bin Sayeed, *Western Dominance*; Persian Outpost, "Iranian History"; Ali, *Clash of Fundamentalisms;* Dankof, "Review."

35. Said, *Covering Islam;* MESA, "Evaluation."

36. Ali, *Clash of Fundamentalisms;* Persian Outpost, "Iranian History"; Armstrong, "Islam Agonistes."

37. Y. Kamalipour, "Windows of Opportunity: Images of Iranians in the U.S. Media," *The Iranian,* http://www.iranian.com/opinion/aug98/media/; Said, *Covering Islam.*

38. MESA, "Evaluation."

39. Quoted in Kamalipour, "Windows of Opportunity."

40. MESA, "Evaluation."

41. Said, *Covering Islam.*

42. Halliday, "Islam in Danger"; Bin Sayeed, *Western Dominance*; J. Bockmeir, "Understanding and Countering Western Islamophobia," http://www.muslimedia.com/archives/features01/islamophob.htm.

43. Bin Sayeed, *Western Dominance*; Said, *Covering Islam.*

44. Byrne, "Twenty Years"; Ali, *Clash of Fundamentalisms;* Bin Sayeed, *Western Dominance.*

45. C. Sudetic, "The Betrayal of Basra," *Utne Reader* 110 (2002), pp. 45–49; Ali, *Clash of Fundamentalisms.*

46. Bin Sayeed, *Western Dominance;* Sudetic, "Betrayal of Basra."

47. L. Hadar, "The 'Green Peril': Creating the Islamic Fundamentalist Threat," *Cato Policy Analysis* 177 (1992), http://www.regulationmagazine.com.pubs. pas.pa-177.html; Armstrong, "Islam Agonistes"; Bin Sayeed, *Western Dominance;* Ali, *Clash of Fundamentalisms.*

48. J. Alterman, "The Gulf States and the American Umbrella," *Middle East Review of International Affairs* 4, no. 4 (December 2000), http://meria.idc.ac.il/ journal/2000/issue4/jv4n4a8.html; R. Ramazani, "The Shifting Premise of Iran's Foreign Policy: Towards a Democratic Peace?" *Middle East Journal,* 1998, http://www.geocities.com/capitolhill.loby.3163/articles.html.

49. Walsh, "Report Details."

50. A. Whitten, "Letter to America—for a Change," 2002, http://zena/secure forum.com/interactive/content/display_item.cfm?itemid = 3154; Ali, *Clash of Fundamentalisms;* Ramazani, "Shifting Premise"; Walsh, "Report Details."

51. Kamalipour, "Windows of Opportunity"; Said, *Covering Islam.*

52. Said, *Covering Islam;* Whitten, "Letter"; Kamalipour, "Windows of Opportunity."

53. Peterson, "In Iran."

54. Ibid.

55. Ibid.

56. Rabi, "Divergence of Beliefs."

57. C. Recknagel and A. Gorgin, "Iran: Reformists See New Crackdown in Row Over Poll on U.S. Ties," http://www.rferl.org/nca/features/2002/ 10/101020021.asp; Rabi, "Divergence of Beliefs"; *Common Ground,* "Persian Gulf Update," September 3, 2002, http://www.commonground radio.org/ shows/02/0236.shtml.

Chapter 5

1. H. Lindemann Nelson, *Damaged Identities: Narrative Repair* (Ithaca, NY: Cornell University Press, 2001).

2. Norman K. Denzin, *Interpretive Interaction* (Newbury Park, CA: Sage Publications, 1989), p. 23.

3. Elliot Eisner, *The Enlightened Eye: Qualitative Inquiry and the Enhancement of Educational Practice* (New York: Macmillan, 1990).

4. Edward Said, *Orientalism* (Harmondsworth, UK: Penguin, 1978, reprinted 1985).

5. Jack G. Shaheen, *The TV Arab* (Bowling Green, OH: Bowling Green State University Popular Press, 1984).

6. Jack G. Shaheen, *Reel Bad Arabs* (New York: Olive Branch Press, 2001).

7. Jack G. Shaheen, "The Comic Book Arab," *Link* 24, no. 5 (1991).

8. Shaheen, *Reel Bad Arabs.*

9. Noam Chomsky, *9-11* (New York: Seven Stories Press, 2001).

10. Samuel P. Huntington, *The Clash of Civilizations and The Remaking of World Order* (New York: Simon & Schuster, 1996).

11. Shaheen, *Reel Bad Arabs.*

12. Fredrick Barth, *Ethnic Groups and Boundaries: The Social Organization of Cultural Differences* (1969; Long Grove, IL: Waveland Press, 1998).

13. Joane Nagel, *American Indian Ethnic Renewal* (New York: Oxford University Press, 1996).

14. Ibid., p. 7.

15. Adam Fortunate Eagle, *Alcatraz! Alcatraz!* (Berkeley, CA: Heyday Books, 1992), pp. 37–38.

16. Stephen Cornell, *The Return of the Native: American Indian Political Resurgence* (New York: Oxford University Press, 1988).

17. Shaheen, *TV Arab.*

18. Marilyn Cochran-Smith, "Blind Vision: Unlearning Racism in Teacher Education," *Harvard Educational Review* 70, no. 2 (2000): pp. 157–90.

19. S. R. Steinberg and J. L. Kincheloe, "Setting the Context for Multi/Interculturalism: The Power Blocs of Class Elitism, White Supremacy, and Patriarchy," in *Multi/Intercultural Conversations,* ed. S. Steinberg, pp. 3–30 (New York: Peter Lang, 2001).

20. Neil Bissoondath, *Selling Illusions* (Toronto: Penguin Books, 1994), p. 111.

21. "A Class Divided," produced by William Peters and Yale University Films for *Frontline,* PBS, Washington, DC, 1985.

22. Linda Tuhiwai Smith, *Decolonizing Methodologies* (London: Zed Books, 1999), pp. 8–9.

23. Edward Said, "Impossible Histories: Why the Many Islams Cannot Be Simplified," *Harper's* (July 2002), http://www.findarticles.com/cf_dis/m1111/1826_305/88998674/p1/article.jhtml.

24. Ibid.

25. Alan C. Cairns, *Citizens Plus: Aboriginal Peoples and the Canadian State* (Vancouver: UBC Press, 2000), p. 11.

26. "Detained Florida Med Students Speak Out," transcript, *Larry King Live,* CNN, September 16, 2002, http://www.cnn.com/transcripts.

27. Shaheen, *Reel Bad Arabs,* p. 590.

28. Ushma Shah, "Creating Space: Moving from the Mandatory to the Worthwhile," in *Creating Democratic Classrooms,* ed. L. Beyer (New York: Teachers College Press, 1996), p. 52.

29. Ibid.

Chapter 6

1. Noam Chomsky, *Necessary Illusions: Thought Control in Democratic Societies* (Boston: South End Press, 1989), pp. 205–6.

2. Ibid., p. 54.

3. Ibid., p. 207.

4. Noam Chomsky, *Deterring Democracy* (New York: Hill and Wang, 1992), p. 378.

5. This is the modern definition of terrorism given in the *Oxford English Dictionary.* To find this word in the online version of the OED go to dictionary.oed.com/cgi/entry/00249603.

6. Chomsky, *Deterring Democracy*, p. 392.

7. Edward W. Said, *The End of the Peace Process: Oslo and After* (New York: Vintage Books, 2001).

8. From a speech given by Cornel West December 18, 2001, in the San Francisco Bay area. To listen to the entire speech go to www.webactive.com/webactive/pacifica/demnow.html

9. Edward W. Said and Christopher Hitchens, *Blaming the Victims: Serious Scholarship and the Palestinian Question* (London: Verso, 1988).

10. Chomsky, *Deterring Democracy*, p. 421.

11. Chomsky, *Necessary Illusions*, p. 288.

12. Ibid., pp. 289–90.

13. Said and Hitchens, *Blaming the Victims*, pp. 204–5.

14. Chomsky, *Necessary Illusions*, p. 290.

15. Ibid., p. 290.

16. Ibid., p. 314.

17. Ibid., p. 315.

18. Said, *End of the Peace Process*, p. 61.

19. Ibid., p. 190.

20. Chomsky, *Necessary Illusions*, p. 275.

21. Ibid., p. 319.

22. Yossi Alpher, "Bush's Dedication to the Cause," June 9, 2003, http://www.bitterlemons.org.

Chapter 7

1. Richard Moore, *The Name "Negro" Its Origin and Evil Use* (Baltimore: Black Classic Press, 1992; originally published in 1960).

2. Gomez Eannes de Azurara, *Chronicle of the Discovery and Conquest of Guinea*, cited in Ulrich Bonnell Phillips, *American Negro Slavery* (Blackmask online, 2004), http://www.blackmask.com.

3. Moore, *The Name "Negro"*; Dana Reynolds, "The African Heritage and Ethnohistory of the Moors: Background to the Emergence of Early Berber and Arab Peoples, from Prehistory to the Islamic Dynasties," in *Golden Age of the Moor*, ed. Ivan Van Sertima (New Brunswick, NJ: Transaction Publishers, 1992).

4. Abdulwahid Dhanun Taha, *The Muslim Conquest and Settlement of North Africa and Spain* (New York: Routledge, 1989).

5. Titus Burckhardt, *Moorish Culture in Spain*, translated by Alissa Jaffa (New York: McGraw-Hill, 1972).

6. H. T. Norris, *The Berbers in Arabic Literature* (United Kingdom: Longman Group, 1982), p. 63.

7. E. W. Bovill, *The Golden Trade of the Moors* (New York: Oxford University Press, 1968; Bernard Lewis, *Race and Slavery in the Middle Ages* (New York: Oxford University Press, 1990); Ferdinand Gregorovious, *History of Rome, Vol. 3: 800–1002 A.D.* (London: George Bell, 1903).

8. Norman Daniel, *The Arabs and Medieval Europe* (London: Longman, 1979).

9. Martin Bernal, *Black Athena: The Afroasiatic Roots of Classical Civilization*, vol. 1 (New Brunswick, NJ: Rutgers University Press, 1987); George G. M. James, *Stolen*

Legacy: The Greeks Were Not the Authors of Greek Philosophy, but the People of North Africa, Commonly Called the Egyptians (New York: Philosophical Library, 1954).

10. Anwar Chejne, *Muslim Spain: Its History and Culture* (Minneapolis: University of Minnesota Press, 1974); Jan Read, *The Moors in Spain and Portugal* (London: Faber, 1974).

11. Stanely Lane Poole, *The Story of the Moors in Spain* (Baltimore: Black Classic Press, 1990; originally published in 1886).

12. S. D. Goitein, *Jews and Arabs: Their Contacts through the Ages* (New York: Schocken Books, 1955), and *A Mediterranean Society: The Jewish Communities of the Arab World as Portrayed in the Documents of the Cairo Geniza* (Berkeley: University of California Press, 1967); Felix Reichmann, *The Sources of Western Literature: The Middle Eastern Civilizations* (Westport: Greenwood Press, 1980).

13. Jan Carew, "Moorish Culture-bringers: Bearers of Enlightenment," in *Golden Age of the Moor,* ed. Ivan Van Sertima (New Brunswick, NJ: Transaction Publishers, 1992).

14. George Sarton, *Introduction to the History of Science,* vol. 1 (New York: Krieger, 1975).

15. Ibid., p. 1.

16. Francis Ghiles, "What Is Wrong with Muslim Science," *Nature* 24 (March 1983): 1.

17. Angela Fisher, *Africa Adorned* (New York: Harry N. Abrams, 1984).

18. Abraham L. Udovitch, "At the Origins of Western Commenda: Islam, Israel, Byzantium?" *Speculum: The Journal of Medieval Studies* 37 (1962): 198–207, and *Partnership and Profit in Medieval Islam* (Princeton, NJ: Princeton University Press, 1970).

19. R. S. Mackensen, "Four Great Libraries of Medieval Baghdad," *Library Quarterly* 2, no. 3 (1932): pp. 279–99; P. M. Holt, ed., *Cambridge History of Islam,* vol. 2 (Cambridge, UK: Cambridge University Press, 1970), pp. 581, 748.

20. T. Hamilton, "The African Heritage in European Expansion," *Journal of Ethnic Studies* 4 (1976): pp. 217–38.

21. David MacRitchie, *Ancient and Modern Britons,* vol. 1 (London: Kegan, Paul, Trench, and Trubner, 1884); Joel Rogers, *Sex and Race,* vol. 1 (Helga M. Rogers, New York, 1967).

Chapter 8

1. Quoted in Yusof Progler, "Destroying and Rebuilding Islam in the Image of the West," *Muslimedia,* March 16–31, 1999, www.muslimedia.com/archives/features99/dest_west.htm.

2. Jonathon Berkey, *The Transmission of Knowledge in Medieval Cairo: A Social History of Islamic Education* (Princeton, NJ: Princeton University Press, 1992), p. 57.

3. Ibid., p. 57.

4. Ibid., p. 101.

5. Ibid., p. 101.

6. Ibid., p. 101.

7. Ibid., p. 101.

8. Ibid., p. 101.

9. David F. Noble, *A World without Women: The Christian Clerical Culture of Western Science* (New York: Oxford University Press, 1992).

10. Berkey, *Transmission of Knowledge.*, p. 105

11. Ibid., p. 105.

12. Ibid., p. 105.

13. Erving Goffman, *Asylums: Essays on the Social Situation of Mental Patients and Other Inmates* (New York: Doubleday, 1961), p. xiii.

14. Michel Foucault, *Discipline and Punish: The Birth of the Prison* (New York: Vintage, 1979), p. 186.

15. Ibid., p. 176.

16. Ibid., pp. 178–81.

17. Ibid., p. 184.

18. Ibid., p. 194.

19. Timothy Mitchell, *Colonising Egypt* (Berkeley: University of California Press, 1991), p. 35.

20. Edward W. Said, *Orientalism* (New York: Vintage, 1979), p. 87.

21. Ibid., p. 80.

22. Ibid., p. 82.

23. Ibid., p. 85.

24. Ibid., p. 89.

25. Ibid., p. 89.

26. Ibid., p. 92.

27. William McNeill, *The Pursuit of Power: Technology, Armed Force, and Society since A.D. 1000* (Chicago: University of Chicago Press, 1982).

28. Alfred W. Crosby, *The Measure of Reality: Quantification and the Western Society, 1250–1600* (Cambridge, UK: Cambridge University Press, 1997).

29. McNeill, *Pursuit of Power*, p. 64, n. 2.

30. Ibid., p. 61.

31. Ibid., p. 62.

32. Cf. Jonathan Feldman, *Universities in the Business of Repression: The Academic-Military-Industrial Complex in Central America* (Boston: South End Press, 1989).

33. Yvonne Dion-Buffalo and John Mohawk, "Thoughts from an Autochthonous Center: Postmodernism and Cultural Studies," *Cultural Survival Quarterly* 17, no. 4 (1993): pp. 16–21.

34. Ibid., p. 35.

35. E. J. Hobsbawm, *The Age of Revolution: Europe 1789–1848* (London: Cardinal, 1991), p. 177.

36. Mitchell, *Colonising Egypt*, p. 35.

37. Ibid., p. 42.

38. Joseph S. Szyliowicz, *Education and Modernization in the Middle East* (Ithaca, NY: Cornell University Press, 1973), p. 104.

39. See, for example, Albert Hourani, *Arabic Thought in the Liberal Age, 1789–1939* (Cambridge University Press, 1962).

40. Trevor J. Le Gassick, *Major Themes in Modern Arabic Thought: An Anthology* (Ann Arbor: University of Michigan Press, 1979), p. 2.

41. Trevor Mostyn, *The Cambridge Encyclopedia of the Middle East* (Cambridge, UK: Cambridge University Press, 1988), p. 149.

42. Hourani, *Arabic Thought*, pp. 53–54.

43. J. Heyworth-Dunne, *An Introduction to the History of Education in Modern Egypt* (London: Luzac & Company, 1938), p. 105.

44. Hourani, *Arabic Thought*, p. 138.

45. Hobsbawm, *Age of Revolution*, p. 293.

46. Ibid., p. 59.

47. Ibid., p. 296.

48. Ibid., p. 330.

49. Mitchell, *Colonising Egypt*, p. 16.

50. Charles Issawi, *Egypt at Mid-Century: An Economic Survey* (London: Oxford University Press, 1954), p. 18, n. 1.

51. Isaiah Berlin, *The Crooked Timber of Humanity: Chapters in the History of Ideas* (New York: Vintage, 1992), p. 160.

52. Ibid., p. 160.

53. Ibid., p. 240.

54. Ibid., p. 240.

55. Hobsbawm, *Age of Revolution*, p. 178.

56. Berlin, *Crooked Timber*, p. 240.

57. Hobsbawm, *Age of Revolution*, p. 318.

58. In Robert C. Tucker, *The Marx-Engels Reader* (New York: Norton, 1978), p. 82.

59. Ibid., pp. 688–89.

60. Hourani, *Arabic Thought*, p. 53.

61. Heyworth-Dunne, *Introduction*, pp. 132, 137, 142, 187.

62. Ibid., pp. 144–45, 188.

63. Said, *Orientalism*, p. 92.

64. Ibid., p. 90.

65. Heyworth-Dunne, *Introduction*, pp. 1184–86.

66. Ibid., pp. 186, 189.

67. Ibid., p. 190.

68. Ibid., pp. 190, 192, 194, 204, 208–9, 210.

69. Hourani, *Arabic Thought*, p. 54.

70. Ibid., p. 76.

71. Abdul Rahman Jabarti, *Napoleon in Egypt: Chronicle of the French Occupation, 1798* (New York: Markus Wiener, 1993; trans. Shmuel Moreh).

72. Heyworth-Dunne, *Introduction*, p. 235.

73. Ibid., p. 137.

74. Charles Issawi, *An Economic History of the Middle East and North Africa* (London: Methuen, 1982), p. 80.

75. E.R.J. Owen, *Cotton and the Egyptian Economy, 1820–1914* (London: Oxford University Press, 1969), pp. 28–30.

76. Mitchell, *Colonising Egypt*, p. 16.

77. Marshall G.S. Hodgson, *The Venture of Islam: Conscience and History in a World Civilization* (Chicago: University of Chicago Press, 1974), p. 218.

78. Mitchell, *Colonising Egypt*, p. 39.

79. E.W. Lane in Heyworth-Dunne, *Introduction*, p. 101, n. 1.

80. Mitchell, *Colonising Egypt*, p. 85.

81. Ibid., p. 84.

82. Ibid., p. 69.

83. Ibid., p. 71.

84. Szyliowicz, *Education and Modernization*, p. 127.

85. Mitchell, *Colonising Egypt*, p. 78.

86. Ibid., p. 71.

87. Ibid., p. 132.

88. Ibid., p. 171.

89. Ibid., p. 125; cf. Hourani, *Arabic Thought*, pp. 139–40.

90. Hourani, *Arabic Thought*, pp. 154–55.

91. Mitchell, *Colonising Egypt*, p. 163.

92. Cf. Allan Christelow, *Muslim Law Courts and the French Colonial State in Algeria* (Princeton, NJ: Princeton University Press, 1985), on Algeria.

93. Said, *Orientalism*, pp. 322–33.

Chapter 9

Special thanks go to Joan Russell and Melanie Bennett-Stonebanks, from the faculty of education at McGill University, for editing earlier drafts of this chapter.

1. D. Lamb, *The Arabs: Journey Beyond the Mirage* (New York: Random House, 1987); M. Salloum, "Casting Out Evil," *Montreal Gazette*, Feb. 8, 1993; M. Wingfield and B. Karaman, "Arab Stereotypes and American Educators," *Social Studies and Young Learners*, Journal of the National Council for Social Studies (1995): 7–10; W. Schwartz, *Arab American Students in Public Schools*, report no. EDO-UD-99-2, Institute for Urban and Minority Education ERIC Document Reproduction Service no. ED 429 1444 (New York: Colombia University, 1999).

2. Lamb, *The Arabs*, p. 126.

3. J. Shaheen, *Arab and Muslim Stereotyping in American Popular Culture* (Washington, DC: Centre for Muslim-Christian Understanding, 1997), p. 21.

4. E. Ghareeb, ed., *Split Vision: The Portrayal of Arabs in the American Media* (Washington, DC: American-Arab Affair Council, 1983); M. Suleiman, *The Arabs in the Minds of America* (Brattleboro, VT: Amana Books, 1988); Salloum, "Casting Out Evil"; M. Nydell, *Understanding Arabs* (Yarmouth, ME: Intercultural Press, 1987).

5. J. Goodwin, *Price of Honor: Muslim Women Lift the Veil of Silence on the Islamic World* (New York: Little, Brown and Company, 1994), p. 9.

6. Suleiman, *Arabs in the Minds*, pp. 150–51.

7. T. Sergent, P. Woods, and W. Sedacek, "University Student Attitudes towards Arabs: Intervention Implications," *Journal of Multicultural Counseling and Development* 20 (1992): 123–31.

8. A. Richardson, *East Comes West: Asian Religions and Cultures in North America* (New York: Pilgrim Press, 1985), p. 165.

9. P. Hitti, *History of the Arabs from Earliest Times to the Present* (New York: St. Martin's Press, 1970).

10. Shaheen, *Reel Bad Arabs*.

11. Ann Coulter, "Future Widows of America: Write Your Congressman," September 27, 2001, http:www.anncoulter.org/columns/2001/092701/htm.

12. *Patterns of Global Terrorism*, www.usis.usemb.se/terror/rpt2000/index.html.

13. J. Rahme, "Ethnocentric and Stereotypical Concepts in the Study of Islamic and World History," *History Teacher* 32 (4)(1999): 473–94.

14. Charles, Prince of Wales, "Islam and the West," *American Journal of Islamic Social Sciences* 10 (1993): 562–71, p. 564.

15. S. Wayland, "Religious Expression in Public Schools: Kirpans in Canada, Hijab in France," *Ethnic and Racial Studies* 20 (1997): 545–61.

16. Wingfield and Karaman, "Arab Stereotype."

17. D. Burke, "Analysis of School Textbooks on Islam," *Muslim Education Quarterly* 3 (1986): 75–98.

18. Ibid., p. 88.

19. S. Abu-Absi, "Stereotypical Images of Arab Women," *Phi Beta Delta: International Review* 37 (6) (1996): 60–65.

20. L. Kenny, "The Middle East in Canadian Social Sciences Textbooks," in *Arabs in America*, ed. B. Abu-Laban (Wilmette, IL: Medina University Press International, 1975), p. 144.

21. S. Nanda and R. Warms, *Cultural Anthropology* (Albany, NY: International Thomson Publishing Company, 1998).

22. G. Ferraro, *Cultural Anthropology: An Applied Perspective* (St. Paul, MN: West Publishing Company, 1995).

23. William McGee, 1895, quoted in Ferraro, *Cultural Anthropology.*

24. Nanda and Warms, *Cultural Anthropology.*

25. J. Laffin, *The Arab Mind Considered: A Need for Understanding* (New York: Taplinger, 1975), pp. 98–109.

26. Raphael Patai, *The Arab Mind* (New York: Scribners, 1983).

27. Ibid.

28. E. Said, *Orientalism* (New York: Pantheon Books, 1978), and *Covering Islam: How the Media and Experts Determine How We See the Rest of the World* (New York: Vintage Books, 1997); H. Barakat, *The Arab World: Society, Culture and State* (Berkeley, CA: University of California Press, 1993).

29. For example, Said, *Orientalism*; E. Said, *Culture and Imperialism* (New York: Random House, 1993); Said, *Covering Islam*; R. Kabbani, *Imperial Fictions: Europe's Myths of the Orient* (London: Pandora, 1994); A. Hussain, *Western Conflict with Islam: Survey of the Anti-Islamic Tradition* (Leicester, UK: Volcano Books, 1990).

30. As described by Patai, *The Arab Mind*; and Laffin, *The Arab Mind Considered.*

31. Charles, "Islam and the West"; Hitti, *History of the Arabs.*

32. Qur'an 49: 13.

33. Qur'an 2:256.

34. Qur'an 5:32.

35. Qur'an 16:125.

36. Shaheen, *Arab and Muslim Stereotyping*; T. Ali, *The Book of Saladin* (London: Verso, 1999).

Chapter 10

1. L. Grossberg, "What's in a Name? (One More Time)," *Taboo: The Journal of Culture and Education* (Spring 1995): 1–37.

2. Ibid.

3. J. Kincheloe, "McDonald's, Power, and Children: Ronald McDonald (aka Ray Kroc) Does It All for You," in *Kinderculture: The Corporate Control of Childhood,* ed. Shirley R. Steinberg and Joe L. Kincheloe (Boulder, CO: Westview Press, 1997), p. 260.

4. McDonald's Customer Relations Center, 1994.

5. Kincheloe, "McDonald's."

Index

About the Editors and the Contributors

IBRAHIM ABUKHATTALA is a doctoral student in the Department of Integrated Studies in Education at McGill University in Montreal.

MORDECHAI GORDON is an associate professor of education at Quinnipiac University in Connecticut.

DOUGLAS KELLNER is the George F. Kneller Philosophy of Education Chair at UCLA.

HAROON KHAREM is an assistant professor of education at Brooklyn College.

JOE L. KINCHELOE is a professor of education at the CUNY Graduate Center and Brooklyn College.

YUSEF J. PROGLER is professor of international and cultural studies and education at Zayed University in Dubai.

LOUBNA SKALLI is an assistant professor of communications at the University of Morocco.

SHIRLEY R. STEINBERG is an associate professor of education at Brooklyn College.

CHRISTOPHER D. STONEBANKS is a doctoral student in the Department of Integrated Studies in Education at McGill University in Montreal.